DISBIS

Dissertationen zu Datenbanken und Informationssystemen

Mit Unterstützung des Fachausschusses 2.5 „Rechnergestützte Informationssysteme" der Gesellschaft für Informatik e.V. herausgegeben von

Transactional Process Management over Component Systems

Heiko Schuldt

AKA

Heiko Schuldt
Database Research Group
Institute of Information Systems
Swiss Federal Institute of Technology (ETH)
CH-8092 Zürich
schuldt@inf.ethz.ch

A dissertation submitted to the
Swiss Federal Institute of Technology Zurich
for the degree of
Doctor of Technical Sciences

Accepted on the recommendation of
Prof. Dr. H.-J. Schek, examiner
Prof. Dr. G. Alonso, co-examiner

Diss. ETH No. 13976

2000

Die Deutsche Bibliothek – CIP-Einheitsaufnahme

Schuldt, Heiko
Transactional Process Management over Component Systems / Heiko
Schuldt. – Berlin : Akad. Verl.-Ges. Aka; Amsterdam : IOS Press, 2001
(Dissertationen zu Datenbanken und Informationssystemen ; Bd. 73)
Zugl.: Zürich, ETH, Diss., 2000
ISBN 3-89838-473-X
ISBN 1-58603-176-7

„infix“ is a joint imprint of Akademische Verlagsgesellschaft Aka GmbH (Berlin) and IOS Press BV (Amsterdam)

Reproduced from camera ready copy supplied by the author
Printing and Binding: Hundt Druck GmbH, Köln
Printed in Germany

ISSN 0949-0183
ISBN 3-89838-473-X
ISBN 1-58603-176-7

Geleitwort

Die Arbeit von Heiko Schuldt ist transaktionellen Prozessen gewidmet, die oberhalb von Komponenten–Systemen angesiedelt sind und daher diese Komponenten systemübergreifend verbinden. Dies ist ein sehr aktuelles Thema und ich möchte dazu einige übergeordnete Gesichtspunkte darstellen. Anwendungsentwicklung mit Zugriff auf grosse Datenmengen findet heute nicht mehr, wie es der klassischen Lehrmeinung entspricht, auf der Basis eines einzigen Datenbanksystems statt, in dem ein unternehmensweites, für alle Anwendungen verbindliches Datenmodell vorliegt. Vielmehr möchte man Anwendungen entwickeln, die in zusammengesetzten Systemen ablaufen, wobei die Komponenten wieder Datenbanksysteme sein können, oder auch allgemeiner als Ressourcen–Verwalter oder Dienstanbieter auftreten. Manche sprechen auch von "Megaprogrammierung" (Wiederhold, Stanford). Es geht in allen Fällen um die Verwendung, also das Aufrufen und Ausführen wohlverstandener Bausteine und um deren Zusammenfügen zu einer wohldefinierten grösseren Einheit. Hierfür hat man auch Begriffe wie Workflow–Management oder Prozessmanagement eingeführt und stellt sich solche neuen Plattformen für zukünftige Anwendungsentwicklung als Bestandteil einer Middleware–Schicht in einer mehrstufigen Systemarchitektur vor.

In einer solchen Umgebung besteht daher ein Programm auch nicht mehr nur aus einer Transaktion oder aus einer Sequenz von Transaktionen, die alle auf der gleichen Datenbank ausgeführt werden. Vielmehr werden viele Transaktionen als Bausteine, als "Schritte" oder "Aktivitäten" zu einem transaktionellen Prozess zusammengefasst, der in mehreren Datenbanksystemen ausgeführt wird und durch einen Transaktionskoordinator überwacht wird. Einzelne Schritte in gewissen Komponentensystemen können erfolgreich durchgeführt werden, bei anderen können sich Ausnahme– oder Fehlersituation einstellen. Je nach Erfolg oder Misserfolg der bislang gestarteten Schritte ergibt sich die Notwendigkeit, weitere Transaktionen, darunter auch Kompensationstransaktionen, zur Ausführung zu bringen oder alternative Schritte auszuführen. In jedem Fall, auch im Fehlerfall, soll ein transaktioneller Prozess zu einem wohldefinierten, vorgesehenen Ende führen. Zwischen den einzelnen Schritten eines transaktionellen Prozesses gibt es Abhängigkeiten, die berücksichtigt werden müssen. Beispielsweise möchte man garantieren, dass zwei Schritte innerhalb eines Prozesses entweder sequentiell ausgeführt werden müssen, oder dass bei paralleler Ausführung die Richtung eines möglichen Informationsflusses vorgeschrieben ist. Weitere Eigenschaften einzelner Schritte wie Kompensierbarkeit oder Wiederholbarkeit müssen berücksichtigt werden. So macht es z.B. keinen Sinn, die Ausführung eines Schrittes zu beenden, wenn nicht sicher ist, ob man diesen Schritt wieder rückgängig machen kann. Auch Interprozess–Abhängigkeiten, also Abhängigkeiten zwischen parallel laufenden Prozessen erfordern Koordinationsmassnahmen. So muss garantiert werden, dass ein zweiter Prozess nie einen nicht–kompensierbaren Schritt ausführt, wenn eine Abhängigkeit von einem kompensierbaren Schritt eines anderen transaktionellen Prozesses besteht, dessen Ausgang noch ungewiss ist. Dagegen kann eine Abhängigkeit von einem nicht–kompensierbaren Schritt eines anderen Prozesses durchaus erlaubt werden.

Die Ähnlichkeiten aber auch die Unterschiede zu der Laufzeitumgebung eines Datenbanksystems werden deutlich: Die Schritte einer DB–Transaktion sind Lese– oder Schreiboperationen auf persistenten Speicherobjekten. Ein Schritt eines transaktionellen Prozesses dagegen ist eine Aktivität, die als DB–Transaktion auf einer DB–Komponente ausgeführt wird. Jede Aktion einer DB–Transaktion ist kompensierbar. Dagegen kann ein Schritt eines transaktionellen Prozesses entweder kompensierbar oder wiederholbar oder beides sein, oder er ist ein "Pivotschritt", d.h. weder kompensierbar noch wiederholbar. Bei einer DB–Transaktion gibt es zwei wohldefinierte Ausgänge, den erfolgreichen Abschluss oder den Abbruch, der keine Spuren hinterlässt. Diese beiden Ausgänge werden einem Programmierer garantiert. In einem transaktionellen Prozess dagegen werden weitere Ausgänge garantiert, die durch den Programmierer durch alternative Ausführungen spezifiziert werden.

In Analogie zu Datenbanken kann man daher auch von der Weiterentwicklung der Datenbanktechnologie auf höherer Ebene sprechen, von der aus man nicht Daten, sondern ganze Datenbanken anspricht und durch transaktionelle Prozesse als verallgemeinerte Transaktionen Garantien für die korrekte Ausführung in mehreren Komponentensystemen bekommt. Die Infrastruktur heute verfügbarer Middleware–Produkte in Form von Transaktionsmonitoren oder Transaktionsservern, etwa auch in COM+, ist hinsichtlich der oben aufgestellten Forderungen recht bescheiden. Man bekommt lediglich verteilte DB–Transaktionen, die durch ein Zweiphasen–Commit–Protokoll koordiniert werden. Es gibt daher nur eine "Alles–oder–Nichts"–Garantie, keine Alternativen und daher keine flexible Fehlerbehandlung, keine Berücksichtigung von Kompensations– oder Wiederholungsaktivitäten, keine Berücksichtigung semantischer Kommutativität und daher keine Unterstützung offen geschachtelter Transaktionen.

Diese unbefriedigende Situation zu ändern, bedurfte einer Reihe grundlagenorientierter Arbeiten, auf denen die Arbeit Schuldt zunächst aufsetzt und die er sehr gekonnt und überzeugend weiterentwickelt hat. In den Kernkapiteln der Arbeit stellt H. Schuldt präzise aber ohne übertriebenen Formalismus dar, was man genau unter einem transaktionellen Prozesse versteht. Er unterscheidet folgerichtig "Process Program" als Spezifkation eines transaktionellen Prozesses von seiner Ausführung, die er kurz "Process" nennt. Das "Process Program" ist die statische Spezifikation eines Prozesses, die man vor der Ausführung auf Wohlgeformtheit überprüfen möchte. Hierbei wird festgestellt, ob die Spezifikation erlaubt, einen der gewünschten alternativen Ausgänge zu erreichen, wobei man die Terminierungseigenschaften der einzelnen verwendeten Aktivitäten in Betracht zieht. Die Definition der korrekten parallelen Ausführung eines oder mehrerer Prozesse ist dann die konsequente Verallgemeinerung eines traditionellen Transaktionsschedulers. Neu wird jetzt nicht nur die Kommutativität von Aktivitäten eingebracht, sondern der Scheduler bekommt auch die Kenntnis über die Kompensation einer ausgeführten Aktivität und die Terminierungseigenschaft einer Aktivität. H. Schuldt hat diese Grundlagen äusserst sorgfältig und ausführlich zusammengestellt und das sehr erwünschte Ziel erreicht, unter präzise gegebenen Voraussetzungen zu beweisen, dass mit seinem Prozess–Scheduler alle parallel ausgeführten Prozesse garantiert terminieren und korrekt ausgeführt werden. Die Theorie hierzu ist leider nicht sehr einfach, aber H. Schuldt geht sehr konsequent vor und unterscheidet sorgfältig mehrere mögliche Korrektheitskriterien, die sich vor allem durch die Behandlung der Recovery, d.h. durch die Berücksichtigung von Fehlerfällen unterscheiden. Man sieht deutlich, dass die Theorie hierdurch sehr viel komplizierter wird als nur durch das alleinige Behandeln der Korrektheit paralleler Ausführung. Selbst dies wird bei transaktionellen Prozessen komplexer, weil beispielsweise im Konfliktfall ein einzelner Prozess eine alternative Ausführung einschlagen kann. Im traditionellen Modell dagegen ist hier nur ein vollständiges Rücksetzen möglich.

Nach dieser wichtigen Grundlagenarbeit kommt der Informatik–Ingenieur Schuldt zum Zug. Er gibt Protokolle an, die relativ einfach zu implementieren sind. Sehr bemerkenswert ist dabei die Verwendung eines Protokolls von El Abbadi, das unter dem Namen "Ordered Shared Locks" bekannt geworden ist. H. Schuldt sieht aber bei der Anwendung dieses Protokolls allein Nachteile und kombiniert dieses geschickt mit Zeitstempelverfahren. Er entwickelt daher beinahe so nebenbei auch ein neues Lock–Protokoll und baut geschickt die Terminierungseigenschaften in dieses Protokoll ein. H. Schuldt gibt sich ausserdem nicht damit zufrieden, dass eine Aktivität beispielsweise kompensierbar ist oder nicht. Vielmehr schlägt er vor, Ausführungskosten, insbesondere auch Kosten für die Kompensation zu berücksichtigen und damit den Scheduler "kostenbewusst" arbeiten zu lassen. Diese Idee ist deswegen bemerkenswert, weil in der Vergangenheit ein unnötiger Streit entstand über die Frage, ob man denn immer eine Kompensation habe. Im neuen Modell hat man immer eine Kompensation, nur kann sie sehr teuer sein, so teuer, dass sich ihre Ausführung aus Kostengründen verbietet.

Es sind damit die Voraussetzungen geschaffen für zukünftige Produkte, die einen solchen Prozessmanager und daher eine deutlich bessere Infrastruktur für die Entwicklung verteilter Anwendungen zur Verfügung stellen, in der flexible Ausführung mit Ausführungsgarantie ermöglicht werden kann.

Zürich, den 28. Februar 2001 Prof. H.-J. Schek

Vorwort

Die vorliegende Dissertation entstand während meiner Tätigkeit als wissenschaftlicher Mitarbeiter an der Datenbankgruppe des Instituts für Informationssysteme der Eidgenössischen Technischen Hochschule (ETH) Zürich. Eingebettet war die Arbeit in die Projekte WISE und INVENT, die vom Schweizer Nationalfonds (SNF) im Rahmen des Schwerpunktprogramms Informations– und Kommunikationsstrukturen gefördert wurden sowie in das Projekt "Computer Integrated Methods based on Federated Databases to Improve Product Modularity and Document Flow in Design Processes", gefördert von der Schweizer Kommission für Technologie und Innovation (KTI).

Mein besonderer Dank gilt meinem Doktorvater Prof. Hans-Jörg Schek, der mir einen großen Freiraum für die Arbeit gewährte und mir in jeder Phase das benötigte Vertrauen entgegen brachte. Seiner Weitsicht ist es zu verdanken, daß die Arbeit die lange Tradition der Datenbankgruppe auf dem Gebiet der Transaktionsverwaltung fortsetzen konnte. Des weiteren gilt mein Dank Prof. Gustavo Alonso für die Übernahme des Korreferats und die sehr angenehme und überaus fruchtbare Zusammenarbeit in den von ihm geleiteten Projekten WISE und INVENT. Die Hinweise und Anregungen wie auch die konstruktive Kritik beider Referenten haben sicherlich zur konzeptionellen Klarheit der Arbeit beigetragen. Ebenso möchte ich Prof. Catriel Beeri für die zahlreichen Diskussionen in der Zeit seines Forschungssemesters in Zürich und die daraus entstandenen Anregungen meinen Dank aussprechen.

Bedanken möchte ich mich auch bei allen derzeitigen und ehemaligen Mitgliedern der Datenbankgruppe, die stets für ein sehr angenehmes Klima gesorgt haben, in dem es Spaß gemacht hat zu arbeiten. Natürlich hatten auch die Kolleginnen und Kollegen, mit denen ich in gemeinsamen Projekten Ideen austauschen konnte, maßgeblichen Einfluss auf die Arbeit. Hier möchte ich mich vor allem bei Claus Hagen, der gerade in meiner Anfangsphase jederzeit ein wichtiger Ansprech– und Diskussionspartner war, für die sehr kooperative und angenehme Zusammenarbeit bedanken. Weiterhin möchte ich auf diesem Wege Uwe Röhm, Christoph Schuler und Markus Tresch sowie Amaia Lazcano und Andrei Popovici für ihre Diskussionsbereitschaft danken. Ein herzliches Dankeschön gebührt vor allem auch Antoinette Förster für ihre vorbildliche Unterstützung in sämtlichen administrativen und organisatorischen Fragen sowie Marco Schmidt für seinen fundierten technischen Support.

Die vorliegende Arbeit wurde auch durch den Einsatz und Eifer zahlreicher Studenten, die im Rahmen ihrer Diplom– bzw. Semesterarbeit einen Teil der Prototyp–Implementierung übernommen haben, vorangebracht. An dieser Stelle sei daher Daniel Bacher, Peter Brantschen, Rolf Locher, Stefan Middendorf, André Naef, Florian Nussberger, Christoph Schuler, Kuno Stöckli und Andreas Weiss für ihre Mithilfe gedankt.

Holger Frietsch und Gerald Witzel, die beide die doch sehr zeitraubende Arbeit des Korrekturlesens auf sich genommen haben, möchte ich auf diesem Wege ebenfalls herzlich danken.

Meinen Eltern bin ich zu sehr großem Dank verpflichtet. Sie haben alle meine Pläne immer sehr wohlwollend und vorbehaltlos unterstützt und mir damit auch die Ausbildung, die ich genießen durfte, ermöglicht. Schließlich möchte ich mich von ganzem Herzen bei Birgit bedanken, die mit ihrer Liebe und Ermunterung ein beständiger Rückhalt in allen Phasen der Arbeit war. Den oftmals leider viel zu kurzen gemeinsamen Wochenenden und den langen Arbeitswochen in großer geografischer Entfernung hat sie während der ganzen Jahre unendlich viel Verständnis entgegen gebracht.
Ohne meine Eltern und ohne Birgit wäre diese Arbeit nicht möglich gewesen!

Zürich, im Februar 2001 Heiko Schuldt

Contents

Abstract

Composite systems are collections of distributed, heterogeneous, and autonomous application systems, connected by a network. Such composite systems support a new paradigm for the development of large-scale, truly distributed applications spanning multiple, originally independent stand-alone components. While the proliferation of network technology has substantially increased the accessibility of previously isolated stand-alone application systems, sophisticated frameworks for the development and the control of distributed applications over component systems are still lacking, especially when these applications have to be enriched by dedicated transactional execution guarantees.

In this thesis, we develop the concept of transactional processes as a means for supporting distributed applications on top of the components of a composite system. A process thereby consists of arbitrary sequences of activities specified in a process program. Each activity, in turn, corresponds to a transactional service invoked within a component.

The goal of this thesis is to provide a powerful and comprehensive framework for the correct concurrent and fault-tolerant execution of transactional processes over independent component systems. In particular, this framework has to provide generic support for the application of transactional process management in various environments. To this end, the thesis addresses and combines the following key aspects.

First, we elaborate a theory of transactional process management. We treat processes as transactions at a higher level of semantics, on top of transactions provided by the individual components. Starting with the correctness of single process programs based on ideas of the flexible transactions model, we derive appropriate correctness criteria for the correct concurrent and fault-tolerant execution of process programs by applying a generalized unified theory of concurrency control and recovery to transactional processes. In addition, these correctness criteria account for the special semantics that can be found in processes, imposed by the layered architecture and the kind of interactions between systems as well as by the characteristics of services provided by the individual components. In terms of the interactions between systems, we aim at allowing as much parallelism as possible by applying ideas of the composite systems theory. In terms of service characteristics, our correctness criteria take into account that not all activities of a process might be compensatable once they have been committed.

Second, we develop the necessary protocols needed to implement a process manager which dynamically controls the execution of transactional processes with respect to the criteria imposed by the theory of transactional process management. Moreover, these protocols encompass sophisticated concepts which allow the flexible optimization of process program executions by considering failure probabilities and execution costs of single activities.

Third, we extend the applicability of the theory of transactional process management to arbitrary non-transactional component systems. Although the theory requires each component to provide dedicated transactional functionality, this is in general not met by the kind of systems that can be found in practice. To this end, we introduce the concept of transactional coordination agents which act as database wrappers for arbitrary application systems. These agents provide key transactional functionality on top of such non-transactional components so as to meet the requirements imposed by transactional process management.

Zusammenfassung

Die Verbreitung von vernetzten Rechnerarchitekturen führt dazu, dass der Zugriff auf ursprünglich unabhängige und isolierte Anwendungssysteme in zunehmendem Maße verbessert wird. Daraus entstehen sogenannte zusammengesetzte Systeme, die aus einer Menge von unabhängigen verteilten, heterogenen und autonomen Anwendungssystemen gebildet werden. Diese zusammengesetzten Systeme und insbesondere die darin verwendeten Netzwerktechnologien schaffen die technologische Basis für die Entwicklung neuer Arten von verteilten Anwendungen. Allerdings besteht derzeit noch grosser Bedarf an geeigneter Systemunterstützung für die Entwicklung und Ausführung von verteilten Anwendungen in zusammengesetzten Systemen, speziell in Fällen, in denen diese Anwendungen dezidierte transaktionale Ausführungsgarantien erfordern.

In dieser Arbeit wird der Begriff der transaktionalen Prozesse für die Entwicklung verteilter Anwendungen oberhalb der Komponenten eines zusammengesetzten Systems eingeführt. Ein Prozess wird als eine in einem Prozessprogramm spezifizierte Folge von Aktivitäten betrachtet. Jede dieser Aktivitäten wiederum entspricht dem Aufruf eines transaktionalen Dienstes, der in einem der Komponentensysteme ausgeführt wird.

Das Ziel der vorliegenden Arbeit ist die Entwicklung einer umfassenden Systemunterstützung für die korrekte parallele und fehlertolerante Ausführung transaktionaler Prozesse in zusammengesetzten Systemen. Eine wesentliche Randbedingung dabei ist, diese Systemunterstützung möglichst generisch zu gestalten, um das Prinzip der transaktionalen Prozessverwaltung für die Entwicklung verteilter Anwendungen in den unterschiedlichsten Bereichen einsetzen zu können. Die vorliegende Arbeit betrachtet daher die folgenden Aspekte im Detail und stellt Lösungen für die damit assoziierten Probleme vor.

Zunächst wird eine Theorie der transaktionalen Prozessverwaltung entwickelt. Dabei werden Prozesse, die Transaktionen der unterliegenden Komponentensysteme als Basiseinheiten verwenden und kombinieren, als Transaktionen auf einer semantisch höheren Abstraktionsstufe betrachtet. Für das Modell der Prozessprogramme werden Konzepte des Modells flexibler Transaktionen angewandt. Dies ermöglicht die Spezifikation flexibler Fehlerbehandlungsstrategien innerhalb eines Prozessprogramms und erlaubt es, Kriterien für die inhärente Korrektheit einzelner Prozessprogramme aufzustellen. Darauf aufbauend werden Korrektheitskriterien für die korrekte parallele und fehlertolerante Ausführung solcher Prozessprogramme entwickelt. Zu diesem Zweck wird die vereinheitlichte Theorie der Mehrbenutzerkontrolle und Fehlererholung in erweiterter und verallgemeinerter Form angewandt. Diese Korrektheitskriterien berücksichtigen dabei die besondere Semantik der Dienstaufrufe in den einzelnen heterogenen und autonomen Komponetensystemen, da unter anderem nicht notwendigerweise jeder dieser Dienste als kompensierbar angesehen werden kann. Zudem wird der Stufenarchitektur und den daraus resultierenden Interaktionen Rechnung getragen indem, durch die Anwendung von Konzepten der Theorie zusammengesetzter Systeme, ein möglichst hoher Grad an Parallelität erlaubt wird.

Darauf aufbauend werden Protokolle entwickelt, welche die Implementierung eines Prozessmanagers ermöglichen. Dieser Prozessmanager erlaubt die dynamische Ausführung von Prozessprogrammen gemäß den Korrektheitskriterien der Theorie der transaktionalen Prozessverwaltung. Darüber hinaus beinhalten diese Protokolle weitergehende Konzepte zur flexiblen Optimierung von Prozessprogramm–Ausführungen durch die Berücksichtigung von Fehlerwahrscheinlichkeiten und Ausführungskosten einzelner Aktivitäten.

Schließlich wird das Prinzip der transaktionalen Prozessverwaltung auf nicht-transaktionale Komponentensysteme ausgedehnt. Obwohl die zugrunde liegende Theorie dezidierte Transaktionsunterstützung für jede einzelne Komponente fordert, ist dies in den Systemen, die in der Praxis anzutreffen sind, zumeist nicht gegeben. Daher wird der Begriff des transaktionalen Koordinationsagenten eingeführt. Koordinationsagenten erweitern einzelne Anwendungssysteme und stellen transaktionale Funktionalität für deren Dienste bereit. Damit werden die Voraussetzungen geschaffen, auch nicht-transaktionale Anwendungen in transaktionale Prozesse zu integrieren ohne das eigentliche Ziel, Prozesse als verteilte Anwendungen um transaktionale Ausführungsgarantien anzureichern, aufgeben zu müssen.

1 Introduction

"Wer sich über die Wirklichkeit nicht hinauswagt, der wird nie die Wahrheit erobern."

Friedrich Schiller,
Über die ästhetische Erziehung des Menschen

The increasing trend towards linking originally independent, stand-alone application systems by networks necessitates sophisticated support for the development of distributed applications spanning these systems. Such environments, consisting of distributed, heterogeneous, and autonomous application systems are referred to as composite systems. Applications on top of composite systems allow for the cooperation between and coordination of individual components by relating and combining services provided by these components, thereby implicitly integrating the latter at a higher semantical level. This kind of applications allows to materialize and automate the enforcement of arbitrary dependencies between these components which require that services are executed in a certain order.

The basic motivation of this thesis is to support such distributed applications over the components of composite systems by means of processes. The main contribution is the development of a sound theory of *transactional process management* which addresses the correct concurrent and fault-tolerant execution of processes. Each of these processes comprises activities which correspond to the invocation of transactional services within the components of a composite system. Distributed applications in composite systems are specified by process programs. Processes reflect the execution of process programs by a process manager. In a nutshell, processes can be considered as complex structured higher level transactions, encompassing transactions of the underlying subsystems, i.e., the components of a composite system, as basic units of execution.

The work presented in this thesis concentrates on a couple of salient features of transactional processes management. First, it considers the special semantics of activities. In particular, unlike traditional transactions, these activities may have different termination properties and may not necessarily be compensatable once they have been executed. Second, process programs consider sophisticated strategies for failure handling purposes, by allowing the specification of alternative executions. Most importantly, these alternative executions, together with the termination properties of single activities, induce constraints on the structure of correct process programs and allow for sophisticated correctness validation. Such correct process programs guarantee that a process terminates in a well-defined state, even in the presence of failures, thereby considerably extending and generalizing the "all-or-nothing" semantics of atomicity that can be found in conventional transactions. Third, when executing process programs in parallel, the process manager exploits ideas of the composite systems theory in that conflicting activities are treated by the weak conflict order so as to increase the degree of parallelism. Finally, concurrency control and recovery for transactional processes are treated uniformly within the same framework, by generalizing and applying the unified theory of concurrency control and recovery to transactional processes.

A further challenge met in this thesis is the practical realization of a process manager following the correctness criteria established by the theory of transactional process management. To this end, a dynamic scheduling protocol, termed process locking, has been developed (and has actually been implemented). Process locking takes into account the special semantics of transactional processes on top of the components of composite systems and jointly provides for correct concurrency control and recovery in the execution of these transactional processes. In addition, more detailed information on the execution cost of single activities can be exploited to apply interesting extensions to the basic process locking protocol (cost-based process scheduling) so as to minimize execution costs in multi-process executions.

Although the theory of transactional process management requires all services to be executed as part of processes to provide key transactional functionality, typical composite systems comprise both transactional and non-transactional components. Hence, a further goal of this thesis is to broaden the applicability of transactional process management by allowing arbitrary non-transactional components to take part in composite systems such that their services can be deployed within transactional processes. To this end, all these non-transactional application systems are wrapped by transactional coordination agents which enrich these systems and provide the transactional functionality required by a process manager.

The main benefit of all the above concepts is that they can be seamlessly integrated into a coherent whole. This leads to a powerful and comprehensive framework for the support of correct concurrent and fault tolerant applications on top of independent component systems by combining the theory of transactional process management, the dynamic scheduling protocol that has been designed based on the correctness criteria established by this theory, and the concept of transactional coordination agents that broadens the applicability of transactional process management to arbitrary components of composite systems. This framework then provides generic support for transactional processes and can be deployed in diverse environments. In effect, it has actually been successfully used in various applications, e.g., for subsystem coordination or for the development of distributed applications in electronic commerce.

Organization

The thesis is organized as follows. Chapter 2 presents a detailed motivation and highlights the contributions of the thesis on the basis of a practical example. Then, basic notions and notation are introduced and current trends in the area of transaction management, reflected and continued in transactional process management, are outlined (Chapter 3).

The above discussed goals are reflected in the three parts (illustrated in Figure 1.1) which form the core of this thesis. The first part, consisting of Chapters 4 and 5, is dedicated to the theoretical foundations of transactional process management. Chapter 4 first introduces the model of transactional process management. Then, Chapter 5 identifies appropriate correctness criteria for the concurrent and fault-tolerant execution of process programs.

The second part, which comprises Chapters 6 and 7, presents how the theoretical concepts can be implemented. In Chapter 6, we introduce process locking, a dynamic scheduling protocol that

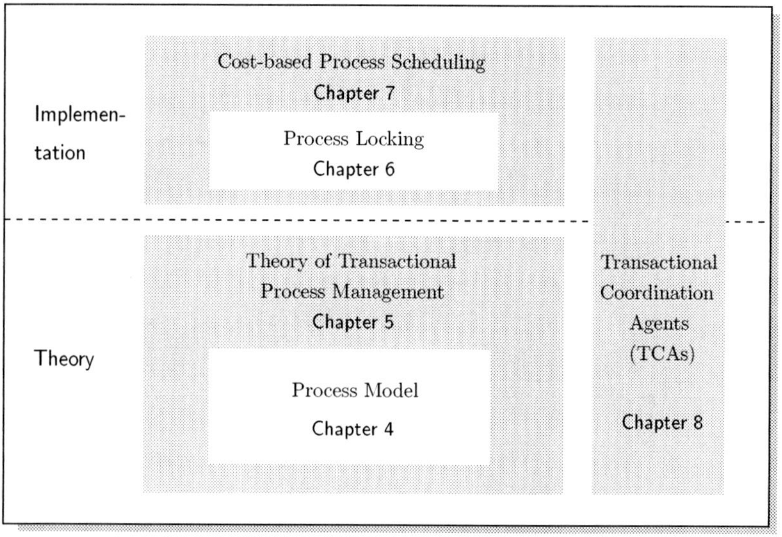

Figure 1.1: Structure of the Core Part of the Thesis

provides the basis for the implementation of a transactional process manager, thereby accounting for the specific notions of correctness of transactional processes. This core protocol can be refined, in case additional information on the execution costs of process activities is available, so as to exploit this information to determine the degree of concurrency within a process schedule on a per-process level (Chapter 7).

The third part, consisting of Chapter 8, addresses the application of transactional process management to arbitrary, non-transactional components. In here, the basic requirements of subsystems are outlined and their extension by transactional coordination agents is discussed.

In Chapter 9, we present a detailed and comprehensive discussion and classification of related approaches from advanced transaction models, transactional workflows, and multiagent systems for process support. Moreover, we compare these approaches to transactional process management.

Finally, Chapter 10 summarizes the contribution of this thesis and provides an outlook to open problems and potential future work in this area.

2 Motivation

"Ein edles Beispiel macht die schweren Taten leicht."

Johann Wolfgang von Goethe,
Paläophron und Neoterpe

Today's IT infrastructures are mostly characterized by highly specialized application and information systems. Large organizations, for instance, typically own a set of these independent, stand-alone applications, also called legacy systems, which can be considered as "islands of competence" in certain domains. Such environments have grown over time by successively improving and extending single applications. Although these islands are well-suited in case they can be operated independently, this paradigm reaches its limits when they have to be bridged, i.e., when cooperation among stand-alone systems is required.

Interconnectivity, however, is becoming increasingly important for several reasons. In terms of organizational structures, the trend towards globalization has as a consequence that the frontiers that existed when islands were developed disappear. Cooperation between as well as within organizations requires the cooperation and coordination of diverse application and information systems. This goes along with the demand for automating mostly manually controlled inter-application dependencies, i.e., induced by business processes, in order to increase efficiency. In terms of technical development, the proliferation of network technologies allows to link independent stand-alone computer systems and to integrate them into networked computing platforms. This, in turn, has made these primarily isolated islands globally available such that the technical burden for crossing their borders dissolves.

2.1 Distributed Applications by Means of Processes

For several reasons, the organizational and application-specific demands for more sophisticated applications, exceeding the complexity of existing systems by orders of magnitude, cannot be coped with physically integrating all functionality and all data into one single system. Most importantly, this would be far from being feasible since it would imply enormous effort and cost. Yet, viable practical solutions have to cope with existing systems as they are and establish means for cooperation and coordination without requiring their modification. Rather, comprehensive frameworks are needed which implicitly integrate existing application systems that were not necessarily designed for cooperation, by combining computational services provided by these systems into a coherent whole [AHST97a, AHST97b].

Such configurations consisting of independent stand-alone systems are referred to as composite systems [ABFS97]. Aside of a powerful execution environment for distributed applications in composite systems, i.e., applications on top of the individual component systems, appropriate support for modeling and developing such applications is an important aspect. In contrast to traditional application development based on a set of basic language primitives, this paradigm, also termed "megaprogramming" [WWC92], allows to build applications at a higher level of abstraction and has to cope with services as basic units of execution. Each component of a composite system is considered as black box. In particular, each component interacts with its environment only by the services it provides. Hence, composite systems induce a couple of problems that have to be taken into account, especially in terms of heterogeneity, distribution, and autonomy. Considerable efforts have been devoted to these problems and have resulted in middleware systems and frameworks for distributed application development and distributed processing, such as distributed object management platforms [OMG, OHE96, Box98], workflow management systems [GHS95, JB96, CHRW98], or process support systems [AM97, AHST97b, Hag99]. Distributed object management approaches like CORBA [OMG] or COM+ [Box98] provide support for distribution and, in the case of CORBA, also for heterogeneity by transparently hiding the location of single systems and the platform they are relying on. But, they nevertheless require enormous efforts for the implementation of applications over the components of a composite system which have to be coded explicitly in some high level programming language [Red96], although the basic computational services provided by the single components are already in place.

In contrast, workflow management systems [GHS95, JB96, CHRW98] or process support systems [AM97, AHST97b, Hag99], respectively, provide a more straightforward framework for the combination of services offered by the components of composite systems. While workflow management systems rather focus on business process support and office automation by integrating human and non-human tasks, process support systems provide a more general approach to distributed processing. Central to these systems is the notion of *process* as a well-defined, ordered sequence of service invocations which has to be executed in a controlled and coordinated manner [AHST97b]. Processes facilitate the development of higher level applications and are considered as a highly appropriate concept to express distributed applications over component systems in a generic way. In a nutshell, this approach allows to glue together different computational services of the components of a composite system and only requires to make application logic explicit by specifying flow of control and flow of data between them. Hence, process-based approaches are much more open compared to hardwired distributed applications and considerably exceed the latter in terms of extensibility, manageability, and maintenance. Process management then has to account for the control and the execution of processes, i.e., the invocation of services in given order.

For these reasons, processes impose a new paradigm for the development of truly distributed, large-scale information systems [AS96a, Alo97]. By their modular structure, induced by the underlying application systems that were glued together, these high-level information systems allow for new kinds of applications which could not be supported by any of the underlying subsystems, i.e., the components of a composite system, especially in terms of complexity and expressiveness. In addition, processes also support the bottom-up development of applications materializing and automating dependencies between originally stand-alone applications. Dependencies may span a broad spectrum and may range from rather simple data-driven dependencies to complex business processes. Data dependencies, e.g., induced by replicated or semantically related data of different applications, may require that, whenever an object is updated in one system, it also has analogously to be updated in another one so as to enforce a globally consistent state of the overall system. Typically, these dependencies were controlled manually, by explicitly invoking the appropriate services in the corresponding systems. Hence, processes allow these dependencies to be automated so as to enforce them without explicit intervention. The support for business processes makes use of similar ideas, i.e., the automation of steps that have to be executed in a coordinated manner to achieve some goal. In contrast to data-driven dependencies, however, business processes are far more complex. In particular, they require sophisticated tool support for specification, i.e., business process modeling [VB96]. Independent of the complexity of the resulting processes, the enforcement of data dependencies as well as the automation of business processes allows to seamlessly relate and combine originally independent applications, thereby providing appropriate support for the coordination of components of composite systems.

In the following example, we introduce a set of applications and the dependencies that exist between them in order to motivate the need for coordination by means of processes.

Example 2.1 *Consider the following scenario taken from computer integrated manufacturing (CIM): the IT infrastructure of a mechanical engineering company comprises several departments, each of which exploiting specialized information and application systems for their specific tasks to be accomplished. In order to construct and design a new product, various steps have to be executed, thereby requiring the cooperation of different departments and the coordination of their independent application systems. First, a computer aided design (CAD) has to be produced in the construction department, electronically supported by some CAD tool. Subsequently, information about the newly designed product has to be transferred in order to be stored within a central product data management (PDM) system. This data is then further exploited for testing purposes which takes place based on data stored in some material characteristics and norm database. This step again has to be initiated manually and is conducted by a separate department. After successful testing, a technical documentation has to be provided, yet based on additional applications and document repositories. The different steps to be accomplished for construction purposes along with the corresponding application services, the required data exchanges, and notifications are depicted in Figure 2.1. Obviously, when the diverse application service invocations are grouped into an appropriate process, all dependencies can be tracked automatically, thereby coordinating the diverse systems involved while freeing users from manual notifications and data transfers.* □

The scenario introduced in Example 2.1, although being presented at a rather coarse-grained level, reflects real-world problems and stems from a joint project conducted at ETH together with Schindler Ltd., a Swiss mechanical engineering company [SST98, MLZ+98]. In particular, it highlights the crucial open problems associated with processes as higher-level applications. First, process executions may be subject to various kinds of failures (e.g., due to erroneous single application services, failure-prone applications, communication failures, etc.) that have to be handled correctly. Moreover, when multiple processes are executed concurrently, the manipulation of and access to shared resources has to be controlled. Hence, transactional guarantees with respect to concurrency control and failure recovery for the execution of processes are required. But, due to the higher level semantics of processes, the application of the traditional criteria for isolation and atomicity may have to be generalized and to be adapted. Second, the provision of transactional execution guarantees for processes would require all components and all services they offer to be transactional in nature. Since this is, in general, not the case, appropriate mechanisms have to be applied in order to extend, yet not to modify, existing components and make them fit for the support of transactional execution guarantees for processes defined on top of them.

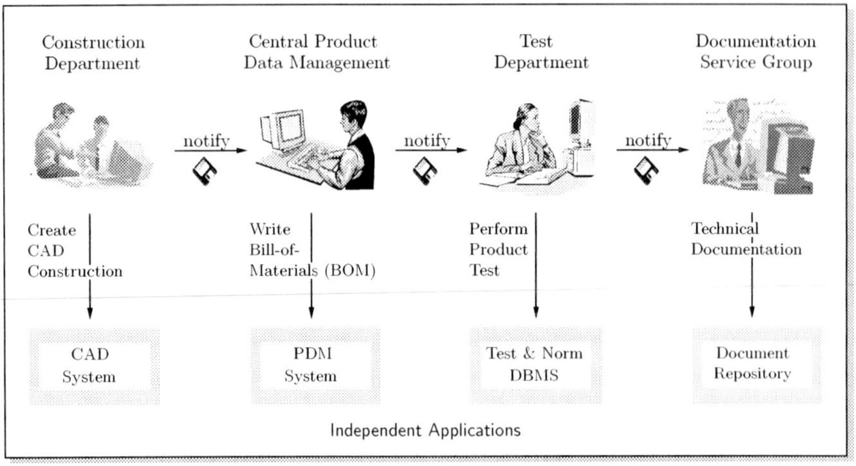

Figure 2.1: Dependencies between Applications in the Sample CIM Scenario

2.2 The Need for Higher Order Transactions

Process management considers the control and the execution of processes by some process support system. However, in order to establish processes as reliable concurrent and fault-tolerant applications, these systems have to be enhanced by transactional functionality. In particular, special effort is required so as to provide correct process executions even in the presence of failures and concurrency, the latter being present both within and between processes. Yet, it has be guaranteed that each process, once started, terminates in a well-defined state.

In the context of transaction support for distributed applications, dedicated middleware systems in the form of TP-monitors have been developed [GR93, BN97]. However, all these TP-monitors rely on two phase commit (2PC) protocols [BHG87] and again require applications to be coded explicitly. Due to the inherent complexity and the special semantics of processes, distributed transactions, based on 2PC, are far too restrictive. Hence, although TP-monitors provide for a clear semantics for concurrency control and failure recovery, they cannot be applied to processes. The reason being is that the blocking character of distributed transactions would impose draconian restrictions on the execution of processes which are, in general, characterized by their very long duration, exceeding those of traditional funds transfer or airline reservation transactions by orders of magnitude. This fact has been manifested early by Gray in his observations on the limitations of the traditional transaction model for complex, long-lived transactions [Gra81].

Other middleware approaches that have been proposed under the notion of transactional workflows [LSV95, RS95, WS97] closely rely on the concept of processes. However, they either impose strong restrictions on the black box systems and especially on their services that are combined by processes [WR92], or they provide only for a limited degree of concurrency by encompassing all steps of a process into a single distributed transaction [CD96]. Some approaches even totally neglect the problems induced by concurrency and provide only support for failure handling [Ley95]. Similarly, commercial workflow management systems also lack support for correct concurrency control [MQS99, Ora99].

Process management therefore has to be enriched by transactional functionality so as to provide transactional execution guarantees for processes, leading to the notion of *transactional process management* [SAS99]. This requires the combination of concepts from workflow management and process support as well as from distributed databases and transaction management. However, due to the special structure and semantics of processes and of the services of black box systems acting as individual process steps, processes are far more complex than traditional transactions.

In general, transactions at the level of processes have to cope with additional constraints that cannot be found in traditional transactions. In terms of recovery, the different steps within a process are radically different from operations within a transaction. Each step may have its own termination semantics. Moreover, due to the complexity of single steps, the restrictive "all-or-nothing" semantics of failure atomicity, although being well-suited for conventional, short transactions, is far too restrictive for processes since it would require that the effects of all process steps are undone once a failure occurs. Hence, there is an urgent demand for relaxing the notion of atomicity, e.g., by allowing alternative executions to be applied in case of failures, thereby preventing previous steps from being undone. These ideas have been introduced in the context of flexible transactions [ELLR90, MRSK92, ZNBB94]. Additionally, since all process steps are executed in other systems, the transactional properties of these underlying subsystems must be considered in order to be able to guarantee that each process terminates correctly. In terms of concurrency control, the flow of control introduced by processes as one of their basic semantic elements is much more complex than that of a flat transaction. A process may partially rollback its execution, it may, for instance, follow several alternatives for failure handling purposes, and it might reach a point (not the final one) where the outcome can only be to commit the process. Finally, also the layered configuration of systems in transactional process management has to be exploited so as to increase the degree of concurrency that can be achieved, by applying the weak conflict order of the composite systems theory [ABFS97, AFPS99a, AFPS99b] to processes. Yet, all these different aspects play a significant role and need to be taken into consideration when deciding how to interleave concurrent processes. In particular, all aspects have to be treated jointly, according to the ideas of the unified theory of concurrency control and recovery [AVA+94a, VYBS95, VHBS98]. For all these reasons, processes require several extensions, in terms of transaction models as well as in terms of the environment in which they are executed.

First, transactional execution guarantees have to be enforced by a dedicated component, a *process manager*, on top of transactional components in a composite system. This process manager brings the functionality of process support systems, especially the control and enactment of processes, into a transactional context. Hence, following the paradigm of externalizing database functionality [Sch96b, SZB+96], transactional execution guarantees for processes, i.e., *transactional processes* [SAS99], are provided outside of existing database systems, although the latter may act as individual components and the transactions they provide are the basic units of execution. This externalization of transaction management functionality, materialized in the form of a process manager, follows the philosophy of hyperdatabases (or higher order databases) [SBG+00] which are considered as databases sitting on top of databases and which manage objects being composed of database objects or, as in the case of processes, manage transactions being composed of transactions. Composite systems are well-suited environments in which the concepts of hyperdatabases and especially of higher-order transactions can be applied.

Second, aside of the above mentioned characteristics of processes as long-lived transactions and their special semantics, problems like heterogeneity, i.e., the non-uniformity of components, and distribution are inherent to these environments and prevent the application of traditional criteria for concurrency control and recovery. They rather demand the generalization and extension of traditional notions so as to make these applicable to transactional process management.

Third, processes, when being executed under transactional control, are well-suited for the development of reliable distributed applications [AS96a, Alo97]. However, due to the high level semantics, the correct specification of processes is, in general, difficult to achieve. Hence, a stringent requirement for guaranteeing only acceptable outcomes of concurrent process executions is that each process is provably correct. In particular, by allowing failure handling strategies to be integrated in the process model, users will be freed from manually dealing with unsuccessful outcomes of process executions. Thus, process modeling and development must be supported by a framework that allows for the specification of failure handling strategies in the same way as the regular execution of processes by means of control flow dependencies is specified. This, in turn, even increases the complexity of single processes and demands sophisticated correctness verification procedures to be applied prior to the execution of processes. For this reason, the provable correctness is a crucial feature of processes as high level transactions in hyperdatabase environments. This feature is, in a more general context, also a central aspect of one of the dozen information technology research challenges that have been identified by Jim Gray in his Turing Award lecture [Gra99]. The "Automatic Programmer" aims at facilitating the development of applications by re-using and/or customizing existing programs and applications in the form of an easy, albeit powerful high-level specification language which also supports reasoning about the characteristics of the newly generated applications based on the information about the components used.

By recalling the initial CIM example and the process we have previously identified, we show the need for sophisticated transaction support which extends and generalizes traditional transaction models, both in terms of failure handling and in terms of the correct interleaving of concurrent processes.

Example 2.1 (Revisited) *Although the process as depicted in Figure 2.1 comprises all dependencies that have to be enforced for construction purposes, it may not cover all possible cases. In particular, it does not consider any strategies for failure handling purposes. If, for instance, a failure during the test of a new product is detected, it is certainly not desirable to undo all previous work including the long running design activity. It is more appropriate to undo only the PDM entry and document the CAD drawing so as to facilitate later reuse. This documentation can be alternatively executed instead of the regular completion of the process, thereby allowing considerably more flexibility in terms of failure handling. The so-extended process is depicted in Figure 2.2 as part of the transactional process manager which is located on top of the underlying transactional subsystems, i.e., the components of the composite system. Assume that an additional process exists which controls the production of new products. Starting with the extraction of product data out of the PDM system, the production process includes all manufacturing steps from the ordering of materials to the production floor including the necessary scheduling and the creation of computerized numerical control (CNC) programs. In particular, it contains a dedicated step where the new product is actually fabricated; this step cannot be undone in case of subsequent failures. The concurrent execution of both processes as depicted in Figure 2.2 is important in practice since it considerably reduces the time to market of new products, especially in cases where production does not follow mass-production techniques but aims at customizing each one of the products to deliver. Thus, an important task of the process manager is to guarantee consistent interaction between processes. As illustrated in Figure 2.2, the*

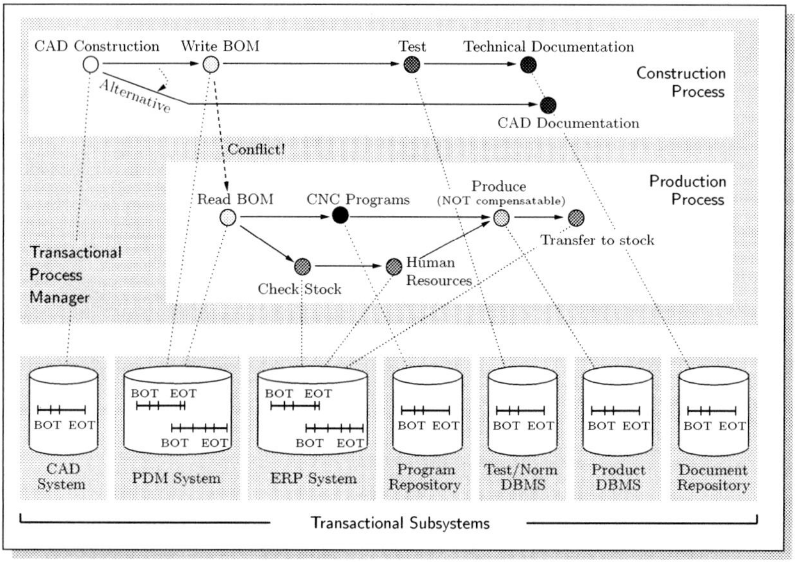

Figure 2.2: Concurrent and Fault-Tolerant Execution of Conflicting Processes in the CIM Scenario

only interaction between both processes takes place by the two services executed within the PDM system since they both operate on shared resources. For concurrency control purposes, imposing an order between these two services would be sufficient. However, when recovery has to be considered, further dependencies exist. As no inverse for the actual production exists, it must not be executed before the test terminated successfully. If the test fails, the PDM entry is compensated within the construction process and the BOM read by the production process is invalidated. Therefore, all effects of the production process would have to be undone, too. However, if production of parts is already performed, this would lead to severe inconsistencies as no valid construction and BOM of these parts exists. □

2.3 Transactional Processes On Top of Arbitrary Non-Transactional Applications

Composite systems comprise arbitrary subsystems. This requires that transactional process management has to deal with heterogeneity, distribution, and autonomy. In the context of enterprise application integration (EAI) [Lin99, Lin00], various tools, so-called adapters, have been introduced. These adapters, in turn, are part of comprehensive frameworks allowing the interconnection of dedicated application systems, extended by adapters. Most of these frameworks are based on message-oriented middleware (MOM) [OHE99] and focus on the reliable transfer of messages between applications. However, only few of them support the notion of processes and, if they do, lack support for transactional execution guarantees.

Transactional processes as higher order transactions, as we have considered them so far, have been based on the implicit assumption that all subsystems are transactional in nature such that the services invoked in these systems provide key transactional functionality. However, as a consequence of the inherent heterogeneity of composite systems, this functionality is not always present. Typical composite systems rather consist of arbitrary legacy applications. A mayor premise on the development of distributed applications by means of processes, we have identified earlier, is that all components have to be left unchanged. Therefore, special treatment is required for such non-transactional applications.

To this end, a *transactional coordination agent (TCA)* [SST98, SSA99] has to be provided for each of these non-transactional applications. Transactional coordination agents have to transparently hide the heterogeneity of individual subsystems they are tailored to so as to allow the process manager to invoke services in subsystems without having to deal with different data structures and application programming interfaces. Most importantly, however, TCAs have to extend and enrich subsystems, by gathering additional information on services that have been invoked, and to provide the transactional functionality required by transactional process management without modifying the underlying system. Hence, TCAs serve as sophisticated database wrappers for their subsystems and make them appear as being conform with the key transactional functionality needed for the correct concurrent and fault-tolerant execution of processes.

A crucial requirement from the point of view of the process manager is that all services invoked in the underlying systems are atomic in the sense that they are either executed completely or not at all. This avoids situations where a process ends up in an inconsistent state due to the undefined outcome of a non-atomic service within a subsystem. Atomicity is trivial in database systems but requires considerable extensions for non-transactional systems. In addition, when services are invoked concurrently, the underlying system has to guarantee that the failure of one service does not affect others being executed in parallel. Moreover, it has to be guaranteed that concurrent services are not arbitrarily interleaved; in particular, if the concurrent invocation of services is constrained by an order given by the process manager, this order must be respected. Again, this functionality has to be added by a TCA in case it is not provided by the underlying system.

Another important aspect is the support for sophisticated failure handling strategies at process level which includes the compensation of already terminated process steps, the execution of alternatives, and the repeated invocation of failed ones. The first task is, however, difficult to achieve if the associated subsystem does not provide an appropriate service for compensation purposes but can, in some cases, be accomplished with additional effort by a TCA.

So far, we have considered coordination in environments involving distributed, heterogeneous, and autonomous subsystems as being the result of some process that is invoked globally, i.e., at process manager level. However, in general, also local operations have to be coped with. Such local operations, when being performed by users which are not necessarily aware of side-effects, may violate consistency by introducing new data dependencies or making old ones disappear. A fundamental aspect of coordination is, thus, to keep track of such dependencies and reestablish overall consistency whenever necessary by invoking appropriate processes subsequently. Hence, processes act both as the core business logic and as the basis for coordination of all the subsystems involved. In order to observe local operations, the interaction patterns of a TCA with its underlying subsystem have to be far more complex than those induced by the exploitation of interfaces for the invocation of services. In particular, local operations have to be monitored such that those which violate global, inter-system dependencies can be identified [NSSW94a, Wun96]. Once such local

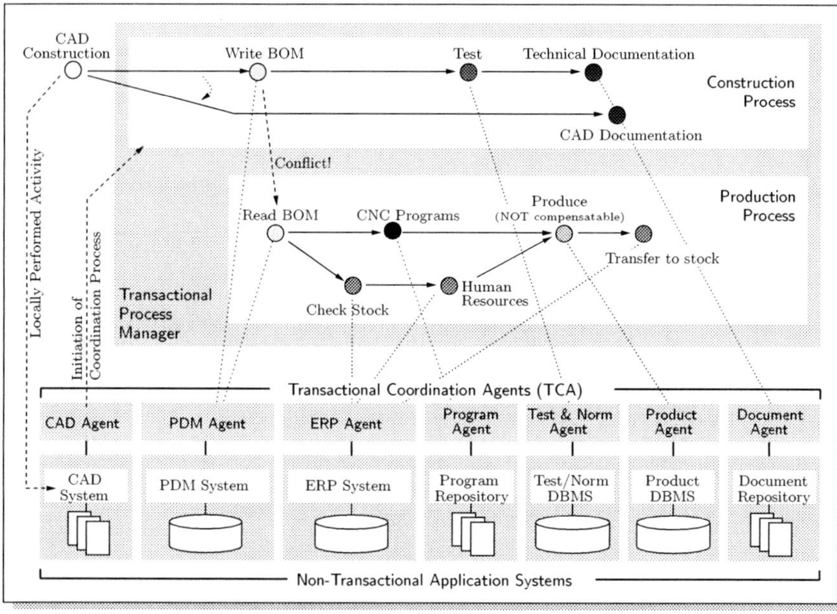

Figure 2.3: Extending the Functionality of Application Systems by Transactional Coordination Agents

operations have been detected, a TCA must be able to initiate corresponding processes that will then reestablish global consistency.

Example 2.1 (Revisited) *Not all subsystems of the initial CIM scenario provide transactional functionality. The document repository, for instance, is based on flat files and does not provide atomic services. Therefore, this task has to be accomplished by its associated TCA (the document agent). The PDM system, although being built on top of a database system, has to be extended since the required services for the compensation of BOM entries, i.e., their deletion, are missing. Yet other systems such as the test and norm database fully provide the required transactional guarantees for their services but nevertheless require appropriate coordination agents. The latter have to exploit the specific APIs of the subsystems to bridge heterogeneity so as to provide a common interface towards the process manager. The extension of all subsystems by transactional coordination agents is depicted in Figure 2.3. In general, a construction process must not necessarily be started explicitly by invoking the corresponding process but can also be triggered by the termination of a locally performed CAD construction. Hence, the CAD agent has to monitor local operations within the CAD system and to invoke, if necessary, the predefined construction process which then enforces the various dependencies that exist between the individual subsystems.* □

3 Transaction Management

"Es ist nichts furchtbarer anzuschauen als grenzenlose Tätigkeit ohne Fundament."

Johann Wolfgang von Goethe,
Maximen und Reflexionen

In this chapter, we present a brief but comprehensive survey of the literature from the field of transaction management. In particular, we focus on the concepts that are relevant for transactional processes. Hence, this chapter introduces the basic notions and notations that can be found in traditional, single-level transactions and the extensions of the traditional model which consider more complex systems and which allow more semantics associated both with the operations that appear in transactions as well as with the transactions themselves.

In Section 3.1, we summarize the basic principles and characteristics of the traditional transaction model and the correctness criteria that have been identified independently for concurrency control and recovery. In this model, the correct concurrent execution of transactions is based on the notion of conflicting operations. Information about conflicts are exploited by a scheduler to decide whether operations can be commuted so as to transform a schedule reflecting a parallel execution of transactions into a serial one.

However, commuting non-conflicting operations only solves the problem of correct concurrency control. For recovery purposes, additional effort is required. Yet, by considering not only commutativity but by providing a scheduler the necessary information that can be exploited to eliminate consecutive pairs of do/undo operations from a schedule, the consideration of correctness can be extended to jointly provide concurrency control and recovery. This is addressed by the unified theory of concurrency control and recovery which is presented in Section 3.2. In addition, the unified theory also provides a framework that allows to generalize the traditional transaction model by considering more complex, semantically rich operations.

The generalization of operations that appear in a schedule goes along with more complex systems in which transactions are executed, as opposed to the basic single-level systems. Work in the field of multilevel transactions has elaborated on the mapping of semantically rich operations, by level-by-level transformations, to the basic operations of the traditional model in the presence of concurrency. Extending the multilevel transaction approach which requires systems to be layered regularly, the composite systems theory considers arbitrarily layered configurations. In addition, by cautiously propagating conflicts along the different hierarchies and by imposing weaker restrictions on the parallelization of operations, the degree of concurrency can be considerably increased. Multilevel transactions and especially their extensions that led to the composite systems theory are presented in Section 3.3.

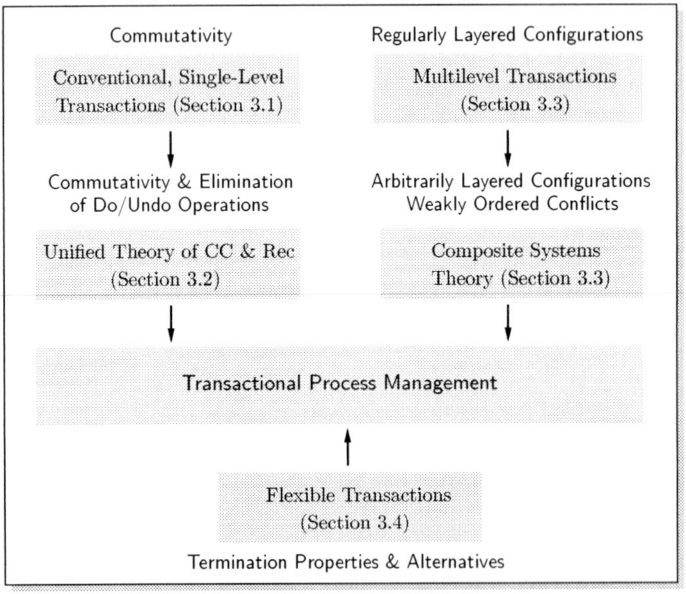

Figure 3.1: Influences of Basic Concepts and Models on Transactional Process Management

While all these approaches strongly influence the information a scheduler exploits for (jointly) determining correct concurrent and fault-tolerant executions, the transaction model implies rather rudimentary and limited failure handling strategies. Hence, adding alternative execution orders that can be effected in the case of failures and distinguishing different termination properties of operations considerably enriches the basic transaction model. These extensions not only allow more flexibility with respect to the recovery strategies that can be applied but they also induce a framework in which the correctness of single transactions can be proven. These ideas have been introduced in the context of the flexible transactions model which is presented in Section 3.4.

In Figure 3.1, all concepts presented in this chapter and their influences on our transactional process management approach are illustrated. First, the process model we consider seamlessly integrates and extends concepts from flexible transactions. Second, the execution of processes jointly provides correct concurrency control and recovery, thereby considering the special semantics of the basic units of execution and the layered systems that can be found in transactional process management.

3.1 Conventional, Single-Level Transactions

This section provides the basic concepts of transaction management and also points out the limitations of this conventional approach that are subject to improvements and extensions in advanced transaction models.

3.1.1 Basic Notions and Notations

A database, $\mathcal{DB}$, consists of a finite set $\mathcal{OBJ}$ of data objects. Access and manipulation of these objects is performed by elements from the finite set $\mathcal{OP}$ of operations. In conventional transaction management, $\mathcal{OP}$ consists of two types of operations: read and write[1] [Pap86]. An instance of a read operation[2] performed on object $x \in \mathcal{OBJ}$, in short $r(x)$, returns the value of x while an instance of a write operation, in short $w(x)$, changes the value of x in the database.

Semantically related and indivisible operations are grouped into *transactions*. Within a transaction T_i, a partial order $\ll_i$ (intra-transaction order) determines the execution order of all operations. This order is a temporal one such that for each pair of operations (o, o') with $o \ll_i o'$, operation o' is not allowed to be executed until o has successfully terminated. Moreover, all operations of T_i have to precede the final transaction operation with respect to $\ll_i$. This termination operation can be either *commit (C)* or *abort (A)* [BHG87]. While the commit C_i of a transaction T_i corresponds to its successful termination, the failure of T_i is denoted by the abort operation A_i. More formally,

Definition 3.1 (Transaction) *A transaction, T, is a tuple $(O, \ll)$ where:*

1. $O = \{o_1, o_2, \ldots, o_n\}$ *is a set of numbered operations with* $o_i \in \mathcal{OP}$ *for* $i \in \{1, \ldots, n-1\}$ *and* $o_n \in \{C, A\}$.
2. *The intra-transaction precedence order $\ll$ is a partial order with $\ll \subseteq (O \times O)$ where all operations must precede the termination operation:* $\forall\ o_i, i \neq n :\ o_i \ll o_n$. □

In general, multiple transactions are executed concurrently in a database system. Furthermore, since in this context failures (of single transactions as well of the database system itself) have to be considered, the following four guarantees, also known as ACID properties [HR83], enforcing the correct concurrent and fault-tolerant execution of transactions have been identified:

Atomicity Either all operations of a transaction are executed completely or none of them. In particular, all previously changes performed by a transaction T_i have to be undone in the case of its abort A_i.

Consistency A transaction has to transform a consistent database state into another consistent state, thus it does not violate the database's integrity constraints.

Isolation Even though transactions are executed concurrently, it has to appear to each transaction as if it is executed in isolation.

Durability Once a transaction is completed successfully (committed), its changes to the database state survive failures.

The isolation property is ensured by the concurrency control component of a database system, while the recovery component addresses atomicity and durability. This separation has led to two different criteria, one for concurrency control, and one for recovery.

[1] This model is therefore also known as *read/write model* in the literature.

[2] In the following, we use the notion of *operation* to denote special instances of operation types, i.e., as they appear within transactions and schedules, respectively.

3.1.2 Concurrency Control

The concurrent execution of transactions in a database system, where operations of different transactions may be interleaved, is reflected by a *schedule* S (sometimes, also the term *history* is used synonymously).

For certain operations, the order in which they are executed matters since this order influences the database state (the operations *conflict*). In the basic read/write model, two operations $o_i(x) \in T_i$ and $o_j(y) \in T_j$ of different transactions ($i \neq j$) conflict, if they are both on the same data object ($x = y$) and at least one of them is a write. Otherwise, if two operations do not conflict, they are said to commute. The above notion of conflict implies that among the four combinations of read and write operations, the following three denote pairs of conflicting activities: $(r_i(x), w_j(x))$, $(w_i(x), r_j(x))$, and $(w_i(x), w_j(x))$.

Definition 3.2 (Schedule) *A schedule, S, is a triple $(\mathcal{T}_S,\ \mathcal{O}_S,\ \ll_S)$ where:*

1. $\mathcal{T}_S = \{T_1, T_2, \ldots, T_m\}$ *is a set of transactions.*
2. $\mathcal{O}_S$ *is a set of numbered operations containing all numbered operations of all transactions of* $\mathcal{T}_S$ *with* $\mathcal{O}_S \subseteq \{o_{j_i} | \ (o_{j_i} \in O_j) \wedge (T_j \in \mathcal{T}_S)\}$.
3. $\ll_S$ *is a partial order between elements of* $\mathcal{O}_S$ *with* $\ll_S \subseteq \mathcal{O}_S \times \mathcal{O}_S$ *that contains the intra-transaction orders of all transactions of* $\mathcal{T}_S$, *that is* $\forall\ T_j \in \mathcal{T}_S : \ll_j \subseteq \ll_S$.
4. *All pairs of conflicting operations have to be ordered in S, that is, for all pairs o_{j_i} and o_{k_l} that do not commute, it must be true that either $o_{j_i} \ll_S o_{k_l}$ or $o_{k_l} \ll_S o_{j_i}$.* □

A *complete schedule* is a schedule where all transactions $T_i \in \mathcal{T}_S$ have terminated (either by C_i or A_i, respectively). The *committed projection* $C(S)$ of a schedule S is obtained from S by deleting all operations of transactions T_i that have not been committed ($C_i \notin \mathcal{O}_S$).

The criterion exploited to reason about the correctness of a schedule S and thus of the compliance of the previously identified isolation property is *conflict equivalence* of S to a *serial schedule* S_{ser} (which trivially follows the isolation requirement), leading to the notion of *conflict-preserving serializability*.

Definition 3.3 (Conflict Equivalence) *Two schedules, S and S' with $S = (\mathcal{T}_S,\ \mathcal{O}_S,\ \ll_S)$ and $S' = (\mathcal{T}_{S'},\ \mathcal{O}_{S'},\ \ll_{S'})$, are* conflict equivalent *if they are defined over the same set of transactions ($\mathcal{T}_S = \mathcal{T}_{S'}$), they contain the same set of operations ($\mathcal{O}_S = \mathcal{O}_{S'}$), and the order of all pairs of conflicting operations are the same in both $\ll_S$ and $\ll_{S'}$.* □

In a serial schedule S_{ser}, for all transactions $T_i, T_j \in \mathcal{T}_{S_{ser}}$, either all operations of T_i have to follow all operations of T_j, or all operations of T_j have to follow all operations of T_i.

Definition 3.4 (Conflict-Preserving Serializability (CPSR)) *A schedule $S = (\mathcal{T}_S,\ \mathcal{O}_S,\ \ll_S)$ is* conflict-preserving serializable (CPSR), *if its committed projection $C(S)$ is conflict equivalent to a serial schedule S_{ser}.* □

The dependencies imposed between conflicting operations of transactions are manifested in the serialization graph of a schedule:

Definition 3.5 (Serialization Graph SG(S)) *The* serialization graph *$SG(S)$ of a schedule $S = (\mathcal{T}_S,\ \mathcal{O}_S,\ \ll_S)$ is a directed graph whose nodes are the committed transactions $T_i \in \mathcal{T}_S$ and whose edges are all (T_i, T_k) for which a pair of conflicting operations o_{i_j}, o_{k_l} exists in S with $o_{i_j} \in O_i$, $o_{k_l} \in O_k$, and $o_{i_j} \ll_S o_{k_l}$.* □

The correctness of a schedule S with respect to CPSR can be checked based on the analysis of its serialization graph:

Theorem 3.1 (Serializability Theorem [Pap86]) *A schedule S is CPSR if and only if its serialization graph $SG(S)$ is acyclic.* □

In order to avoid unintuitive executions where a transaction T_i is completely executed before another transaction T_j in a schedule S but appears after T_j in an equivalent serial schedule, the CPSR criterion is further restricted leading to the notion of order-preserving serializability, also introduced in the literature as *strict serializability* [BSW79] and *serializability in the strict sense* [Pap79]:

Definition 3.6 (Order-Preserving Serializability (OPSR)) *A schedule, $S = (\mathcal{T}_S,\ \mathcal{O}_S,\ \ll_S)$, is* order-preserving serializable (OPSR) *if S is CPSR and if each pair of transactions T_i, T_k that are completely ordered in S (all operations o_{i_j} of T_i precede all operations o_{k_l} of T_k, $o_{i_j} \ll_S o_{k_l}$) are ordered in the same way in its conflict-equivalent serial schedule S_{ser}, that is $o_{i_j} \ll_{S_{ser}} o_{k_l}$.* □

Another restriction of CPSR that has shown to be of high practical relevance addresses the *order of commits* in a schedule [Raz92]. The commitment ordering criterion is also known as *strong recoverability* [BGRS91].

Definition 3.7 (Commitment Ordering (CO)) *A schedule, $S = (\mathcal{T}_S,\ \mathcal{O}_S,\ \ll_S)$, fulfills the property of* commitment ordering (CO), *if for each pair of conflicting operations o_{i_j}, o_{k_l} of transactions T_i, T_k that are committed in S (that is $o_{i_j} \in \mathcal{O}_S$, $T_i \in \mathcal{T}_S$, $o_{k_l} \in \mathcal{O}_S$, $T_k \in \mathcal{T}_S$, $C_i \in \mathcal{O}_S$, and $C_k \in \mathcal{O}_S$) with $o_{i_j} \ll_S o_{k_l}$ the following holds: $C_i \ll_S C_k$.* □

It has been shown that both the class OPSR of order-preserving schedules and the class CO of schedules fulfilling the commitment ordering property are proper subclasses of CPSR, the class of conflict-preserving schedules: CPSR $\supset$ OPSR [Pap79] and CPSR $\supset$ CO [Raz92].

3.1.3 Recovery

According to the atomicity property, all effects of transactions that are aborted have to be undone [Had83, Pap86, BHG87]. These effects do not only contain changes performed on data objects but also affect other transactions that have read values written by an aborted transaction. The latter dependency can be formalized using the notion of reads-from relation:

Definition 3.8 (Reads-From Relation) *Let $S = (\mathcal{T}_S,\ \mathcal{O}_S,\ \ll_S)$ be a schedule with $T_i \in \mathcal{T}_S$ and $T_k \in \mathcal{T}_S$. A transaction T_k* reads from *T_i if a data object $x \in \mathcal{OBJ}$ exists for which a write operation $w_{i_j}(x) \in O_i$ exists in S which is followed by a read operation $r_{k_l}(x) \in O_j$ in S, that is $w_{i_j}(x) \ll_S r_{k_l}(x)$ with $A_i \not\ll_S r_{k_l}(x)$, and all other write operations $w_{p_q}(x)$ in S either precede $w_{i_j}(x)$ in S ($w_{p_q}(x) \ll_S w_{i_j}(x)$) or succeed $r_{k_l}(x)$ in S ($r_{k_l}(x) \ll_S w_{p_q}(x)$).* □

Definition 3.9 (Recoverability (RC)) *A schedule $S = (\mathcal{T}_S,\ \mathcal{O}_S,\ \ll_S)$ is* recoverable (RC), *if for all pairs of transactions (T_i, T_k) with $T_i, T_k \in \mathcal{T}_S$ where T_k reads from T_i holds: when the commit C_k of T_k is in S ($C_k \in \mathcal{O}_S$), then it has to succeed the commit of T_i in S ($C_i \ll_S C_k$).* □

The recoverability criterion takes the above mentioned dependencies existing between transactions into account but also considers the durability property which implies that only effects of non-committed transactions can be undone. Although RC is the basic criterion guaranteeing correct recovery, its drawbacks include the fact that the abort of a single transaction in a schedule S may cause the cascading abort of other transactions. This is addressed by a more restrictive criterion:

Definition 3.10 (Avoiding Cascading Aborts (ACA)) *A schedule $S = (\mathcal{T}_S,\ \mathcal{O}_S,\ \ll_S)$* avoids cascading aborts (ACA) *when each transaction T_i only reads values that were written by committed transactions, that is for each pair of transactions (T_i, T_k), $T_i, T_k \in \mathcal{T}_S$ where T_i reads from T_k ($w_{k_l}(x) \ll_S r_{i_j}(x)$, $i \neq k$), $C_k \ll_S r_{i_j}(x)$ has to hold.* □

The further restriction that only committed values of data objects may be read or overwritten leads to the notion of *strict* schedules. When additionally all transactions that have read some data object must have either been committed or aborted before the value of this data object is allowed to be overwritten, schedules are said to be *rigorous* [BGRS91]. More formally,

Definition 3.11 (Strictness (ST)) *A schedule $S = (\mathcal{T}_S,\ \mathcal{O}_S,\ \ll_S)$ is* strict (ST), *if for each pair of conflicting operations $(w_{i_j}(x),\ o_{k_l}(x)) \in \mathcal{O}_S$ with $w_{i_j}(x) \ll_S o_{k_l}(x)$ and $i \neq j$ either $A_i \ll_S o_{k_l}(x)$ or $C_i \ll_S o_{k_l}(x)$ holds where $o_{k_l}(x) \in \{r_{k_l}(x),\ w_{k_l}(x)\}$.* □

Definition 3.12 (Rigorousness (RG)) *A schedule $S = (\mathcal{T}_S,\ \mathcal{O}_S,\ \ll_S)$ is* rigorous (RG), *if for each pair of conflicting operations $(o_{i_j}(x), o_{k_l}(x))$ with $o_{i_j}(x) \in \mathcal{O}_S$, $o_{k_l}(x) \in \mathcal{O}_S$, $o_{i_j}(x) \ll_S o_{k_l}(x)$, and $i \neq j$ either $A_i \ll_S o_{k_l}(x)$ or $C_i \ll_S o_{k_l}(x)$ holds where $o_{i_j}(x) \in \{r_{i_j}(x),\ w_{i_j}(x)\}$ and $o_{k_l}(x) \in \{r_{k_l}(x),\ w_{k_l}(x)\}$.* □

Bernstein et al. [BHG87] have shown that the class RC of recoverable schedules contains ACA, the class of schedules avoiding cascading aborts which, in turn, contains the class ST of strict schedules: RC $\supset$ ACA $\supset$ ST. Additionally, ST contains the class RG of rigorous schedules: ST $\supset$ RG [BGRS91].

3.1.4 Limitations of the Conventional Approach

In the classical database theory, recovery is treated independently from concurrency control. This is reflected in the fact that the classes (CPSR and RC), (CPSR and ACA), and (CPSR and ST) are pairwise incomparable. Only rigorousness, the most restrictive access to recovery, also provides correct concurrency control with respect to CPSR since for the class RG, the following holds: RG $\subset$ CPSR [BGRS91]. Breitbart et al. have additionally shown that RG is even contained in CO, that is RG $\subset$ CO [BGRS91]. But since RG is a proper subclass of CPSR, it is too restrictive in order to be exploited as correctness criterion for recovery and concurrency control. This drawback therefore necessitates the simultaneous consideration of both problems in a joint framework leading to a correctness criterion that is less restrictive than RG.

This need is even reinforced when no longer only simple read and write operations at page level are considered but semantically rich operations, such as, for instance, the deposit or withdraw of money from an account. In these more general cases, the notion of conflict and therefore also the notion of commutativity is more complex than in the traditional read/write model. The *unified theory of concurrency control and recovery* which can be applied both to the traditional read/write model and to semantically rich operations overcomes these problems by providing one single criterion for both problems.

Since these semantically rich operations finally have to be mapped to page level operations, concurrency control and recovery mechanisms have to be extended to layered systems where scheduling takes place at each level separately. Based on these ideas, even more general cases consisting of independent transactional components in arbitrarily layered configurations have to be included within a conceptual framework addressing transaction management in multilevel systems. The *composite systems theory* not only provides such a framework but also aims at maximizing the degree of parallelism that can be achieved.

As a consequence of considering more complex operations and also arbitrary configurations of independent systems, the traditional assumption that the effects of each operation of an active transaction can be undone at any point in time before the transaction commits must no longer be true. This, however, requires more sophisticated and more flexible strategies for recovery and failure handling than in the traditional approach. The model of *flexible transactions* considers operations that cannot be undone once they are executed and also encompasses flexible failure handling by alternative executions in order to cope with this kind of operations.

3.2 Bringing Isolation and Atomicity Together: The Unified Theory of Concurrency Control and Recovery

The arbitrary separation of correctness criteria for concurrency control and recovery leads to an unnecessarily restrictive class of schedules covering both problems. The aim of the *unified theory of concurrency control and recovery* [SWY93, AVA+94a, VYBS95, VHBS98] is therefore to identify and formalize more permissive classes of schedules accounting simultaneously for correct parallelization and fault tolerance. This is achieved by establishing a framework where recovery related operations are made explicit in a schedule which, in turn, allows to jointly reason about atomicity and serializability.

3.2.1 Unified Theory in the Read/Write Model

One aspect of recovery is to undo changes that have been effected by aborted transactions. In the basic model introduced in Section 3.1.1, only two types of operations, read and write, were allowed. Since a read operation does not change the database state, nothing has to be undone for it when its corresponding transaction aborts. Therefore, the inverse $r^{-1}(x)$ of a read operation $r(x)$ is the null operation (called λ in the following). However, in the case of a write, the effects of this operation have to be wiped out (e.g., by restoring the before image of the associated data object), thus effecting another write operation in the database. This is reflected in the commutativity matrix depicted in Table 3.1: while $r^{-1}(x) = \lambda$ commutes with all other operations, the inverse $w^{-1}(x)$ has the same commutativity characteristics than its corresponding regular operation $w(x)$.

The basic idea of the unified theory of concurrency control and recovery [SWY93, AVA+94a, AVA+94b] is to replace each abort A_i in a schedule S by the operations that are required for

	read	write	read^{-1}	write^{-1}
read	+	−	+	−
write	−	−	+	−
read^{-1}	+	+	+	+
write^{-1}	−	−	+	−

Table 3.1: Commutativity Matrix of Do and Undo Operations in the Read/Write Model

recovery purposes. These undo operations have to be in reverse order of the corresponding regular operations. In order to cope with system crashes where all active transactions (those transactions that are neither committed nor aborted in a schedule S) have to be aborted, a set-oriented *group abort* $A(T_{i_1}, \ldots, T_{i_n})$ is introduced [AVA+94a] with $T_{i_1}, \ldots, T_{i_n} \in \mathcal{T}_S$. This group abort indicates that each transaction from $\{T_{i_1}, \ldots, T_{i_n}\}$ is to be aborted and that all these aborts are performed concurrently. The schedule $\tilde{S}$ that results from the replacement of all aborts by the associated undo operations is called *expanded schedule* [SWY93, AVA+94a]:

Definition 3.13 (Expanded Schedule $\tilde{S}$) *Let $S = (\mathcal{T}_S, \mathcal{O}_S, \ll_S)$ be a schedule. The* expansion, *or* expanded schedule, *$\tilde{S}$ of S is a triple $(\tilde{\mathcal{T}}_S, \tilde{\mathcal{O}}_S, \tilde{\ll}_S)$ where:*

1. *$\tilde{\mathcal{T}}_S$ is a set of transactions with $\tilde{\mathcal{T}}_S = \mathcal{T}_S$.*
2. *$\tilde{\mathcal{O}}_S$ is a set of operations which is derived from $\mathcal{O}_S$ in the following way:*
   (a) *For each transaction $T_i \in \mathcal{T}_S$, if $o_i \in \mathcal{O}_S$ and o_i is not an abort operation, then $o_i \in \tilde{\mathcal{O}}_S$.*
   (b) *Active transactions are treated as aborted transactions by adding a group abort $A(T_{i_1}, \ldots, T_{i_k})$ at the end of S where $T_{i_1}, \ldots, T_{i_k}$ are all active transactions in S.*
   (c) *For each aborted transaction $T_j \in \mathcal{T}_S$ and for every operation $o_j(x) \in \mathcal{O}_S$, there exists an inverse (backward) operation $o_j^{-1}(x) \in \tilde{\mathcal{O}}_S$ which is used to undo the effects of the corresponding forward operation. An abort operation $A_j \in \mathcal{O}_S$ is changed to $C_j \in \tilde{\mathcal{O}}_S$. Operation $A(T_{i_1}, \ldots, T_{i_k})$ is replaced with a sequence of $C_{i_1}, \ldots, C_{i_k}$.*
3. *The partial order, $\tilde{\ll}_S$, is determined as follows:*
   (a) *For every two operations $o_i \in \mathcal{O}_S$ and $o_j \in \mathcal{O}_S$, if $o_i \ll_S o_j$ in S, then $o_i \tilde{\ll}_S o_j$ in $\tilde{S}$.*
   (b) *If $A(T_{i_1}, \ldots, T_{i_k}) \in \mathcal{O}_S$, then every two conflicting undo operations of transactions from the set $\{T_{i_1}, \ldots, T_{i_n}\}$ are in $\tilde{S}$ in a reverse order of the two corresponding forward operations in S.*
   (c) *All undo operations of every transaction T_i that does not commit in S follow the transaction's original operations and must precede C_i in $\tilde{S}$.*
   (d) *Whenever $o_n \ll_S A(T_{i_1}, \ldots, T_{i_k}) \ll_S o_m$ and some undo operation o_j^{-1} with $j \in \{i_1, \ldots, i_k\}$ conflicts with o_m (o_n), then it must be true that $o_j^{-1} \tilde{\ll}_S o_m$ ($o_n \tilde{\ll}_S o_j^{-1}$).*
   (e) *Whenever $A(\ldots, T_i, \ldots) \ll_S A(\ldots, T_j, \ldots)$ for some $i \neq j$, then for all conflicting undo operations of T_i and T_j, o_i^{-1} and o_j^{-1}, it must be true that $o_i^{-1} \tilde{\ll}_S o_j^{-1}$.* □

Once a given schedule is expanded, reasoning about correct concurrency control and recovery can be performed based on the *reducibility* of the expanded schedule [SWY93, AVA+94a]:

Definition 3.14 (Reducibility (RED)) *A schedule* $S = (\mathcal{T}_S, \mathcal{O}_S, \ll_S)$ *is* reducible (RED), *if its expanded schedule* $\tilde{S} = (\tilde{\mathcal{T}}_S, \tilde{\mathcal{O}}_S, \tilde{\ll}_S)$ *can be transformed into a serial schedule by applying the following two transformation rules in arbitrary order a finite number of times:*

1. **Commutativity Rule:** *If two operations* o_i *and* o_j *do not conflict in* $\tilde{S}$, *and there is no* o_k *such that* $o_i \tilde{\ll}_S o_k \tilde{\ll}_S o_j$, *then the ordering* $o_i \tilde{\ll}_S o_j$ *can be replaced by* $o_j \tilde{\ll}_S o_i$.

2. **Undo Rule:** *If* $o_i(x)$ *and* $o_i^{-1}(x)$ *are in* $\tilde{\mathcal{O}}_S$ *with* $o_i(x) \tilde{\ll}_S o_i^{-1}(x)$ *and there is no* $o_j \in \tilde{\mathcal{O}}_S$ *such that* $o_i(x) \tilde{\ll}_S o_j \tilde{\ll}_S o_i^{-1}(x)$, *then* $o_i(x)$ *and* $o_i^{-1}(x)$ *can be removed from the expanded schedule* $\tilde{S}$. □

Unfortunately, the class RED of reducible schedules is not prefix-closed. In order to make the reduction technique applicable in dynamic scheduling, the following more restrictive criterion has been introduced [SWY93, AVA+94a]:

Definition 3.15 (Prefix-Reducibility (PRED)) *A schedule* $S = (\mathcal{T}_S, \mathcal{O}_S, \ll_S)$ *is* prefix-reducible (PRED), *if every prefix of S is reducible.* □

Since PRED, the class of prefix-reducible schedules, is a proper subclass of CPSR-RC (which is the class of schedules that are both conflict-preserving serializable and recoverable), obviously only correct schedules with respect to both concurrency control and recovery are allowed. Additionally, PRED is more permissive than the traditional rigorousness criterion and also even more permissive than the class CPSR-ST of schedules that are both conflict-preserving serializable and strict, that is: CPSR-RC $\supset$ PRED $\supset$ CPSR-ST $\supset$ RG [SWY93].

However, prefix-reducibility is based on the notion of expanded schedule and therefore very complex to evaluate. This drawback is addressed by the criterion *serializability with ordered termination* proposed in [AVA+94a]:

Definition 3.16 (Serializability with Ordered Termination (SOT)) *A schedule* $S = (\mathcal{T}_S, \mathcal{O}_S, \ll_S)$ *is* serializable with ordered termination (SOT), *if S is serializable (CPSR), and for every two transactions* $T_i \in \mathcal{T}_S$, $T_j \in \mathcal{T}_S$ *and every two operations* $o_i \in \mathcal{O}_S$ *and* $o_j \in \mathcal{O}_S$ *such that* $o_i \ll_S o_j$, A_i *does not precede* o_j *in S,* o_i *is in conflict with* o_j, *and* o_i^{-1} *is in conflict with* o_j, *the following conditions hold:*

1. *If* T_j *commits in S, then it commits after* T_i *commits* ($C_i \ll_S C_j$)

2. *If* o_i^{-1} *and* o_j^{-1} *are in conflict, and* T_i *aborts in S then either it aborts after* T_j *aborts* ($A_j \ll_S A_i$) *or S contains a group abort* $A(\ldots, T_i, \ldots, T_j, \ldots)$. □

In [AVA+94a], it has been shown that PRED and SOT, the class of schedules that are serializable with ordered termination, are equivalent in the traditional read/write model: PRED $\equiv$ SOT. That is, SOT can be exploited as basis for the definition of protocols for dynamic scheduling guaranteeing both transaction atomicity and serializability in a uniform way.

A related approach towards a unified treatment of concurrency control and recovery proposed by Beeri [Bee00] is based on a notion of schedule that considers all operations as they occur, thus it encompasses not only regular operations but also the recovery related ones. The advantage of this approach is that it avoids the complex expansion of a schedule. It exploits, however, the same

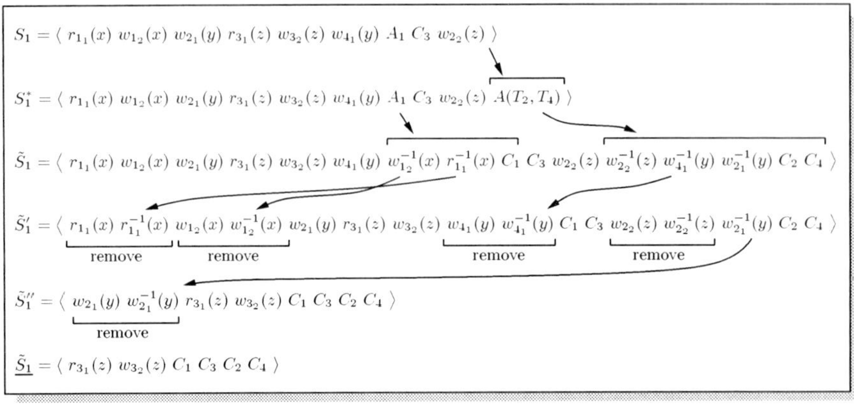

Figure 3.2: Process of Expanding (Schedule $\tilde{S}_1$) and Reducing (Schedule $\underline{\tilde{S}_1}$) Schedule S_1 of Example 3.1

reduction rules for permutation and elimination of operations (see Definition 3.14) than the original unified theory does.

Lechtenbörger and Vossen extend the unified theory in another direction: In [LV00], a family of strategies for write operations (update strategies) is considered, where each of these strategies leads to different commutativity characteristics and thus, also to different unified correctness criteria.

Example 3.1 *Consider schedule* $S_1 = \langle\ r_{1_1}(x)\ w_{1_2}(x)\ w_{2_1}(y)\ r_{3_1}(z)\ w_{3_2}(z)\ w_{4_1}(y)\ A_1\ C_3\ w_{2_2}(z)\ \rangle$ *depicted in Figure 3.2. Since transactions* T_2 *and* T_4 *are active, a group abort* $A(T_2, T_4)$ *has to be added to* S_1 *leading to the schedule* S_1^**. Then, each abort operation (that is, the group abort* $A(T_2, T_4)$ *and* A_1*) has to be expanded by adding the associated undo operations to* S_1^* *leading to the expanded schedule* $\tilde{S}_1$*. By applying the commutativity rule, the following pairs of do/undo operations can be brought in consecutive order:* $(r_{1_1}(x), r^{-1}_{1_1}(x))$, $(w_{1_2}(x), w^{-1}_{1_2}(x))$, $(w_{4_1}(y), w^{-1}_{4_1}(y))$ *and then be eliminated with respect to the undo rule (note that* $r^{-1}_{1_1}(x) = \lambda$*; therefore, it commutes with all other operations). In this newly emerged schedule, also* $w_{2_1}(x)$ *and* $w^{-1}_{2_1}(x)$ *can be removed after they have been brought in adjacency leading to the reduced schedule* $\underline{\tilde{S}_1}$*. Since* $\underline{\tilde{S}_1}$ *is serial, the initial schedule* S_1 *is in class RED. By analyzing each prefix of* S_1*, it is furthermore possible to show that* S_1 *is also in PRED. However, according to the equivalence of PRED and SOT, it is also possible to show that* S_1 *fulfills the SOT properties which then implies also the conformance with respect to PRED in a less complex and less costly way.* □

3.2.2 Unified Theory for Semantically Rich Operations

In the traditional read/write model, it is intuitively clear which operations (including inverses) do commute and which do conflict, leading to the commutativity matrix depicted in Table 3.1. When more complex operations settled at a higher semantical level than read or write operations of data objects are considered, this is no longer true [VYBS95, Has96, HS96, VHBS98]. In this general case, reasoning about commutativity is based on the return values of single operations [VHBS98]:

Definition 3.17 (Effect-Freedom) *Let $\sigma = \langle o_i \; o_j \ldots o_n \rangle$ be a sequence of operations from $\mathcal{OP}$. The sequence σ is* effect-free *if, for all possible sequences of operations α and ω from $\mathcal{OP}$, the return values of α and ω in the concatenated operation sequence $\langle \alpha \; \sigma \; \omega \rangle$ are the same as in the operation sequence $\langle \alpha \; \omega \rangle$.* □

Intuitively, two operations commute if their order does not affect any return value of other operations in all possible operation sequences. More formally,

Definition 3.18 (Commutativity) *Two operations $p \in \mathcal{OP}$ and $q \in \mathcal{OP}$* commute *if for all possible sequences of operations α and ω from $\mathcal{OP}$, the return values of all operations in the operation sequence $\langle \alpha \; p \; q \; \omega \rangle$ are the same as in the operation sequence $\langle \alpha \; q \; p \; \omega \rangle$.* □

Based on Definition 3.18, two operations o_i and o_j are said to be *in conflict* if they do not commute. However, in the general case when considering arbitrary semantically rich operations, the equivalence between SOT and PRED no longer holds.

Theorem 3.2 (PRED $\subseteq$ SOT [VHBS98]) *Every prefix-reducible schedule is also serializable with ordered termination, that is PRED $\subseteq$ SOT.* □

Out of the variety of possible commutativity relations, the following two classes, which differ in the symmetry of commutativity behavior between a forward operation and the related backward operation, have been identified since they encompass the most relevant cases found in practice: the symmetric, *perfect*, commutativity relation and a special case of an asymmetric variant, called *normal* commutativity. The differentiation of these two classes then allows for a refinement of the relationship between the classes PRED and SOT when considering semantically rich operations [VHBS98].

Definition 3.19 (Normal Commutativity) *A commutativity relation is* normal, *if for every two operations $p \in \mathcal{OP}$ and $q \in \mathcal{OP}$ the following holds: if p does not commute with q and p^{-1} is not the null operation λ, then p^{-1} does not commute with q. If, in addition q^{-1} is not the null operation λ, then p^{-1} also does not commute with q^{-1}.* □

Definition 3.20 (Perfect Commutativity) *A commutativity relation is* perfect, *if for every two operations $p \in \mathcal{OP}$ and $q \in \mathcal{OP}$ the following holds: if p commutes with q, then p^{α} has to commute with q^{β} for all possible combinations of $\alpha, \beta \in \{-1, 1\}$ or, if p and q do not commute, then p^{α} does not commute with q^{β} for all possible combinations of $\alpha, \beta \in \{-1, 1\}$ with the exception of λ as an inverse operation commuting with everything.* □

Example 3.2 *Consider a counter implemented in a database by the operations $Incr(x)$, $Reset(x)$, $Retrieve(x)$, and the associated inverse operations $Incr^{-1}(x, y)$, $Reset^{-1}(x, y)$, $Retrieve^{-1}(x)$ with the following semantics [VHBS98]: if $x > 0$, then $Incr(x)$ increments data object x and returns 1, otherwise x is left unchanged and the return value is 0. The inverse operation $Incr^{-1}(x, y)$, where y is the return value of the corresponding forward operation, decrements x if $y \neq 0$, otherwise it does nothing; in any case, the return value is 0. $Reset(x)$ sets the value of x to 1 and returns the old value of x, $Reset^{-1}(x, y)$ sets the value of x to y which is the old value that has been reset by the forward operation. $Reset^{-1}(x, y)$ always returns 0. Finally, $Retrieve(x)$ returns the*

	Incr	Reset	Retrieve	Incr^{-1}	Reset^{-1}	Retrieve^{-1}
Incr	+	−	−	−	−	+
Reset	−	−	−	−	−	+
Retrieve	−	−	+	−	−	+
Incr^{-1}	−	−	−	+	−	+
Reset^{-1}	−	−	−	−	−	+
Retrieve^{-1}	+	+	+	+	+	+

Table 3.2: Commutativity Matrix for Semantically Rich Operations of Example 3.2

current value of x whereas its inverse $Retrieve^{-1}(x)$ is a λ operation that has no return value. The commutativity matrix of these operations is depicted in Table 3.2. Commutativity in this example is not perfect, since, for instance, two increment operations on the same data object, $Incr_1(x)$ and $Incr_2(x)$, commute while an increment operation does not commute with an inverse increment, that is, $Incr_1^{-1}(x, y)$ and $Incr_2(x)$ conflict. However, it can be shown that commutativity in this example is at least normal. □

Theorem 3.3 ([VHBS98]) *Let a commutativity relation be either normal or perfect. Then the two classes PRED and SOT coincide.* □

According to Definition 3.20, commutativity in the traditional read/write model is perfect and thus, the equivalence between SOT and PRED holds.

Example 3.3 *Consider again the semantically rich operations Incr, Reset, and Retrieve of Example 3.2. Let $S_2 = \langle\ Incr_2(x)\ Reset_1(y)\ Incr_3(y)\ Incr_1(x)\ Retrieve_2(x)\ A_1\ Reset_3(x)\ C_2\ C_3\ \rangle$ be a schedule defined on these operations. Since we already identified the commutativity relation to be normal, the criterion SOT can be exploited to determine the correctness of S_2. Although S_2 is serializable, it is not correct with respect to both concurrency control and recovery. Consider, for instance, the two conflicting operations $Reset_1(y)$ and $Incr_3(y)$ with $Reset_1(y) \ll_{S_2} Incr_3(y)$. Since $Reset_1^{-1}(y, v)$ and $Incr_3(y)$ as well as $Reset_1^{-1}(y, v)$ and $Incr_3^{-1}(y, w)$ pairwise do also not commute, according to Definition 3.16.2, the abort of T_1 would have to be preceded by the abort of T_3, or both would have at least to be performed jointly by $A(T_1, T_3)$. Therefore, $A_1 \ll_{S_2} C_3$ causes a violation of the SOT criterion.* □

The idea of making abort-related operations explicit in a schedule has also been discussed in [GM83]. The model used there, albeit not explicitly introducing the notion of semantically rich operations, allows basic read/write operations to be grouped into so-called steps. In addition, each step is assumed to have a counter-step which semantically undoes its effects, similar to the notion of inverses in the context of semantically rich operations. However, and in contrast to the unified theory for semantically rich operations, the framework established in [GM83] does not consider recovery-related operations, i.e., counter-steps, in the presence of concurrency, thus it does not provide a joint criterion for both problems but rather sticks to the traditional way of treating both aspects independently.

3.3 Scheduling in Layered Systems: From Multilevel Transactions to Composite Transactions

Layered systems supporting semantically rich operations have, in general, to map each of these operations successively and in a level-by-level manner to basic read/write operations at page level. This leads to the notion of nested transactions which define a tree of transactions whose subtrees are either flat transactions, thus consist of basic operations, or are again nested transactions (called subtransactions). Only the leaf nodes of such a nested transaction tree consist of basic operations. In terms of the visibility of subtransactions within a nested transaction, a differentiation between closed nesting and open nesting is made. Closed nested transactions [Mos85, Mos87] restrict the visibility of each subtransaction completely to the scope spanned by its top-level transaction, i.e., each commit of a subtransaction releases its effects to its parent in the transaction tree, but neither to its concurrent siblings nor to the outside, thereby considerably limiting the degree of parallelism. Only when the top-level transaction decides to commit, the results of all its subtransactions are finally committed and made globally available.

Reducing the restrictions imposed on the visibility of subtransactions leads to the notion of *open nested transactions* introduced by Gray [Gra81] and later refined and generalized by Weikum and Schek [WS92]. In this model, the drawbacks of closed nesting are overcome in that subtransactions are allowed to commit and thus to make their effects available —not only to concurrent siblings but also to concurrent nested transactions— prior to the commit of the associated top-level transaction. The price that has to be paid for this gain in concurrency is the consideration of compensation for recovery purposes. Since subtransactions are committed as early as possible leading to a relaxation of the isolation property, an abort of the top-level transaction necessitates all its effects to be (semantically) undone [Gra81, KLS90] in order to enforce the property of atomicity for the complete open nested transaction. To this end, a compensating subtransaction has to be available for each regular subtransaction.

3.3.1 Multilevel Transactions

The most important application of nested transactions, i.e., of the open nesting paradigm, can be found in layered systems offering operations at all different levels of abstraction. Each operation in such layered systems is recursively implemented by a set of operations of the next lower level (encompassed within a subtransaction) down to the leaf level which consists of basic read/write operations on pages. *Multilevel transactions* [BBG$^+$83, Wei87, BSW88, Wei88, BBG89, Wei91] address these kinds of layered systems and consider scheduling at all different layers simultaneously. Compared with the general notion of arbitrary nested transactions, subtransactions of multilevel transactions have special semantical relations to their parent transactions due to the regular, level-by-level composition of operations. The concept of composition of operations in multilevel transactions is illustrated in Example 3.4.

Example 3.4 *Consider the set of semantically rich operations that has been introduced in Example 3.2 of Section 3.2.2. A Reset operation on a counter object, for instance, is mapped to the two SQL statements Select and Update at tuple level which are again mapped to reads and writes of the pages this tuple and its associated indices are located. Figure 3.3 depicts a multilevel transaction* T_1 *consisting of a Retrieve(*$counter_A$*) and a Reset(*$counter_B$*) operation.* □

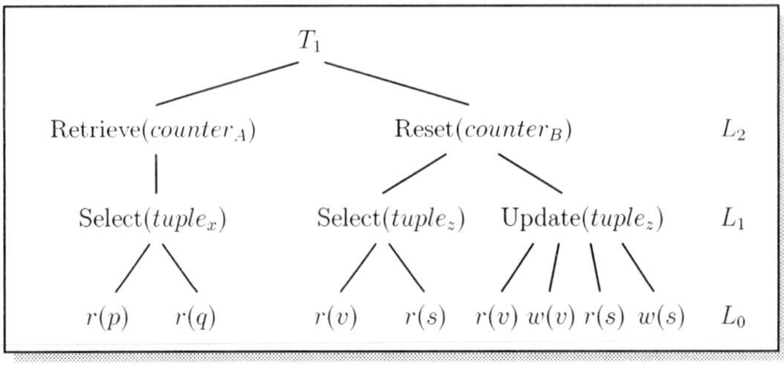

Figure 3.3: Multilevel Transaction T_1 Spanning Three Levels L_2 – L_0

In such multilevel systems, a scheduler is assigned to each layer, that is to each combination of two adjacent levels. A basic prerequisite for all these schedulers is that commutativity between operations at each layer is given (following Definition 3.18 addressing commutativity for semantically rich operations). Obviously, all different schedulers in a layered system are not independent. The question that arises therefore is how to apply and how to generalize the traditional (single-level) notions of correctness, especially those of conflict-preserving serializability, to multilevel systems.

Beeri et al. propose *order preservation* as handshaking mechanism between schedulers in a layered system [BBG+83, BBG89]. To this end, the order on the root transactions has to be respected at each level in an equivalent serial execution. Furthermore, the order between operations at each level must always be compliant with the order between the associated transactions of the next higher level (downward order compatibility). The approach followed is very general in nature since it allows that subtransactions of the same level have different depths. A given multilevel schedule, i.e., a set of schedules, each of them corresponding to one layer, can be proven correct by successively applying reduction techniques from the leaves up to the root level while preserving the root order. This so-called "reduction of fronts" first encompasses the permutation of leaf operations in order to bring their parents in a serial order. The notion of front denotes all nodes within the transaction tree with the same distance from the root level. The permutation step is followed by the pruning of subtrees of the next higher level, that is the replacement of subtransactions by their associated operations.

The approach proposed by Weikum [Wei87, Wei88, Wei91] makes use of the regular composition of operations by imposing the additional constraint that whenever two operations conflict at one level, there must at least be one pair of conflicting operations between both subtransactions at the next lower level. An additional requirement is that all transaction trees have the same depth. The criterion exploited for correct concurrency control is *conflict preservation*; if this holds for each layer, a multilevel schedule is called *level-by-level serializable (LLSR)*. To support this criterion, an order $\lesssim$, called quasi-order, is introduced which captures the order of conflicting operations. This order is propagated from the leaf level up to the root level such that $\lesssim$ encompasses not only all conflicts of a given level but also all conflicts that are observed between subtransactions and thus reflects the composition of schedules.

Both approaches have in common that the analysis of a multilevel schedule is performed bottom-up. Moreover, they require conflicting operations at each level to be ordered which, in the context of multilevel transactions, leads to a total separation of the subtrees associated with these operations.

Due to the exploitation of the open nested paradigm allowing subtransactions to commit prior to the commit of their root transactions, recovery of multilevel transactions does not only encompass undo operations but has also to consider compensating subtransactions. This is the case, for instance, in layered systems applying two phase locking protocols at record level while using only short locks ("latches") for the synchronization of page level operations (e.g., System R [ABC+76, GMB+81], or ARIES [MHL+92]). The joint consideration of concurrency control and recovery for multilevel transactions now requires an extension of the traditional unified theory in order to perform expansion (by undo operations and compensation) and reduction techniques at all different levels simultaneously [Has96], leading to the notion of *multilevel prefix-reducibility (MLPRED)*.

3.3.2 Composite Transactions

Composite systems consist of a set of distributed, heterogeneous, and autonomous applications that can be connected to each other in an arbitrary way [ABFS97, AFPS99a, AFPS99b]. Each component encompasses a transaction manager scheduling the invocation of services provided by the applications of the next lower level. The aim of the composite systems theory is to extend the traditional multilevel transaction model in different ways. First, the kind of systems addressed generalizes the regular configuration that can be found in multilevel transactions. Second and most important, the degree of parallelism, both within single transactions and in the context of concurrent executions of transactions, is increased.

In the traditional transaction model, operations of a transaction T_i are either temporally ordered, i.e., $o_{i_j} \ll_i o_{i_k}$ indicating that o_{i_k} may only be invoked after o_{i_j} has returned (thus, $\ll$ enforces sequential execution), or they are not ordered at all. In the latter case, an unrestricted parallel execution of these operations is allowed. The same classification holds when transactions are executed concurrently: a schedule S either enforces a temporal order between two operations or allows them to be executed concurrently, without any restriction. To overcome the drawback that a temporal order between semantically rich operations which may themselves be inherently complex reduces the degree of parallelism, a more permissive order, $<$, called *weak order*, has been introduced [ABFS97]. Let A and B be two transactions or two operations, respectively. The weak order $A < B$ allows A and B to be executed concurrently but restricts this parallelism in that the effects must be the same as if both would have been executed with respect to the temporal (*strong*) order $A \ll B$.

The weak order can be exploited both as intra-transaction order and as inter-transaction order, the latter one allowing even conflicting operations to be executed concurrently. The gain in concurrency when exploiting the weak conflict order in layered systems is illustrated in Example 3.5.

Example 3.5 *Consider two transactions, T_1 and T_2, defined over the set of semantically rich operations of Example 3.2. According to Table 3.2, the following pair of operations of level L_2 does not commute: Reset(c_B) of transaction T_1 and Incr(c_B) of T_2. In the traditional case depicted in Figure 3.4 (a), a strong order is established between both operations leading to a serial execution of the associated transactions. A weak conflict order established between Reset(c_B) and Incr(c_B), however, allows for a higher degree of concurrency. This case is depicted in Figure 3.4 (b) where the subtrees of both transactions are interleaved. Since the conflicts at all levels are compliant with the weak conflict order Reset(c_B) $<$ Incr(c_B), the result is the same as if both L_2 operations would have been executed strongly ordered.* □

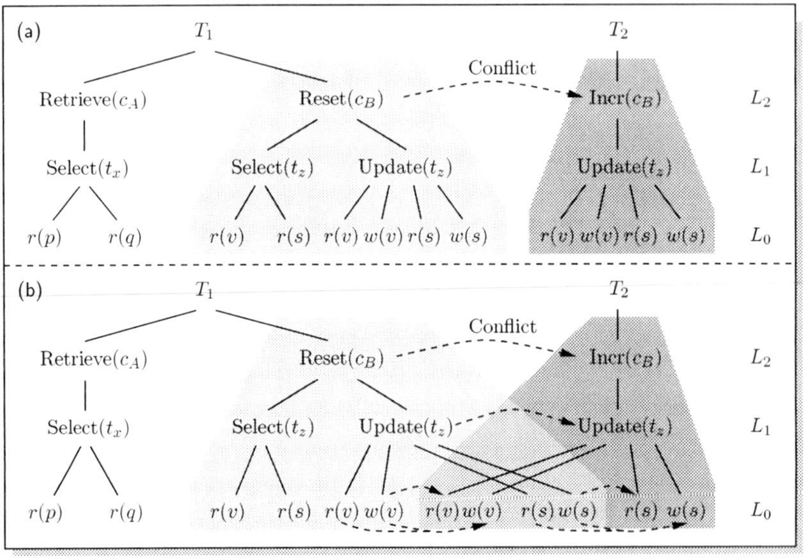

Figure 3.4: Comparison of Strongly (a) and Weakly (b) Ordered Conflicts

In the composite systems theory, constraints imposed on the execution of transactions are made explicit, thereby extending the classical transaction model [ABFS97]. Each schedule encompasses a strong ($\Rightarrow$) and a weak ($\rightarrow$) input order with the additional requirement that ($\Rightarrow \cup \rightarrow$) be acyclic. Analogously, in terms of the execution order (output order) determined by a scheduler, a distinction between strong ($\ll$) and weak ($<$) order is made. The output orders between operations determined by a scheduler are passed to the next lower schedulers which have to respect these orders when executing transactions corresponding to operations of the higher level scheduler. In this way, it is possible to prevent that the order established at one level is ignored by the next lower level which may lead to incorrect executions. While the strong input order between two transactions has to be propagated to a strong output order for each pair of operations of both transactions, the weak input order between two transactions only requires all pairs of conflicting operations to appear in the weak output order (which has to be compliant with the input order). Note that the transmission of orders from one scheduler to the next lower schedulers is strongly related to handshaking mechanisms that are used, for instance, between a transaction manager and a data manager in a database system [BHG87].

The strong input order is respected, when, for instance, all schedulers support order-preserving serializable (OPSR) executions. In terms of the weak input order, protocols supporting commit ordering (CO) can be exploited. In this case, a weak input order constraint between two transactions $T_i \rightarrow T_j$ can be mapped to an appropriate order on the associated commits, $C_i \ll C_j$.

Input orders have additionally to be considered when reasoning about the correctness of a single schedule [ABFS97]:

Definition 3.21 (Conflict Consistency (CC)) *A schedule S is* conflict consistent *it is conflict equivalent to a serial schedule S' which contains the strong and weak input order of S, i.e., $\Rightarrow_S \subseteq \Rightarrow_{S'}$ and $\rightarrow_S \subseteq \rightarrow_{S'}$.* □

Correctness in composite systems, however, requires the consideration of all schedules jointly. To this end, some basic configurations and combinations of those have been analyzed [ABFS97, AFPS99b]. In the most straightforward configuration, all schedulers are regularly layered, one on top of the other. Executions in such systems are captured under the notion of *n-level stack schedule (SS)* which considers the set $S_1, \ldots, S_n$ of n schedules with $\rightarrow_{S_{i-1}} = <_{S_i}$ and $\Rightarrow_{S_{i-1}} = \ll_{S_i}$ for $1 < i \leq n$. In [ABFS97] it has been shown that a stack composite system is globally correct *(stack conflict consistent, SCC)* if each individual schedule S_i is CC. Therefore, in terms of global correctness it is sufficient to consider the local correctness of each single component separately.

Due to the cautious propagation of conflict orders, SCC has been proven to be a more permissive correctness criterion than both conflict preservation [BBG$^+$83, BBG89] and level-by-level serializability [Wei87, Wei88, Wei91].

Fork schedules (FS), another common configuration in composite systems, are characterized by a top level schedule S_F whose output is distributed to several independent lower schedules $S_1, \ldots, S_n$ where every operation of S_F is sent to exactly one schedule S_i, $1 \leq i \leq n$ for execution. Additionally, output orders between operations executed in the same system are present in the input orders of the associated lower level schedule. In analogy to the stack case, a fork schedule can be proven globally correct *(fork conflict consistent, FCC)* if each of the schedules $S_F, S_1, \ldots, S_n$ is locally correct with respect to CC [AFPS99b].

In [Feß99, FS99], the application of the composite systems theory for the parallelization of numerical algorithms has been shown, thereby making intensive use of the higher degree of concurrency composite transactions allow compared to conventional approaches. In addition to these applications, [Feß99] presents an extension of the composite systems theory which considers also recovery aspects by applying the unified theory of concurrency control and recovery to composite transactions.

3.4 Making Failure Handling Strategies Explicit: The Flexible Transaction Model

The combination of the open nested transaction paradigm with the composite systems theory where subtransactions correspond to invocations of arbitrary transactional services requires an appropriate compensating service, i.e., a compensating subtransaction, to be available for each regular service. However, this imposes strong restrictions that are, in general, not met by each system. To this end, a more sophisticated differentiation of termination properties of subtransactions is required which, in turn, also influences failure handling strategies that have inherently to be provided by advanced transaction models.

3.4.1 Termination Properties of Subtransactions

The atomicity requirement of transactions prohibits any effects of aborted transactions to become visible. With the open nested transaction paradigm, this can be generalized in that all committed subtransactions of aborted transactions have to be semantically compensated leading to the notion of *semantic atomicity* [GM83]. A prerequisite, however, is that a compensating subtransaction is provided for each subtransaction.

In general, one non-compensatable subtransaction may exist. But, it has to be deferred until the end of the top-level transaction and, given that all preceding compensatable transactions have committed, determines the outcome of the top-level transaction. This structure even allows several non-compensatable subtransactions which then also have to be deferred [Gra81]. In addition, they have to be committed jointly by applying atomic commit protocols, e.g., two phase commit [BHG87, GR93]. Such top-level transactions consisting of both compensatable and non-compensatable subtransactions are referred to as *mixed transactions* [ELLR90].

A more fine-grained differentiation of termination properties of subtransactions considers, in addition to compensation, the possibility to repeatedly invoke failed subtransactions which are guaranteed to successfully commit after a finite number of attempts. These subtransactions are called *retriable* [LKS91, MRKS92, MRSK92]. All retriable subtransactions are considered as non-compensatable. Moreover, a third category, namely *pivot subtransactions*, which are neither compensatable nor retriable, has been introduced [LKS91, MRKS92, MRSK92]. These different termination properties now imply a certain order between subtransactions and relax the requirement that non-compensatable, i.e., pivot, subtransactions have to be deferred. A correct structure allows one pivot subtransaction which has to be preceded only by compensatable subtransactions and which is followed by a set of retriable subtransactions [MRKS92, MRSK92]. In [LKS91], even multiple pivot subtransactions are allowed which have again to be committed atomically and thus appear as one single entity. Since this structure allows two different recovery strategies, i.e., compensation or retry, and thus further generalizes semantic atomicity, it is denoted as *relaxed atomicity* [LKS91].

3.4.2 Constraints for Alternative Executions

All transaction models we have addressed so far, hence also multilevel and composite transactions, only consider execution orders based on the successful termination of operations or subtransactions, respectively. When subtransactions fail, appropriate failure handling strategies have to be provided by the corresponding application. However, in many cases the explicit specification of failure handling strategies, i.e., when failure handling is shifted from the application to the transaction model, allows a scheduler to provide more flexibility and may even be an indispensable requirement when subtransactions with special termination properties have to be considered.

Evidently, in the case of *function replication* [ELLR90], that is when identical types of subtransactions are provided at multiple, i.e., fully replicated, sites, alternative execution dependencies allow to cope with constraints like "at most one out of a bunch of functionally equivalent subtransactions is allowed to commit". To this end, precedence predicates defined over the different termination states of subtransactions (committed or aborted) provide the necessary information on which alternative executions are preferred and allow a scheduler to automatically invoke an equivalent subtransaction when a previously invoked one has failed. This kind of alternative execution constraints has been introduced in [ELLR90] under the term *flexible transactions*.

In general and without restricting failure handling to functionally equivalent subtransactions only, arbitrary *semantically equivalent* subtransactions can be specified as substitutes, replacing failed ones. Again, dependencies on termination states of preceding subtransactions are appropriate means for this purpose [RELL90].

3.4.3 Combining Alternative Executions with Termination Properties

When multiple non-compensatable, i.e., pivot, subtransactions within one transaction exist, they have either to be deferred or they have to be followed by retriable subtransactions only. In any case, however, an atomic commit protocol coordinating all these pivots has to be exploited. In order to loosen the latter restriction, subtransactions with special termination properties require the existence of appropriate alternative executions.

Zhang et al. bring the differentiation of termination properties of subtransactions (compensatable, retriable, and pivot) and alternative executions together [ZNBB94], thereby extending the notion of *flexible transactions*. A flexible transaction, $\mathcal{T}$, encompasses a set T of subtransactions t_i, that is $T = \{t_1, t_2, \ldots, t_n\}$. To specify regular and alternative executions of these subtransactions, a set of *representative partial orders (rpo's)* is additionally required. Each rpo, denoted as $(T_i, \ll_i)$ with $T_i \subseteq T$ specifies an allowed execution of $\mathcal{T}$ with respect to the order $\ll_i$. The union $\ll$ of all rpo orders $\ll_i$ is called *precedence order*[3] of $\mathcal{T}$. The specification of multiple rpo's additionally necessitates an order on the different alternatives, called *preference order*, $\lhd$. This preference order is defined between two elements of the power set $\mathcal{P}(T)$ of T. In order to define alternative executions, two rpo's, $(T_i, \ll_i)$ and $(T_j, \ll_j)$, must have a common prefix and an appropriate preference order $T_i' \lhd T_j'$ between the set of subtransactions T_i' and T_j', respectively, following the common prefix. Then, the set T_i' which is replaced by T_j' in case at least one of its subtransactions definitively fails (i.e., fails and is not retriable) is called *switching set.*

Each rpo may contain more than one pivot subtransaction. Out of these, one dedicated pivot subtransaction, the *critical point*, is chosen (this is either the critical point of a higher priority rpo or the first pivot that is not part of a switching set). All compensatable subtransactions of an rpo succeeding the critical point as well as all other pivot subtransactions of the same rpo are called *abnormal subtransactions*. Out of these abnormal subtransactions of an rpo, the ones that do not immediately succeed a switching set consisting only of compensatable subtransactions are called *blocking points*. Given this classification, a flexible transaction is called *well-formed* if each blocking point of each rpo is member of some switching set whose other members are all compensatable and whose next alternative consists only of retriable or of abnormal subtransactions.

Example 3.6 *Consider a flexible transaction $\mathcal{T}_1$ consisting of subtransactions $t_1, \ldots, t_5$ that are executed at five different sites $S_1, \ldots, S_5$. All these subtransactions are formed out of the set of semantically rich operations that has been introduced in Example 3.2. The two subtransactions $t_1 = Retrieve(x)$ and $t_2 = Retrieve(y)$ are both compensatable. Since site S_3 at which $t_3 = Reset(w)$ is executed does not provide an inverse operation $Reset^{-1}(w)$, t_3 is pivot. Similarly, subtransaction $t_4 = Incr(v)$ cannot be compensated since $Incr^{-1}(v)$ is not available at S_1. Moreover, an upper bound on the value of v exists such that t_4 is even not retriable. Subtransaction $t_5 = Incr(z)$, however, is retriable since at site S_5 no upper bound on the value of z exists. In terms of alternative executions, subtransaction t_1 may be replaced by t_2 upon failure. Similarly, a failure of t_4 can be captured by alternatively executing t_5. This is reflected in the four rpo's of $\mathcal{T}_1$: $rpo_1 = \{t_1 \ll_1 t_3 \ll_1 t_4\}$, $rpo_2 = \{t_1 \ll_2 t_3 \ll_2 t_5\}$, $rpo_3 = \{t_2 \ll_3 t_3 \ll_3 t_4\}$, and $rpo_4 = \{t_2 \ll_4 t_3 \ll_4 t_5\}$. The preference order $\lhd$ of $\mathcal{T}_1$ therefore evaluates to: $\{t_1, t_3, t_4\} \lhd \{t_2, t_2, t_4\}$ and $\{t_4\} \lhd \{t_5\}$. The switching sets of rpo_1 are $SW_{1_1} = \{t_1\}$*

[3] In [ZNBB94], the symbol $\prec$ is used for the precedence order. Since this order corresponds to the standard temporal intra-transaction order we have introduced previously and for reasons of uniformity, we denote the precedence order by $\ll$.

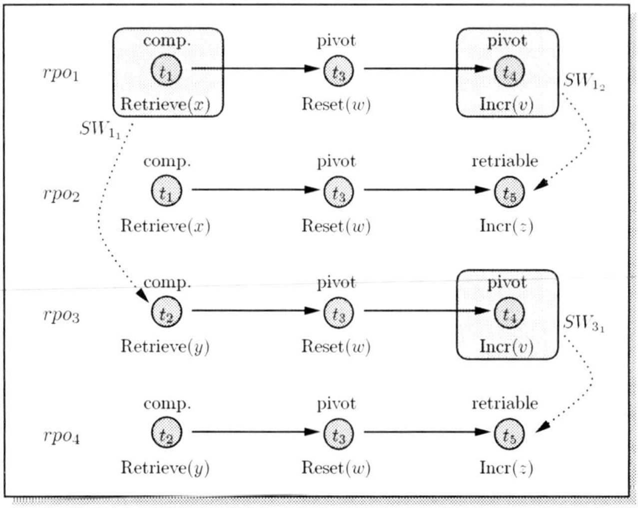

Figure 3.5: Flexible Transaction $\mathcal{T}_1$ with Representative Partial Orders (rpo's) and Switching Sets (SW)

and $SW_{1_2} = \{t_4\}$; *rpo*$_3$ *encompasses one switching set, namely* $SW_{3_1} = \{t_4\}$ *while rpo*$_2$ *and rpo*$_4$ *do not contain any switching set. In Figure 3.5, all subtransactions of* $\mathcal{T}_1$ *together with the precedence order, their associated rpo's, and their switching sets are depicted. With the information on termination properties and switching sets,* t_3 *can be identified as critical point of each of the four rpo's. Since* t_4 *is also pivot, it is an abnormal subtransaction in rpo*$_1$ *and rpo*$_3$ *and yet also a blocking point in these rpo's. However,* t_4 *is part of a switching set both in rpo*$_1$ (SW_{1_2}) *and in rpo*$_3$ (SW_{3_1}). *Therefore,* $\mathcal{T}_1$ *is a well-formed flexible transaction.* □

In [ZNBB94] is has been shown that well-formed flexible transactions guarantee that exactly one rpo is executed correctly while the effects of all other rpo's can be undone. Since the well-formed structure repeatedly considers compensation (i.e., of the successors of a failed blocking point) and alternative executions, the notion of relaxed atomicity which allows for only one pivot subtransaction is further generalized, leading to the notion of *semi-atomicity* [ZNBB94].

Semi-atomic flexible transactions are characterized by the existence of one rpo in which no abnormal subtransactions exist (i.e., in which only retriable subtransactions follow the critical point) and which has no lower priority rpo. According to [ZNBB94], all rpo's of a flexible transaction $\mathcal{T}$ are executed concurrently. In this concurrent execution, all compensatable subtransactions are allowed to commit after termination. However, the commit of pivot and retriable subtransactions has to be deferred in order to respect the preference order.

An execution of a flexible transaction $\mathcal{T}$ is called *F-recoverable* when both $\mathcal{T}$'s precedence and preference orders are respected and when no two retriable or pivot subtransactions of different rpo's commit simultaneously. A failure of a subtransaction t_i in an F-recoverable execution of some flexible transaction $\mathcal{T}$ is treated as follows: if t_i is member of a switching set, then all other subtransactions t_j of this switching set that have already committed are compensated (compensation, however, is done in an additional top-level transaction). Then, according to the preference order, the next rpo is considered. When an rpo is completed correctly, all subtransactions of lower priority rpo's that have already committed are compensated; again, an additional top-level transaction is used for this purpose. Since the lowest priority rpo does not contain any abnormal subtransaction, retriability and thus its successful completion is guaranteed. When a subtransaction t_i fails that is not part of a switching set, the well-formed structure of $\mathcal{T}$ guarantees that no critical point has committed such that all effects of $\mathcal{T}$ can be undone by a compensating transaction $\mathcal{T}'$.

Since all rpo's are invoked concurrently, the additional compensating top-level transaction $\mathcal{T}'$ may even be required when no failure occurs, i.e., when the most preferred rpo with highest priority succeeds.

Example 3.6 (Revisited) *Consider again flexible transaction $\mathcal{T}_1$ depicted in Figure 3.5. In an F-recoverable execution, all four rpo's are considered concurrently, that is, all five subtransactions are invoked. Subtransactions t_1 and t_2 are allowed to commit immediately since both are compensatable. After commitment of at least one of them, the critical point, subtransaction t_3, is allowed to commit. In case of success, according to the preference order on rpo's, subtransaction t_4 is committed. If t_4 fails, execution is switched to t_5 which is guaranteed to successfully terminate. When initially both t_1 and t_2 have committed and when $\mathcal{T}_1$ is successfully executed, the compensation of t_2 is added to the compensating transaction $\mathcal{T}_1'$. When $\mathcal{T}$ fails, i.e., when the critical point t_3 is aborted, $\mathcal{T}_1'$ encompasses even the compensation of t_1 and t_2, if both have previously committed.* □

4 A Model for Transactional Process Management

"Give me some ink and paper in my tent
I'll draw the form and model of our battle."

William Shakespeare, King Richard III.

The evolution of transaction models presented in the previous chapter and, as a consequence thereof, the resulting extensions in diverse directions has accentuated the trend of making transaction schedulers more "intelligent", i.e., making a variety of additional constraints available to them, thereby allowing a more fine-grained control of the execution of complex operations while adding more flexibility and concurrency. However, most of these extensions were motivated by special problems and have been developed independently. Thus, a framework in which more sophisticated, semantically rich transactions, i.e., transactions on top of transactions, can be addressed requires the combination of these different concepts by extracting the particularities of all models from their context accompanied by their generalization and extension.

Transactional process management [SAS99] aims at providing semantically rich transactions in composite systems consisting of a variety of distributed and heterogeneous components. To this end, *process programs* [ABSS00] are exploited as means to group transactions into entities with higher level semantics [AHST97b], thereby relating transactional services offered by components of a composite system and reflecting arbitrary complex dependencies between them. Thus, transactional processes can be seen as a major component of a transaction specification and transaction management environment in higher order databases — hyperdatabases [SBG$^+$00]. Starting with a powerful model for the specification of process programs, we elaborate on the provable inherent correctness of single process programs (guaranteed termination) as well as on the fault-tolerant and correct concurrent execution of these process programs in transactional process management.

This chapter provides a detailed introduction to the model of transactional process management. First, the system model in which transactional processes are executed is clarified (Section 4.1). Second, in Section 4.2, we present the model of transaction programs. These transaction programs are the building blocks of process programs. In here, we discuss the requirements imposed on transaction programs, as well as their concrete semantics and, for the time being, assume that they are executed in transactional applications. Third, the model of process programs is introduced (Section 4.3). This process model not only addresses the special structure of process programs but also the inherent correctness properties of process programs which can be derived from their structure and which can be validated statically, i.e., prior to their execution.

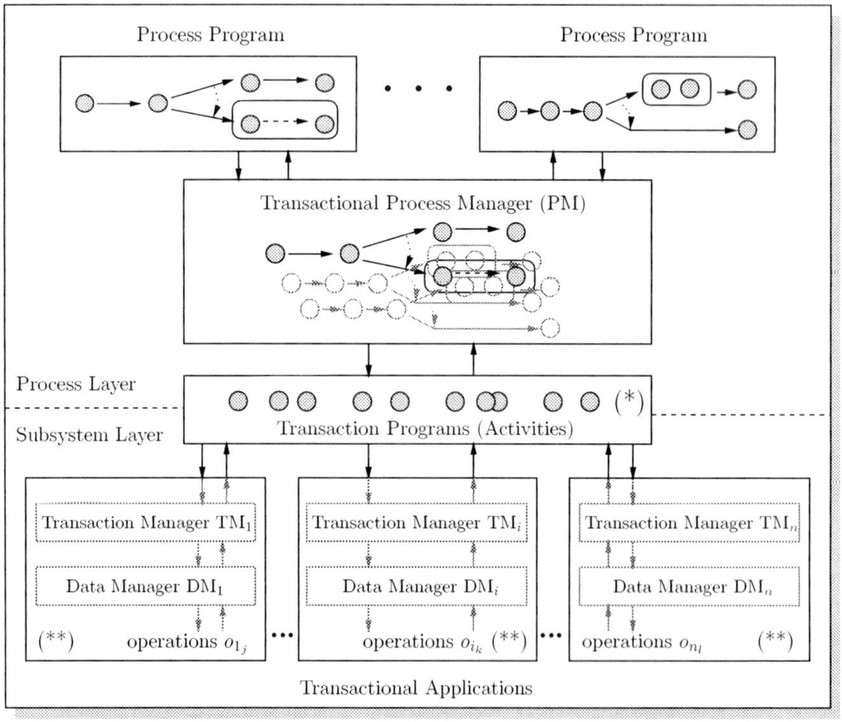

Figure 4.1: System Model: Transactional Processes on Top of Transactional Applications (Components)

4.1 System Model

We consider an architecture with two layers. The top layer controls the execution of *transactional processes*, as specified in *process programs*. Each one of these process programs is a set of partially ordered activities. Each activity, in turn, corresponds to a conventional transaction, or *transaction program*, executed in a transactional application (component system). In addition to the encapsulation of conventional transactions, the process structure is enriched by the possibility of adding more flexibility in the form of alternative executions in which also the concrete semantics associated with the activities of a process is reflected.

The bottom layer of the system model is formed by the universe of all available independent transactional components as depicted in Figure 4.1. Thus, the system model corresponds to a configuration which is referred to as *fork system* in the composite systems theory.

The concurrent execution of transactional processes is controlled by a *transactional process manager (PM)*, which is responsible for scheduling the invocation of the transaction programs in the underlying applications. In here, we present the basic model in order to reason about correct process structures and about correctness at the process level, i.e., of the invocation of transaction programs (marked with $(*)$ in Figure 4.1). For the scheduling, the PM exploits not only information about the commutativity of transaction programs but also about termination properties of these programs (whether there is an inverse or not), and the process structure, i.e., the orders that are imposed between transaction programs.

For the underlying applications, we assume basic transactional functionality. To this end, at a first glance, we assume a conventional architecture [BHG87] where a *transaction manager* (TM_i) executes transactional programs by submitting operations to a *data manager* (DM_i). These components are depicted in light grey color in Figure 4.1. In Chapter 8, we provide a more detailed discussion of the prerequisites that have to be provided by arbitrary application systems given this conventional architecture is not present.

4.2 Transaction Programs Model

Processes are conventionally seen as a collection of activities. In here, a process program which defines the execution of a process is a structured collection of *transaction programs*, or *activities*. Activities are, by definition, atomic and therefore either terminate committing or aborting. Let $\mathcal{A}^*$ be the set of all activities available in the system, i.e., the union of the transaction programs provided by all applications. To account for aborts and commits of processes, we augment $\mathcal{A}^*$ to $\hat{\mathcal{A}} := \mathcal{A}^* \cup \{C, A\}$ where C denotes the commit of a process and A its abort.

4.2.1 Termination Properties

Activities differ in terms of their termination guarantees. According to the flexible transaction model, we consider the three cases: compensatable, retriable, and pivot [LKS91, MRKS92, MRSK92, ZNBB94]. A *compensatable* activity has a compensating activity, namely a compensation transaction, that is provided by the same system, which semantically undoes the effects of the original activity. To this end, we apply the definition of effect-freedom (Definition 3.17) to the level of activities in that we consider a sequence σ of activities as *effect-free* if σ preceded by an arbitrary sequence of activities α from $\mathcal{A}^*$ and followed by another arbitrary sequence β from $\mathcal{A}^*$ produces the same return values as α directly followed by β.

A special case of effect-free activities is the sequence $\sigma = \langle a_i \, a_i^{-1} \rangle$ consisting of a compensatable activity a_i and its compensating activity a_i^{-1}. More formally,

Definition 4.1 (Compensatability and Compensating Activity) *An activity $a_i \in \mathcal{A}^*$ is* compensatable *if there is an activity $a_i^{-1} \in \mathcal{A}^*$ where the activity sequence $\sigma = \langle a_i \, a_i^{-1} \rangle$ is effect-free. Activity a_i^{-1} is called the* compensating activity *of a_i.* □

Compared with the conventional transaction model, a compensatable activity corresponds to a regular operation while a compensating activity corresponds to an inverse operation, respectively.

Moreover, activities a_i for which no effect-free sequence $\sigma = \langle a_i \, a_i^{-1} \rangle$ can be built, that is, for which no compensating activity a_i^{-1} exists, are also considered as special cases:

Definition 4.2 (Pivot Activity) *An activity $a_i \in \mathcal{A}^*$ is* pivot *if it is not compensatable.* □

Activities whose executions are guaranteed to successfully terminate after a finite number of invocations are called *retriable*. Just as transaction consistency is an axiom, but its details and verification are not covered by transaction management, so is retriability a classification of activities provided by the underlying systems.

Definition 4.3 (Retriable Activity) *An activity $a_i \in \mathcal{A}^*$ is* retriable *if each sequence α of activities from $\mathcal{A}^*$ can be expanded to $\langle\ \alpha\ a_i\ \rangle$ by invoking a_i a finite number of times such that the last invocation terminates committing while all the previous ones return with abort.* □

Since each transaction program is required to be atomic, failed invocations of activities do not leave any effect and can be safely discarded. While, in the case of retriable activities, the failure of an invocation can be coped with repeated invocations until the final commitment, this is not possible for non-retriable activities. Hence, when the transaction program corresponding to a non-retriable activity returns with abort, this leads to the failure of the activity. Note that in contrast to the original flexible transaction model, retriability on the one hand and the availability of compensation on the other hand are orthogonal properties. An activity can have both, one of them, or neither.

Note further that the semantics of compensation does not require each compensating activity to be itself compensatable. However, we assume each compensating activity to be retriable and, therefore, guaranteed to succeed.

4.2.2 Basic Requirements for Transaction Programs Executions

Each activity of a process corresponds to a transaction, that is an execution of a transaction program within a subsystem. These transactions follow the conventional model. Hence, they consist of a set of basic operations where each of them is, in contrast to activities of the process model, considered to be compensatable — except for those that are atomically executed after the commit decision.

The following two basic correctness requirements exist for the execution of operations at the data manager (DM) level of each subsystem, marked with (**) in Figure 4.1.

Conflict-Preserving Serializability (CPSR) Even when transaction programs are executed concurrently, the execution must be conflict-equivalent to a serial execution of these programs. In terms of the process level, this criterion enforces that the interleaved execution of conflicting activities is correct. The CPSR criterion, when present at the subsystem level, allows to consider a total order between all activities of this subsystem at process manager level without affecting the effects these activities have in their subsystem.

Avoiding Cascading Aborts (ACA) The ACA property guarantees that the abort of single activities at process manager level will not affect any other activity of the same subsystem and thus, prevents that abort of one activity causes the abort of other processes with activities in common subsystems.

Aside of the basic requirement of CPSR–ACA schedules [BHG87, Bee00], each subsystem additionally must

- provide *order-preserving serializability (OPSR)* [BSW79, Pap79]. This is required since the serialization order of transactions in each subsystem has to coincide with the order imposed between activities at process manager level, i.e., when one activity is invoked after another one has terminated, this order must be reflected in an equivalent serial subsystem execution.

- allow the process manager to determine the serialization order for any pair of activities of the same subsystem and to pass this required order to the subsystem. The order so imposed must be enforced when executing the transactions associated with these activities. To this end, protocols following, for instance, *commit ordering (CO)* [BGRS91, Raz92] have to be applied in all subsystems to order transactions appropriately. This allows the process manager to map the desired serialization order of activities to the commit order of the associated transactions. When commit ordering is provided, the requirement of order preservation as a handshaking mechanism between schedulers (commit-order serializability), in this case between the process manager and the subsystems, as identified in [BBG89] holds.

This brief summary of correctness issues at the subsystem layer is based on the (implicit) assumption that each subsystem corresponds to a database system with conventional architecture [BHG87], as depicted in Figure 4.1. The goal in transactional process management is, however, to apply this type of high level transactions on top of arbitrary distributed and heterogeneous application systems acting as subsystems. This does not affect the basic requirements listed above but needs a considerably deeper analysis of how these basic requirements can be grafted on top of arbitrary applications. For the time being, we restrict this discussion to the analysis of basic requirements that are exploited by a process manager when transactional processes are executed concurrently. In Chapter 8, we will resume and extend this discussion and address the problem of providing the basic subsystem requirements on top of arbitrary applications in detail, thereby loosening the assumption that each subsystem corresponds to a full-fledged database system.

4.3 Process Model

In analogy to the traditional transaction model where the term transaction is used for an execution of a sequence of operations specified in a transaction program, we use the term *process program* for the static specification of semantically related activities and their dependencies. The execution of a process program is then termed *process*.

For the process model, we adopt and refine ideas of the flexible transaction model and extend them by applying the different orderings of the composite systems theory.

4.3.1 Process Programs

A *process program* encompasses a set of activities and executes them according to a given order, possibly also influenced by the results of previous activities. Thus, a process program can be viewed as a tree whose nodes are activities and whose edges correspond to order constraints between these activities. A path in the tree then reflects a possible execution.

This view is generalized as follows. If a process program allows for concurrent execution of activities, we group a partially ordered set of activities as a single (multi-activity) node of the tree, rather than as distinct nodes. All activities of a node, whether this is a singleton or a multi-activity node, are totally ordered with respect to activities of preceding and subsequent nodes in the tree. In this model, branching decisions are present in that a node may have several successors among which one is chosen when the process program is executed. The order between nodes is a temporal one (*strong order*, $\ll$) which has the semantics of a handshake. If node n_1 precedes n_2, then all activities of n_1 must have committed before any activity of n_2 is allowed to be invoked (e.g., to respect the fact that there may be data flow between activities).

In addition to the strong order between nodes in the tree, a process program may allow some activities, say a and b, to be executed concurrently, but *request* that the execution be equivalent to one in which a precedes b (*weak order*, $<$). Ensuring such constraints is a service provided by the underlying systems, and can be accomplished by, e.g., using commit-order serializability [BBG89] based on commit ordering protocols. Recalling that a multi-activity node is a partially ordered set of activities, we represent such requests by associating a weak order request and a partial strong order with each multi-activity node. Thus, if activities are strongly ordered in a multi-activity node, they will be executed in this order, since the process program will invoke the second only after the first one has returned. If they are weakly ordered, the necessary ordering will be enforced by the underlying system. When activities are allowed to be executed in parallel, without any restriction, they have to appear in the same multi-activity node, but neither strongly nor weakly ordered.

Hence, the temporal, strong order between activities of a process program is defined as the union of all partial strong orders within multi-activity nodes and the order induced on activities by the edges of the process program tree. The weak order of a process program is the union of the weak order requests of all multi-activity nodes.

These ideas are formalized in the following definition:

Definition 4.4 (Process Program (PP)) *A* process program, *PP, is a tuple* $(N, E, \ll, <, Piv, \lhd)$, *where*

1. *N is a set of nodes. Each node $n \in N$ consists of a set $\mathcal{A}_n \subseteq \mathcal{A}^*$ of activities. If $card(\mathcal{A}_n) = 1$, a node is called singleton node, otherwise, n is called multi-activity node. Associated with each multi-activity node $n \in N$ are two different orders on the corresponding activities: a partial strong order, $\ll_n$, and a partial weak order, $<_n$, where the union of both orders, $\ll_n \cup <_n$, is acyclic.*
2. *E is a set of directed edges which, together with the set of nodes N, forms a directed tree. Each edge $e = (n_1, n_2) \in E$ corresponds to a strong order constraint.*
3. *The acyclic partial strong order, $\ll$, is the union of the order induced on activities by the edges and of all partial strong orders $\ll_n$, $n \in N$, within multi-activity nodes.*
4. *The acyclic partial weak order, $<$, is the union of all weak orders $<_n$, $n \in N$, of all multi-activity nodes.*
5. *Piv is a set of distinguished singleton nodes in the tree: each singleton node in the tree containing an activity that is not compensatable is in Piv.*
6. *The* preference order, *$\lhd$, defines a partial order on the children of each node $n \in N$.* □

The universe $\mathcal{A}_{PP} \subseteq \mathcal{A}^*$ of all activities explicitly encompassed in a process program PP is the union of all activities of all nodes, that is $\mathcal{A}_{PP} := \bigcup_{n \in N} \mathcal{A}_n$. While the weak order between activities from $\mathcal{A}_{PP}$ is only present within multi-activity nodes, the specification of PP's strong order is spread over multi-activity nodes and the edges of the process program tree.

Optionally, branching decisions may be present in a process program PP in that conditions on the execution of a child node n_k of some node n_i are specified. To this end, a condition, $cond_k$, has to be attached to the edge $e = (n_i, n_k)$ leading from n_i to n_k. Let n_{k_l} with $1 \leq l \leq m$ be the m children of n_i in a process program PP. Then, $j \leq m$ different conditions may exist. In order to avoid indeterminism, these conditions have to be pairwise disjoint, that is $\forall\ l, q \in \{1, \ldots, m\}$, $l \neq q : cond_{k_l} \wedge cond_{k_q} = FALSE$. When several children of n_i have the same condition restricting their execution, then these nodes are considered as alternatives, hence they are ordered with respect to the preference order $\lhd$.

The flexible transaction model has shown that the differentiation of termination properties of subtransactions has a strong impact on the structure of correct (well-formed) transactions. Analogously, the different termination properties of transaction programs and thus, of the corresponding activities, also affect the structure of the associated process programs and lead to the notion of *process programs with guaranteed termination.*

The first non-compensatable activity on a path from the root in the tree of a process program with guaranteed termination is called *primary pivot* of the process. Note that this primary pivot is not necessarily unique in a given process program. The possibility of branching decisions that can be taken prior to the execution of a pivot activity may cause the existence of several candidates for primary pivots. In any case, the primary pivot is a "point-of-no-return" of the corresponding process: if it commits, the process cannot rollback any more; it must be able to complete. Pivots have always to be represented as singleton nodes, rather than as members of a multi-activity node. This captures the fact that no other activity of a process may be executed in parallel to a pivot activity. To be able to complete after a pivot commits, there must be at least one path, encompassed in the *assured termination tree* rooted at a child node of the pivot, which consists only of retriable activities. More formally,

Definition 4.5 (Assured Termination Tree) *An* assured termination tree *is a subtree in a process program that consists only of retriable activities (either in multi-activity or in singleton nodes).* □

After successfully executing a pivot, the process program may try different alternatives, and only if they fail, execute the one whose termination is assured. Therefore, an assured termination tree must be rooted at one of the children of a pivot. Note that, although it is sufficient to restrict assured termination to a flat path of retriable activities from a pivot to a leaf node, we generalize this view and allow a complete subtree of retriable activities such that branching decisions may be taken during execution without limiting the property of assured termination (since all activities of the assured termination tree are required to be retriable).

Generally, a pivot may have an *ordered* set of children, each a process program with guaranteed termination while the last one of these children (the one with lowest priority) must be the root of an assured termination tree and all previous ones have (recursively) the same properties as the process program itself. These children will also be referred to as *subprocess programs.* In particular, each of these may have their own pivots, assured termination trees, and so on.

While the children of a singleton node encompassing a pivot activity inevitably have to be totally ordered, this is not required for the children of non-pivot nodes. If they are not ordered at all, the program selects *one* of them, according to results of previous activities. A partial order on the children of non-pivot nodes, however, can be exploited for failure handling purposes in that this order specifies which alternative has to be taken in case of failure.

The structure of process programs with guaranteed termination is formalized in the following definition:

Definition 4.6 (Process Program with Guaranteed Termination) *A process program PP with $PP = (N, E, \ll, <, Piv, \lhd)$ has* guaranteed termination *property when*

1. *Piv encompasses* all *pivot activities of $\mathcal{O}_{PP}$. That is, no pivot activity must appear in a multi-activity node. The first nodes of Piv on a path from the root of the tree are called* primary pivots.

2. *The preference order, $\lhd$, is acyclic and defines a* total *order on the children of each member of Piv.*

3. *For each member p of Piv, the following has to hold: if p is not a leaf node, at least one of its children, a^r, must be the root of an assured termination tree. All other children a' are the roots of process programs with guaranteed termination, called subprocess programs. Furthermore, a^r must follow all other children of p with respect to $\lhd$, that is $a' \lhd a^r$ for all a'.* □

Note that a process program with guaranteed termination may have no pivot, in which case it has the same properties as a regular transaction. Even in case pivot activities exist, but only as leaf nodes in the tree, correspondence to conventional transactions is present since the latter require all non-compensatable steps to be deferred.

When branching conditions are present in a process program with guaranteed termination PP, the following has to hold: as before, all constraints $cond_{k_l}$ on the children n_{k_l} with $1 \leq l \leq m$ of a node n_i must be pairwise disjoint, and, in addition, the disjunction of all these constraints must evaluate to true, that is $\bigvee_{l=1}^{m} cond_{k_l} = TRUE$. Then, it is guaranteed that, in any case, a child can be determined that is allowed to be executed with respect to the associated condition. In terms of the above rules of process programs with guaranteed termination, these branching conditions require that all subprocess programs succeeding a node n_p from Piv having the same condition are grouped, leading to j different groups with $j \leq m$, m being the number of children of n_p. The extension of constraint 2 of Definition 4.6 then does no longer require $\lhd$ to be total on all children of n_p but it has to be total on all members of each of these groups. Analogously, the adaptation of constraint 3 of Definition 4.6 requires an assured termination tree for each of these groups that follows all other nodes of its associated group with respect to $\lhd$.

In the following, when depicting process programs, we will use solid arcs for strong order constraints and dashed arcs for weak order constraints. The preference order, $\lhd$, will be depicted by dotted arcs. The superscripts of activities denote their termination property (compensatable, pivot, or retriable). Although retriability on one hand and (non-)compensatability on the other hand are considered to be orthogonal and thus may appear simultaneously (an activity may be compensatable *and* retriable or it may be pivot *and* retriable), we focus on one property, the one that is significant for the guaranteed termination property of the associated process program. Activities that are both compensatable and retriable are denoted as compensatable if they precede the primary pivot of a (sub-)process program and are denoted as retriable if they appear in an assured termination tree. Analogously, activities that are pivot and retriable are treated as pivot if they are not preceded by any non-compensatable activity in their (sub-)process program and are denoted as retriable otherwise. The unique id of process programs is denoted by a superscript, i.e., PP^k.

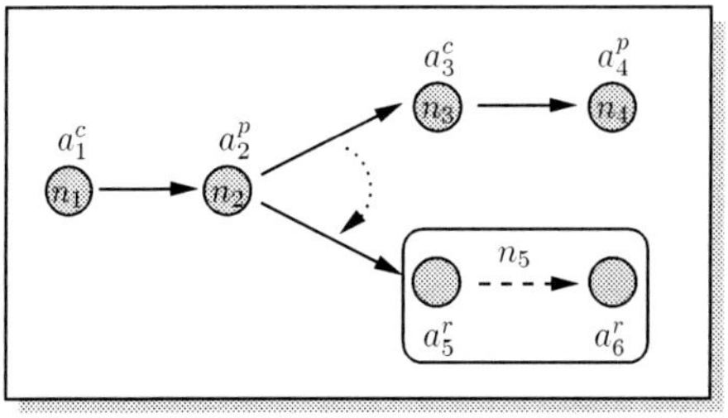

Figure 4.2: Process Program PP^1 with Strong and Weak Order Constraints and Preference Order

Example 4.1 *Consider process program PP^1 depicted in Figure 4.2. PP^1 consists of five nodes: four of them are singleton nodes (n_1 encompassing activity a_1^c, n_2 with activity a_2^p, n_3 with activity a_3^c, and n_4 with activity a_4^p), and the multi-activity node n_5 encompassing activities $\mathfrak{A}_{n_5} = \{a_5^r, a_6^r\}$. The strong order, $\ll$, is given by $\ll = \{(a_1^c \ll a_2^p), (a_2^p \ll a_3^c), (a_3^c \ll a_4^p), (a_2^p \ll a_5^r), (a_2^p \ll a_6^r)\}$ and the weak order, $<$, of PP^1 by $< = \{(a_5^r < a_6^r)\}$. Finally, the alternative executions following the commit of the primary pivot, a_2^p, are given by an order on its children $\lhd = \{PP_1^1 \lhd PP_2^1\}$ where PP_1^1 is the subprocess program consisting of nodes n_3 and n_4 while PP_2^1 is the subprocess program consisting of node n_5. In PP^1, no conditions on the children of n_2 —that would allow to take branching decisions— are present. According to Definition 4.6, PP^1 is a process program with guaranteed termination. Activities a_2^p and a_4^p, the only pivot activities of PP^1, are both encompassed within a singleton node, n_2 and n_4, respectively. Moreover, all children of n_2 are totally ordered with respect to $\lhd$. Since n_4 is a leaf node, this requirement is trivially fulfilled. Finally, PP_1^1 is a subprocess program with guaranteed termination, and n_5 is the root of an assured termination tree (all its activities are retriable) which follows all other children of n_2, that is $n_3 \lhd n_5$ holds.* □

While we included the node identifiers in the process program tree depicted in Figure 4.2, in what follows, we will only attach to each node its associated activities and omit the node identifiers.

4.3.2 Process Executions

Following conventional notations where the execution of a transaction program is denoted by the term "transaction", we will call an execution of a single process program a *process*. We consider partial executions in which a process may not have terminated. Although executions are in general concurrent, the underlying system guarantees serializability at the activity level. In such executions, we require that all activities of a node are executed in an order compatible with the strong and weak orders defined within the node and that the order implied by the edges of the process program tree is respected.

A process execution is not a path in the tree. It may contain aborted activities, compensating activities for the process or for its subprocesses, and it may contain aborted executions of subprocesses. This is illustrated in Figure 4.3 where a possible execution of a process program including regular activities (denoted by the forward transfer of nodes) and compensating activities (denoted by the backward transfer of nodes) is highlighted. The latter is necessary in order to cope with failures of single activities (denoted by flashes in Figure 4.3).

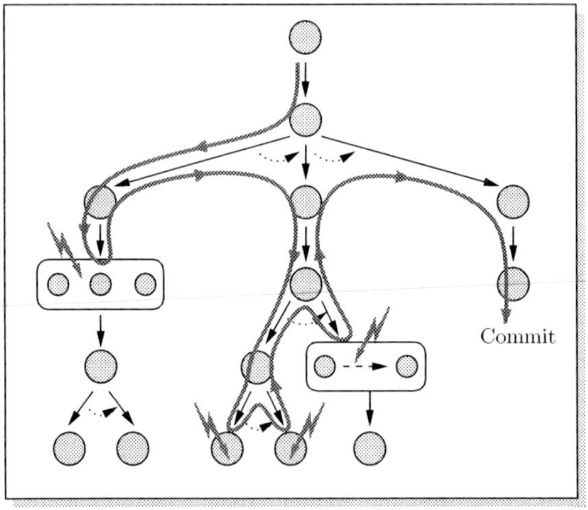

Figure 4.3: Execution of a Process Program Including Regular and Compensating Activities

In what follows, we consider only executions of process programs with guaranteed termination since we have already identified these process programs as the ones with correct structure. It is convenient to explain processes in terms of the states of their associated process program. In contrast to the flexible transaction model, however, we do not invoke alternative activities concurrently. Rather, the invocation of activities follows both the precedence and the preference order, that is an alternative is only effected when the previous alternative has failed.

In anticipation of multiprocess executions, i.e., the concurrent execution of several process programs with guaranteed termination, a process is assumed to have a unique identifier as subscript and, as a superscript, the id of the process program whose execution it reflects, e.g., process P_i^k corresponds to PP^k. The latter index may be omitted when the associated process program is not relevant. Activities within P_i^k are denoted as $a_{i_1}^c$, $a_{i_2}^p$, ..., $a_{i_n}^r$. The superscript again denotes the termination property of an activity, the subscripts are the process id and a unique id for the activity. Superscripts are omitted when not relevant or interesting. The commitment of process P_i is denoted by C_i, its abort by A_i.

In what follows, we summarize the possible states of processes. The states and the associated state changes are also illustrated in Figure 4.4.

1. Once instantiated, a process is in the state *running*.
2. Prior to the commit of a primary pivot p_{i0}, an abort, of a compensatable activity or of the primary pivot, changes the state to *aborting*, where compensating activities are executed.
3. After finally having compensated each activity, a process is in the state *aborted*.
4. The commit of a primary pivot p_{i0} causes a state change from *running* to *completing*. The program may now try several alternatives. The failure, i.e., abort of an alternative, causes it

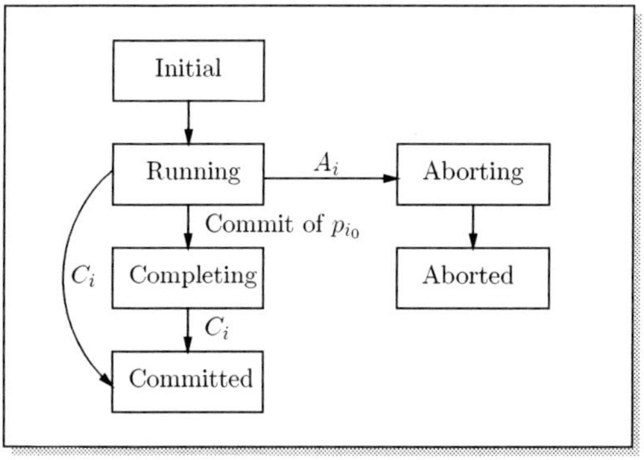

Figure 4.4: Possible States of a Process P_i

to try the next one. In here, the total order on the children of pivot activities that is required for process programs with guaranteed termination is important. Thus, the state of a process specifies the alternative, say j, in which it is now, and the state within the subprocess of this alternative.

5. Finally, if an alternative commits, then the subprocess completes and so does the process, which then contains the commit activity C_i. The process changes to the final state *committed.*

6. When no primary pivot exists, the commit of a process changes its state directly from *running* to *committed.*

A process that is either running or completing is called *active.*

According to Figure 4.3, a process encompasses (a subset of) the regular activities defined by the nodes of the associated process program (since each activity is atomic, we restrict the consideration to those activities that terminate successfully; in particular, only the last invocation of retriable activities is taken into account) and eventually also compensating activities for some of the regular ones, all appearing in an order compliant to those defined in the process program. Thus, not all activities of a process P_i^k are explicitly given by its process program since it also encompasses compensating activities which are only implicitly present in PP^k. More formally:

Definition 4.7 (Process) *A process, P_i^k, is a quadruple $(\mathcal{A}_i, \ll_i, <_i, \prec_i)$ reflecting the execution of a process program with guaranteed termination property $PP^k = (N^k, E^k, \ll^k, <^k, Piv^k, \lhd^k)$ where*

1. *$\mathcal{A}_i \subseteq \hat{\mathcal{A}}$ is a set of activities that contains regular activities of PP^k, but may also encompass compensating activities for some of them. Additionally, $\mathcal{A}_i$ contains at most one of C_i or A_i: $\mathcal{A}_i \subseteq \Big(\mathcal{O}_{PP^k} \cup \{a_{i_j}^{-1} \mid a_{i_j}^c \in \mathcal{O}_{PP^k}\} \cup \{C_i, A_i\}\Big)$.*

2. *The order $\ll_i \subseteq (\mathcal{A}_i \times \mathcal{A}_i)$ encompasses the strong order constraints between activities of $\mathcal{A}_i$ and extends the strong order of PP^k by also relating regular and compensating activities.*

(a) *First, the strong order explicitly specified in* PP^k *(either within multi-activity nodes or by edges in the process program tree) is present:*
$(\{a_{i_k}, a_{i_l}\} \in \mathcal{A}_i \ \wedge \ (a_{i_k} \ll^k a_{i_l})) \ \Rightarrow \ a_{i_k} \ll_i a_{i_l}$.

(b) *Moreover,* $\ll_i$ *also contains strong order constraints between regular activities and their compensating activities* ($\{a_{i_k}, a_{i_k}^{-1}\} \in \mathcal{A}_i \ \Rightarrow \ a_{i_k} \ll_i a_{i_k}^{-1}$) *as well as between pairs of compensating activities whose regular activities are strongly ordered:*
$\Big(\{a_{i_k}, a_{i_l}, a_{i_k}^{-1}, a_{i_l}^{-1}\} \in \mathcal{A}_i \ \wedge \ (a_{i_k} \ll_i a_{i_l})\Big) \ \Rightarrow \ a_{i_l}^{-1} \ll_i a_{i_k}^{-1}$.

(c) *Additionally, the preference order has to be respected. If one child of a pivot has been successfully compensated, the next one according to* $\lhd$ *is executed:*
$\Big(\{a_{i_j}, a_{i_k}, a_{i_k}^{-1}, a_{i_l}\} \subset \mathcal{A}_i \ \wedge \ (a_{i_j} \lll^k a_{i_k}) \ \wedge \ (a_{i_j} \ll^k a_{i_l}) \ \wedge \ (a_{i_k} \lhd^k a_{i_l})\Big) \Rightarrow a_{i_k}^{-1} \ll_i a_{i_l}$.

(d) *Finally, if one of either* C_i *or* A_i *is in* $\mathcal{A}_i$*, then it has to be after all other activities of* $\mathcal{A}_i$ *with respect to* $\ll_i$.

3. *The order* $<_i \subseteq (\mathcal{A}_i \times \mathcal{A}_i)$ *comprises the weak order constraints between activities of* $\mathcal{A}_i$.

   (a) *It encompasses the weak order constraints defined within multi-activity nodes of* PP^k*:*
   $(\{a_{i_k}, a_{i_l}\} \in \mathcal{A}_i \ \wedge \ (a_{i_k} <^k a_{i_l})) \ \Rightarrow \ a_{i_k} <_i a_{i_l}$.

   (b) *It requires two compensating activities to be weakly ordered when their corresponding regular activities are in the same multi-activity node and appear in the weak order request*
   $\Big(\{a_{i_k}, a_{i_l}, a_{i_k}^{-1}, a_{i_l}^{-1}\} \in \mathcal{A}_i \ \wedge \ (a_{i_k} <_i a_{i_l})\Big) \ \Rightarrow \ a_{i_l}^{-1} <_i a_{i_k}^{-1}$.

4. *The* required *order* $\prec_i \subseteq (\mathcal{A}_i \times \mathcal{A}_i)$ *with* $\prec_i = (\ll_i \cup <_i)$ *summarizes both strong and weak order constraints of a process.* □

If $\mathcal{A}_i$ contains one of the two termination activities C_i or A_i, respectively, then process P_i is said to be *complete*, otherwise, P_i is called *partial*.

Since, in general, a process P_i^k includes not only activities that are present in the associated process program PP^k and since the order constraints explicitly specified in PP^k only consider regular activities, the order constraints of P_i^k are much more complex. According to Definition 4.7, an order between compensating activities and their regular activities as well as among compensating activities (given that the corresponding regular activities are also ordered) has to be imposed in a process. All order constraints of a process P_i^k are summarized by the *required order*, $\prec_i$, which contains the extensions of the process program's strong and weak order constraints to the compensating and termination activities. This required order has to be included in any execution order (which may additionally order activities that are considered as parallel in the associated process program).

A multi-activity node n_i is executed correctly if all activities of $\mathfrak{A}_{n_i}$ have committed. But, when any of these activities fail and given it is not retriable, then all activities of $\mathfrak{A}_{n_i}$ that have already committed are compensated in backward order with respect to $<_i$ and $\ll_i$. Compensating activities associated with activities of n_i that are neither ordered by $<_i$ nor by $\ll_i$ can also be executed in parallel. Note that, according to Definition 4.6, a multi-activity node does not contain any pivot activity.

In order to discuss the characteristics of a process, i.e., the execution of a process program with guaranteed termination, its possible states are best suited:

1. If a process is running, its execution is a sequence of compensatable activities, corresponding to a path from the root.

2. When a process is aborting, its execution consists of a sequence of committed activities, followed by one aborted activity (that may be the primary pivot or a preceding activity), followed by a sequence of compensating activities, in reverse order.

3. The execution of an aborted process consists of a sequence as in case 2, where each committed activity has a corresponding compensating activity, and the final activity is A_i. We refer to such an execution as an *abort process execution* of the process program.

4. After a process has changed its state from running to completing, it contains the activities on the path from the root to the primary pivot, followed by abort process executions for alternatives $1, \ldots, j-1$, and an execution for alternative j compatible with its state.

5. When a process is committed and when it has changed its state from completing to committed, before committing, retriable activities of the assured termination tree (of the process or of a subprocess) may abort, but then they are retried, so a process execution may contain a subsequence of m aborted instances of a retriable activity, followed by a committed one. Note that in a committed process (even when it has changed from completing to committed), no retriable activity must be present. This might be the case when subprocesses with higher priority than the assured termination tree successfully commit. When the commit is executed in state running, C_i is preceded only by compensatable activities.

We note that as long as the primary pivot on the selected path has not committed, the process can always abort (if executed in isolation). When P_i is either running or aborting, it is said to be *backward-recoverable*. The sequence of activities to be executed in one of these states is called its *backward recovery path*. All activities of P_i preceding each primary pivot are compensatable. Therefore, if a primary pivot or one of its predecessors definitively fails, or if an abort A_i of P_i is requested for some other reason, backward recovery can be performed by successively applying compensation activities.

Once a primary pivot has terminated successfully, the process is in the state completing. Since, by the existence of the assured termination tree, it has a final alternative consisting only of retriable activities, and since all previous alternatives are smaller subprocesses with the same properties, a process in this state is guaranteed to complete. A process, P_i, is said to be *forward-recoverable* when it is completing. The sequence of activities leading from any activity succeeding a primary pivot to the well-defined termination of a process is the *forward recovery path*.

The set of activities of a process P_i executed for recovery purposes (either forward or backward) after the abort A_i, i.e., all activities that need to be executed to correctly terminate a partial process, is called the *completion* of P_i, and denoted by $\mathcal{C}(P_i)$. Note that in the case of P_i being in state running, $\mathcal{C}(P_i)$ consists only of compensating activities. If P_i is in state completing, the structure of $\mathcal{C}(P_i)$ is more complex. If the process is in the subprocess corresponding to its assured termination tree, then it consists of a path of retriable activities; this is also the case if a subprocesses of P_i is in its assured termination tree. If the process is now in another subprocess, and the deepest subprocess is completing, the completion of P_i is determined by the completion of that subprocess. If this deepest subprocess is aborting, then it consists of its completion (bringing it to the aborted state), followed by the assured termination tree of its parent. Hence, $\mathcal{C}(P_i)$ may consist of both compensating activities (for backward recovery of an aborting subprocess) followed by a path of retriable activities.

Although the model of process programs with guaranteed termination is based on the flexible transaction model, it augments the latter in several directions:

i.) it allows for a higher degree of concurrency within a process by considering not only a strong order between activities but also by allowing activities to be weakly ordered,

ii.) by requiring a total order on the children of each pivot, it avoids the indeterminism the flexible transaction model allows for the preference order between different rpo's,

iii.) it provides an intuitive structure, the process program tree, which encompasses all properties of a process program, thereby preventing the repeated specification of common activities. While the flexible transaction model requires shared prefixes of possible executions to be present in each corresponding rpo, these common prefixes have to be specified exactly once in the process program tree (such that the possible completions are subtrees starting from the common prefix),

iv.) it allows branching conditions associated with edges in the process program tree such that child nodes can be chosen dynamically, while this extension can, at the same time, be seamlessly integrated into the core process program model and does not affect the guaranteed termination property.

In addition, processes denoting the execution of process programs with guaranteed termination provide a clear semantics in that they explicitly encompass recovery related activities and the orders that have to be applied between them and between regular and compensating activities. Finally, processes avoid unnecessary redundancy since alternatives are tried in preference order only while the flexible transaction model considers the concurrent invocation of all possible rpo's, along with the necessary clean-up actions required for all others when one of them commits.

In [ZNBB94] it has been shown that a flexible transaction with well-formed structure always guarantees the existence of one possible execution (rpo) that can be executed correctly while all other rpo's leave no effects. Similarly, the execution of process programs with guaranteed termination ensures in any case the existence of a path along which a process can be terminated correctly. More formally,

Theorem 4.1 (Guaranteed Termination and Correct Execution) *Each complete process executed in isolation is guaranteed to terminate in a well-defined state, that is, it is ensured that the process either does not leave any effects or that exactly one path from the root to a leaf node of the associated process program with guaranteed termination is executed completely while all other activities do not leave any effects.* □

Proof (Theorem 4.1) *Consider a complete process P_i^k reflecting the execution of PP^k, a process program with guaranteed termination. In case no failure occurs, the execution path with highest priority, according to $\lhd^k$, is completely effected, with respect to the orders given by Definition 4.7.2a and 4.7.3a, and no other activity which does not belong to this path is invoked. Hence, P_i^k, terminates in a semantically correct and well-defined state. In order to show that P_i^k also terminates in a well-defined state in the presence of failures, the following cases have to be distinguished:*

i.) *Assume that an activity* a_{i_j} *preceding the primary pivot or that the primary pivot itself fails.*

(a) *If* a_{i_j} *is retriable, then, according to Definition 4.3, it cannot fail such that* $a_{i_j} \in \mathcal{A}_i$

(b) *If* a_{i_j} *is not retriable, then* $a_{i_j} \notin \mathcal{A}_i$. *If* a_{i_j} *is the first activity, then* $\mathcal{A}_i = \emptyset$ *which implies that* P_i^k *is aborted leaving no effects, thus terminates in a well-defined state. When* a_{i_j} *is not the first activity, then* $\mathcal{A}_i$ *comprises, for each regular activity* $a_{i_h} \in \mathcal{A}_i$, *the corresponding compensating activity* $a_{i_h}^{-1}$ *in the order* $a_{i_h} \ll_i a_{i_h}^{-1}$ *required by Definition 4.7.2b. Since* PP^k *is a process program with guaranteed termination (Definition 4.6), all these* a_{i_h} *are actually compensatable. In addition, each* $a_{i_h}^{-1}$ *is itself retriable, which means that it cannot fail. Moreover, according to Definition 4.7.2b and 4.7.3b, the sequence of regular activities of a* P_i^k *is followed by their compensating activities in reverse order which is referred to as abort process execution. Since an activity directly succeeded by its compensating activity forms an effect-free sequence, this abort process execution does not leave any effects (by repeatedly applying Definition 4.1). Hence, the state in which* P_i^k *terminates in this case is well-defined and correct.*

ii.) *Assume that some activity* a_{i_j} *succeeding the primary pivot fails.*

(a) *If* a_{i_j} *belongs to some assured termination tree, then it is retriable and* $a_{i_j} \in A_i$. *Since all activities of the assured termination tree are retriable, all of them that are effected appear in* $\mathcal{A}_i$ *in the order given by Definition 4.7.2a and 4.7.3a, and* P_i^k *commits.*

(b) *If* a_{i_j} *does not belong to an assured termination tree, then it has to precede the primary pivot of some subprocess program, or* a_{i_j} *is the primary pivot of some subprocess program. Then, according to i.) either* a_{i_j} *cannot fail or it leads to an abort subprocess execution such that all effects of that subprocess are completely undone. In the latter case, the preference order* $\lhd^k$ *is applied (Definition 4.7.2c) and leads to the next alternative. If this is an assured termination tree, a path will be effected correctly. Hence, since all effects of the abort subprocess execution are undone and since the path within the assured termination tree succeeds,* P_i^k *consists of all activities of exactly one allowed execution path and no other activity that does not belong to this path is committed without its effects being undone. Thus,* P_i^k *terminates in a well-defined state.*

If, by $\lhd^k$, *an alternative is chosen which is not an assured termination tree, then ii.(b) can be applied repeatedly in the case of failures.*

Assume that the failure of a_{i_j} *leads to an abort subprocess execution which, according to* $\lhd^k$, *cannot be continued by any alternative. However, since* PP^k *is a process program with guaranteed termination, Definition 4.6 requires that the last alternative given by* $\lhd^k$ *is an assured termination tree such that this case cannot happen.*

In all cases, P_i^k *terminates in a correct and well-defined state, even in the presence of failures. To this end, the basic properties of process programs with guaranteed termination are exploited, i.e., that all aborted (sub-)process executions do not leave any effects, that an assured termination tree exists as alternative for each pivot, and that a path of an assured termination tree is guaranteed to be executed successfully.* □

A classical transaction may abort as long as not all its operations have been executed. Actually, even after all of them were executed, the commit request may be denied. Operations without an inverse receive special treatment, and are always deferred to be executed after the commit decision, where

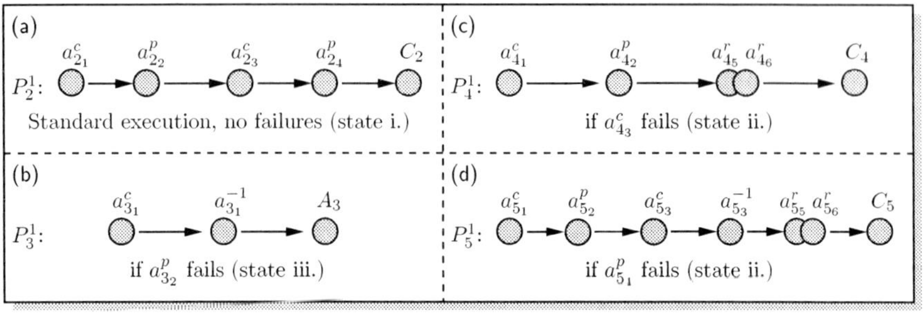

Figure 4.5: Possible Executions of Process Program PP^1

the transaction management system takes responsibility for their eventual execution. Analogously, transaction programs do not deal with the issue of how to continue after an abort since it is typically assumed that in transactional systems, inverse operations are, if needed, requested by the transaction manager (TM). However, in a transactional process, a non-compensatable activity may occur in the middle of execution, and cannot be deferred. After this activity, the process can no longer abort. Consequently, the responsibility for correct completion, by using retriable activities, now shifts to the process program which has to explicitly consider alternative executions.

Therefore, the guaranteed termination property of transactional processes is a generalization of the "all-or-nothing" semantics of traditional ACID transactions. While the all-or-nothing semantics only allows two possible outcomes of a transaction, several possibilities exist for transactional processes (there are, in effect, $m + 1$ possibilities where m is the number of leaf nodes in the process program tree; in addition to the m paths from the root to a leaf, the null execution where all activities are undone is also possible as long as no primary pivot has committed) and it is guaranteed that exactly one of these possibilities is completely and correctly executed. Moreover, since the guaranteed termination property of transactional processes is inherently present in the structure of the associated process program, it can be statically verified whether or not a given program can be executed correctly *prior* to its execution, by analyzing its structure. This is an important feature which supports and even eases the specification of higher-order transactions in the kind of framework, i.e., hyperdatabase environments, we consider in transactional process management.

Example 4.1 (Revisited) *Consider again process program PP^1 depicted in Figure 4.2. We have already shown that PP^1 is a process program with guaranteed termination. Due to the precedence order, $\lhd^1$, a^r_5 and therefore also a^r_6 can only be executed after a^c_3 has failed or after a^p_4 has failed and a^c_3 has been compensated by a^{-1}_3. PP^1 contains $m = 2$ leaf nodes. Therefore, three possible final states exist. The first corresponds to a regular execution, without any failure (leading to state i.). The second one (resulting in state ii.) is effected when a failure after the commit of a^p_2, the primary pivot, occurs and contains the completion along the assured termination tree. Finally, the third possibility (state iii.) is the null execution which will be effected when either a^c_1 or a^2_2 fail. Assuming that none of the activities not belonging to the assured termination tree starting from*

a_2^p is retriable, five different complete processes exist. The four non-trivial executions of PP^1 are depicted in Figure 4.5, along with the final state reached. The most trivial complete process, P_1^1, consists only of A_1 and is present when a_1^c fails. The other process resulting in the null execution, P_3^1, is depicted in Figure 4.2 (b). In P_3^1, the failure of $a_{3_2}^p$ is captured by executing the backward recovery path. Thus, the completion $\mathcal{C}(P_3^1)$ consists only of $\{a_{3_1}^{-1}\}$. In case of a failure after the commit of the primary pivot, the assured termination tree has to be executed. In process P_4^1, depicted in Figure 4.2 (c), activity $a_{4_3}^c$ fails and the execution is switched to the assured termination tree such that $\mathcal{C}(P_4^1) = \{a_{4_5}^r <_4 a_{4_6}^r\}$. The failure of $a_{5_4}^p$, which is considered in process P_5^1 depicted in Figure 4.2 (d), combines backward recovery and forward recovery. Therefore, both compensating and regular activities appear in its completion: $\mathcal{C}(P_5^1) = \{a_{5_3}^{-1} \ll_5 a_{5_5}^r <_5 a_{5_6}^r\}$. Finally, the standard execution in which no failures occur (process P_2^1) is depicted in Figure 4.2 (a). □

5 Concurrency Control and Recovery for Transactional Processes

"Von einem gewissen Punkt an gibt es keine Rückkehr mehr. Dieser Punkt ist zu erreichen."

Franz Kafka, Aphorismen

In the previous chapter, we have introduced the model of transactional process programs and identified a subset of all process programs which, when executed in isolation, are inherently and provably correct: process programs with guaranteed termination. Although concurrency is already present in the notion of process which reflects the execution of a single process program (note that we do not require a total order of all process activities with respect to the strong and weak precedence order), the concurrent execution of process programs introduces a couple of additional constraints that have to be met by a transactional process manager acting as scheduler for processes (see Figure 4.1). These extra constraints of multi-process executions are stemming from the additional semantics encompassed within processes, namely their inherent structure, the different termination properties of activities, the failure handling strategies that are present in process programs by appropriate preference orders, as well as the interaction between hierarchical schedulers in the kind of layered systems the transactional process management approach addresses. Therefore, although concurrency control and recovery are well understood problems in traditional databases, both notions have to be reformulated and extended in order to meet the additional constraints imposed in transactional process management [SAS99].

In terms of concurrency control, the flow of control of a process is far more complex than that of a flat transaction. A process may partially rollback its execution, it may follow several alternatives, and it might reach a point-of-no-return, already in the middle of execution, which requires that the subsequent commit of the process has to be enforced. All these different aspects need to be taken into account when deciding how to interleave processes. In terms of recovery, the different termination properties of activities within a process are also more complex compared with the characteristics of operations within a conventional transaction. These termination properties will introduce additional dependencies between processes in multi-process executions, thereby giving rise to even more constraints that have to be respected by a process scheduler.

In this chapter, we provide a unified model for concurrency control and recovery in transactional processes. To this end, we first introduce the notion of process schedule which, in analogy to the the traditional notion of schedule, reflects the concurrent execution of process programs. Then, we reformulate correctness criteria for concurrency control and recovery in the context of transactional processes and show how these notions, induced by the more complex semantics that can be found in transactional processes, differ from and extend the traditional ones. Finally and most importantly, we provide a joint correctness criterion for both problems.

5.1 Process Schedule

According to the traditional notion of schedule, i.e., the concurrent execution of transactions, a *process schedule* denotes concurrent processes. The main prerequisite we impose on multi-process executions is that each process program itself is inherently correct. Therefore, in all what follows, we consider only executions of process programs with guaranteed termination:

Axiom 5.1 *All process programs fulfill the guaranteed termination property.* □

Given the correct structure of process programs with guaranteed termination, a process schedule reflects concurrent processes, that is, the concurrent execution of process programs. The formalism used here is based on a reformulation of the unified theory of concurrency control and recovery recently proposed by Beeri [Bee00] in the context of conventional, single-level transactions, which is extended and generalized here in order to meet to the special requirements and the special structure of processes in transactional process management. According to [Bee00], the notion of process schedule $\mathcal{S}$, which is defined over a set of processes $\mathcal{P}_\mathcal{S}$, should not only include regular activities (as it is the case in the traditional notion of schedule) but also recovery related activities as they appear in an execution and as they are considered in processes. This avoids the expansion of a given schedule — in contrast to the original unified theory of concurrency control and recovery [SWY93, AVA$^+$94a, VHBS98] which is based on the traditional notion of schedule encompassing only regular operations. Furthermore, a process schedule $\mathcal{S}$ not only includes the observed execution order $<_\mathcal{S}$ between activities, but also the required order $\prec_\mathcal{S}$ which summarizes the strong and weak order constraints explicitly specified for each process in its corresponding process program (and which is further extended about constraints on the execution of compensating activities). The need for including the required order explicitly in a process schedule stems from the fact that a process program may not require any order on some activities, i.e., they are not related by $\prec_i$, yet they are ordered by $<_\mathcal{S}$ in some execution. Therefore, without $\prec_\mathcal{S}$, the requested orders of processes could not be reconstructed from a process schedule. However, in order to apply reduction techniques (Section 5.5) to process schedules, this information is required.

Definition 5.1 (Process Schedule $\mathcal{S}$) *A* process schedule $\mathcal{S}$ *is a quadruple* $(\mathcal{P}_\mathcal{S}, \mathcal{A}_\mathcal{S}, \prec_\mathcal{S}, <_\mathcal{S})$ *where*

1. *$\mathcal{P}_\mathcal{S}$ is a set of (partial) processes $P_i = (\mathcal{A}_i, \ll_i, <_i, \prec_i)$.*
2. *$\mathcal{A}_\mathcal{S} \subseteq \hat{\mathcal{A}}$ with $\mathcal{A}_\mathcal{S} = \{a_{i_j} \mid (a_{i_j} \in \mathcal{A}_i) \wedge (P_i \in \mathcal{P}_\mathcal{S})\}$ is the set of all activities of all processes of $\mathcal{P}_\mathcal{S}$.*
3. *$\prec_\mathcal{S}$ is a partial order between activities of $\mathcal{A}_\mathcal{S}$, called the* required order, *with $\prec_\mathcal{S} \subseteq (\mathcal{A}_\mathcal{S} \times \mathcal{A}_\mathcal{S})$ which is the union of the required orders of all processes of $\mathcal{P}_\mathcal{S}$, that is $\prec_\mathcal{S} = \bigcup_{P_i \in \mathcal{P}_\mathcal{S}} \prec_i$.*
4. *$<_\mathcal{S}$ is a partial order between activities of $\mathcal{A}_\mathcal{S}$, called* execution order, *with $<_\mathcal{S} \subseteq (\mathcal{A}_\mathcal{S} \times \mathcal{A}_\mathcal{S})$ reflecting the observed order in which activities are executed. The required order $\prec_\mathcal{S}$ of $\mathcal{S}$ is contained in the observed execution order $<_\mathcal{S}$, that is $\prec_\mathcal{S} \subseteq <_\mathcal{S}$.* □

This definition of process schedule reflects the invocation of activities at the process manager level as marked with (*) in Figure 4.1. In general, processes do not need to have terminated in $\mathcal{S}$. Therefore, the above definition includes both partial and complete processes. Accordingly, if all processes P_i of a process schedule $\mathcal{S}$ have terminated (either by C_i or A_i), then $\mathcal{S}$ is said to be *complete*, otherwise $\mathcal{S}$ is called *partial.*

Note that since a process schedule is defined at the level of activities, it also includes committed activities of aborted processes. However, since the underlying subsystems guarantee both serializability (CPSR) and atomicity (ACA), activities returning with abort can be omitted in $\mathcal{S}$. In particular, retriable activities appear at most once in a process schedule, namely when they are committed, while all previous failed invocations —which do not leave any effects in the associated subsystem and which, due to the ACA property provided by this system do also not affect other activities— do not need to be considered. Moreover, the CPSR property of subsystems allows to consider all activities of $\mathcal{S}$ that belong to the same subsystem (that correspond to transactions in the same subsystem) as totally ordered.

In accordance to the traditional transaction theory where all transactions are considered to be independent of each other such that flow of information is only possible via shared data objects (in the form of pairs of conflicting operations) we also consider all processes to be independent. Thus, the only possibility for some flow of information between concurrent processes is when conflicting activities share some resources, that is when there is flow of information between the associated transactions of both activities. Hence, a common mechanism to verify the equivalence between schedules that are defined over semantically rich operations or activities, respectively, is *commutativity.* Following [VHBS98], the notion of commutativity is defined using the return values of activities: we assume each activity a_i to provide a return value which includes a description of a_i's outcome (success or failure, respectively). The return value of a process is a function of the return values of all its activities. Given this information, Definition 3.18 can be applied to transactional processes such that two activities, a_{i_k}, $a_{j_l} \in \mathcal{A}^*$ are considered as commuting, if for all activity sequences α and ω from $\mathcal{A}^*$ the return values of all activities in the activity sequence $\langle \alpha\ a_{i_k}\ a_{j_l}\ \omega \rangle$ are identical to the return values of the activity sequence $\langle \alpha\ a_{j_l}\ a_{i_k}\ \omega \rangle$. Conversely, two activities are in conflict if they do not commute.

Information about the commutativity behavior of activities, following Definition 3.18, is crucial for the transactional process manager. Hence, a commutativity relation has to be available to it for scheduling purposes. This commutativity relation specifies, for each pair of activities from $\mathcal{A}^*$, whether or not they commute, thereby also considering predicates on the parameters associated which the invocation of both activities. Yet, a process manager is able to determine pairs of conflicting activities in a concrete context which is indicated by their actual parameters.

Activities may only conflict if they are executed in the same subsystem. This observation is based on the kind of layered architecture that can be found in transactional process management, corresponding to a fork configuration in the terminology of the composite systems theory. As depicted in Figure 4.1, all these subsystems are independent. In particular, the resources on which subsystems operate are pairwise disjoint. Hence, since the conflict behavior of each pair of activities coincides with the conflict behavior of the corresponding transactions, once the necessary information about commutativity of transactions in each subsystem are given, these can be combined so as to derive the global commutativity relation at process manager level, encompassing all activities of $\mathcal{A}^*$.

In practical applications, a common assumption is that commutativity is perfect. According to Definition 3.20 [VHBS98], a commutativity relation between activities is perfect, if, for all pairs of activities $a_{i_k}, a_{j_l} \in \mathcal{A}^*$, either all possible combinations $(a_{i_k}^{\alpha}, a_{j_l}^{\beta})$ for $\alpha, \beta \in \{-1, 1\}$ commute, or all possible combinations of these activities conflict.

With the notion of commutativity, we are now able to extend the traditional definition of *conflict-equivalence* (Definition 3.3) to process schedules as follows:

Definition 5.2 (Conflict Equivalence) *Two process schedules* $\mathcal{S}_i = (\mathcal{P}_{\mathcal{S}_i}, \mathcal{A}_{\mathcal{S}_i}, \prec_{\mathcal{S}_i}, <_{\mathcal{S}_i})$ *and* $\mathcal{S}_k = (\mathcal{P}_{\mathcal{S}_k}, \mathcal{A}_{\mathcal{S}_k}, \prec_{\mathcal{S}_k}, <_{\mathcal{S}_k})$ *are* conflict equivalent, *if they are defined over the same set of processes* ($\mathcal{P}_{\mathcal{S}_i} = \mathcal{P}_{\mathcal{S}_k}$), *contain the same set of activities* ($\mathcal{A}_{\mathcal{S}_i} = \mathcal{A}_{\mathcal{S}_k}$), *and if all pairs of conflicting activities appear in the same order in the observed execution orders* $<_{\mathcal{S}_i}$ *and* $<_{\mathcal{S}_k}$ *of both process schedules.* □

Since two conflict equivalent process schedules, $\mathcal{S}_i$ and $\mathcal{S}_k$, are defined over the same set of processes ($\mathcal{P}_{\mathcal{S}_i} = \mathcal{P}_{\mathcal{S}_k}$) and contain the same set of activities ($\mathcal{A}_{\mathcal{S}_i} = \mathcal{A}_{\mathcal{S}_k}$), also the required orders of both process schedules must be identical, $\prec_{\mathcal{S}_i} = \prec_{\mathcal{S}_k}$. Therefore, when analyzing whether two process schedules are conflict equivalent, only the compliance of conflicting activities with respect to the execution orders $<_{\mathcal{S}_i}$ and $<_{\mathcal{S}_k}$, respectively, has to be verified.

5.2 Process–Serializability

Before introducing a joint criterion for concurrency control and recovery in transactional process management, we first clarify the problem how serializability is affected by the special semantics that can be found in processes. In the traditional model, transactions are either aborted or committed. In the latter case, they contain only regular operations but no recovery related ones. When considering transactional processes, things become more complex. Since partial backward recovery combined with alternative executions is possible, a process may encompass aborted subprocess executions before it is finally committed. When reasoning about correct concurrency control in transactional process management, aborted or aborting processes are neglected, as in the traditional case. In addition, and in analogy to the traditional case where concurrency control is treated independently from recovery, also aborted or aborting subprocesses of completing processes are excluded. Thus, using the notion of conflict equivalence, a process schedule is process-serializable if its projection on all committed and active (running and completing) processes, in which also all activities of aborted or aborting subprocesses are omitted, is conflict equivalent to some serial process schedule.

Definition 5.3 (Committed and Active Projection (CA)) *Let* $\mathcal{S} = (\mathcal{P}_{\mathcal{S}}, \mathcal{A}_{\mathcal{S}}, \prec_{\mathcal{S}}, <_{\mathcal{S}})$ *be a process schedule. The* committed and active projection $CA(\mathcal{S})$ *of* $\mathcal{S}$ *is a process schedule which is defined on all processes that are running, completing, and committed in* $\mathcal{S}$. $CA(\mathcal{S})$ *contains all activities from* $\mathcal{A}_{\mathcal{S}}$ *belonging to these processes, except for the activities of aborted or aborting subprocesses of completing or committed processes. Furthermore,* $CA(\mathcal{S})$ *contains the required orders for all these processes, projected on the activities of* $CA(\mathcal{S})$. *Analogously, the observed order of* $CA(\mathcal{S})$ *is the projection of* $<_{\mathcal{S}}$ *on its activities.* □

In terms of the sketched execution of a single process program depicted in Figure 4.3, the committed and active projection of a process schedule $\mathcal{S}$ considers only a subset of the processes' regular activities, namely those of nodes that are traversed in forward direction but neither any activity of nodes whose (sub-)process is aborted or aborting nor any compensating activity. For committed processes, $CA(\mathcal{S})$ contains only the activities of the execution path, from the process program's root to a leaf node, which is effected completely and correctly.

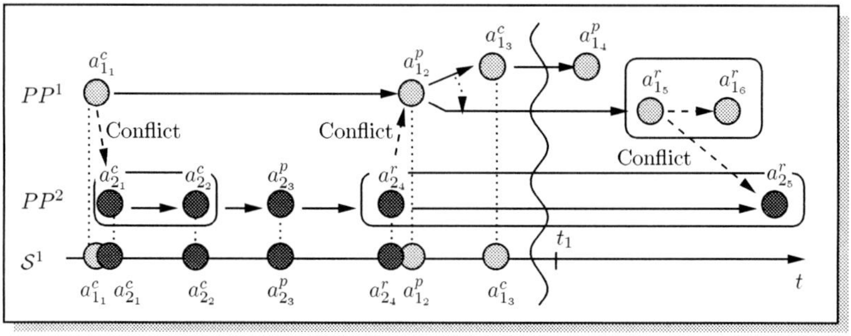

Figure 5.1: Non–P–SR Process Schedule $\mathcal{S}^1_{t_1}$ of Example 5.1

Definition 5.4 (Process–Serializability (P-SR)) *A process schedule* $\mathcal{S} = (\mathcal{P}_\mathcal{S}, \mathcal{A}_\mathcal{S}, \prec_\mathcal{S}, <_\mathcal{S})$ *is* process-serializable (P-SR) *if its committed and active projection* $CA(\mathcal{S})$ *is conflict-equivalent to a serial process schedule* $\mathcal{S}_{ser} = (\mathcal{P}_{\mathcal{S}_{ser}}, \mathcal{A}_{\mathcal{S}_{ser}}, \prec_{\mathcal{S}_{ser}}, <_{\mathcal{S}_{ser}})$. □

Process-serializability is defined on the conflict equivalence between a serial process schedule $\mathcal{S}_{\text{ser}}$ (in which the execution order, $<_{\mathcal{S}_{\text{ser}}}$, is total and serial), and the committed and active projection $CA(\mathcal{S})$ of a given process schedule $\mathcal{S}$. Therefore, it has to be noted that $CA(\mathcal{S})$ may contain both a smaller set of processes compared to $\mathcal{S}$ (analogously to the traditional notion of serializability which considers the committed projection of a schedule in which also a potentially smaller set of transactions is present) and, for these processes, also a possibly smaller set of activities (namely only the ones of subprocesses that are neither aborted nor aborting).

Example 5.1 *Consider two processes,* P_1^1 *and* P_2^2*, being executed in parallel. In Figure 5.1, the associated process programs* PP^1 *and* PP^2 *as well as process schedule* $\mathcal{S}^1$ *reflecting the concurrent execution of* P_1 *and* P_2 *are depicted. While the required order* $\prec_{\mathcal{S}^1}$ *of* $\mathcal{S}^1$ *can be derived from the corresponding process programs, the observed execution order,* $<_{\mathcal{S}^1}$*, is explicitly depicted by projecting both processes to a common timeline. Pairs of activities that are weakly ordered and thus, are executed concurrently, appear overlapped on this timeline. In total, three pairs of activities of* P_1 *and* P_2 *exist that do not commute:* $(a^c_{1_1}, a^c_{2_1})$, $(a^p_{1_2}, a^r_{2_4})$, *and* $(a^r_{1_5}, a^r_{2_5})$. *At time* t_1*, process schedule* $\mathcal{S}^1_{t_1} = (\mathcal{P}_{\mathcal{S}^1_{t_1}}, \mathcal{A}_{\mathcal{S}^1_{t_1}}, \prec_{\mathcal{S}^1_{t_1}}, <_{\mathcal{S}^1_{t_1}})$ *encompasses the set of processes* $\mathcal{P}_{\mathcal{S}^1_{t_1}} = \{P_1, P_2\}$ *and the set of activities* $\mathcal{A}_{\mathcal{S}^1_{t_1}} = \{a^c_{1_1}, a^p_{1_2}, a^c_{1_3}, a^c_{2_1}, a^c_{2_2}, a^p_{2_3}, a^r_{2_4}\}$. *In addition, the required order,* $\prec_{\mathcal{S}^1_{t_1}}$*, results in* $\prec_{\mathcal{S}^1_{t_1}} = \{(a^c_{1_1} \prec_{\mathcal{S}^1_{t_1}} a^p_{1_2} \prec_{\mathcal{S}^1_{t_1}} a^c_{1_3}), (a^c_{2_1} \prec_{\mathcal{S}^1_{t_1}} a^c_{2_2} \prec_{\mathcal{S}^1_{t_1}} a^p_{2_3} \prec_{\mathcal{S}^1_{t_1}} a^r_{2_4})\}$ *and the observed execution order in* $<_{\mathcal{S}^1_{t_1}} = \{(a^c_{1_1} <_{\mathcal{S}^1_{t_1}} a^c_{2_1} <_{\mathcal{S}^1_{t_1}} a^c_{2_2} <_{\mathcal{S}^1_{t_1}} a^p_{2_3} <_{\mathcal{S}^1_{t_1}} a^r_{2_4} <_{\mathcal{S}^1_{t_1}} a^p_{1_2} <_{\mathcal{S}^1_{t_1}} a^c_{1_3})\}$. *However, according to Definition 5.4,* $S^1_{t_1}$ *is not P-SR since no conflict equivalent serial execution of* P_1 *and* P_2 *exists due to a conflict cycle caused by the orders* $(a^c_{1_1} <_{\mathcal{S}^1_{t_1}} a^c_{2_1})$ *and* $(a^r_{2_4} <_{\mathcal{S}^1_{t_1}} a^p_{1_2})$. *Since none of the activities involved in this cycle belongs to an aborted (sub-)process, they are all present in* $CA(\mathcal{S}^1_{t_1})$. *Hence, they must also be present in a conflict equivalent serial process schedule which, however, would in any case have a different ordering of one pair of conflicting activities.* □

Remarkably, process-serializability is not prefix-closed. Even if there is a conflict cycle in the committed and active projection of a given process schedule involving, say two processes, it is possible

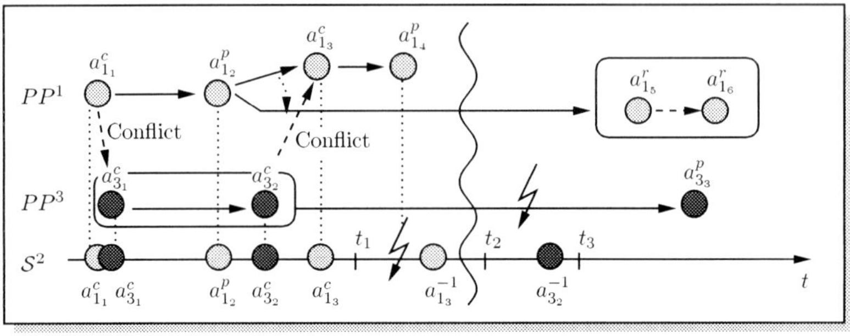

Figure 5.2: Non-Prefix-Closed P–SR Process Schedule $\mathcal{S}^2_{t_2}$ of Example 5.2

that an abort of a subprocess (and a subsequent execution of another alternative subprocess) of one of them will allow both to complete while removing the cycle, such that the resulting process schedule is process-serializable. This is illustrated in the following example.

Example 5.2 *Consider the concurrent execution of P^1_1 and P^3_3 reflected in process schedule $\mathcal{S}^2$ as depicted in Figure 5.2. Activities $a^c_{1_1}$ and $a^c_{3_1}$ as well as $a^c_{3_2}$ and $a^c_{1_3}$ do not commute (denoted by dashed arcs). At time t_1, $\mathcal{S}^2_{t_1}$ is not process-serializable: both P_1 and P_3 are active (P_3 is running and P_1 is completing where its subprocess including $a^c_{1_3}$ is neither aborting nor aborted) but the execution of both processes is not conflict equivalent to any serial execution, due to cyclic conflicts. Assume now that either activity $a^p_{1_4}$ fails or that the process manager decides to abort the subprocess of P_1 containing $a^c_{1_3}$ and $a^p_{1_4}$ in order to break the conflict cycle. Both cases lead to the compensation of $a^c_{1_3}$ and to the execution of the assured termination tree which succeeds the primary pivot $a^p_{1_2}$ of P_1 and which is ordered after the subprocess of $a^3_{1_3}$ and $a^p_{1_4}$ with respect to $\lhd_1$. By changing the state of P_1's subprocess from running to aborting, the conflict in which $a^c_{1_3}$ is involved will be neglected. Yet, the compensating activity $a^{-1}_{1_3}$ undoes the effects of its regular activity. At time t_2, after $a^{-1}_{1_3}$ has committed, process schedule $\mathcal{S}^2_{t_2}$ is P-SR since $CA(\mathcal{S}^2_{t_2})$ is conflict equivalent to a serial execution of P_1 —without its aborted subprocess— followed by P_3.* □

In traditional transactions where only total backward recovery is allowed, this phenomenon cannot occur (at least when commutativity between activities is perfect) since whenever a cycle in a conflict graph exists, there is no way for all involved transactions to finally commit successfully. In process executions where partial backward recovery combined with alternative executions is possible, this may however be the case.

In analogy to the traditional, single-level transaction model where a serialization graph (see Definition 3.5) is used to verify whether a given schedule is serializable or not, a *process serialization graph*, $PSG(\mathcal{S})$, can be used for the verification of the P-SR property of a process schedule $\mathcal{S}$. This process serialization graph contains a node for each running, completing, and committed process. A directed edge from P_i to P_j is inserted whenever a pair of conflicting regular activities $a_{i_k} \in P_i$ and $a_{j_l} \in P_j$ appears in $\mathcal{S}$ with $a_{i_k} <_{\mathcal{S}} a_{j_l}$. Whenever a subprocess is aborted, all edges introduced by activities of this subprocess (that is, all conflicts in which an activity of an aborted subprocess is involved) are removed from $PSG(\mathcal{S})$. More formally,

Definition 5.5 (Process Serialization Graph (PSG)) *Let $\mathcal{S} = (\mathcal{P_S}, \mathcal{A_S}, \prec_{\mathcal{S}}, <_{\mathcal{S}})$ be a process schedule. The* process serialization graph (PSG($\mathcal{S}$)) *of $\mathcal{S}$ is a directed graph whose nodes are the processes of the committed and active projection $CA(\mathcal{S})$ of $\mathcal{S}$ and whose edges are all (P_i, P_j) for which a pair of conflicting activities a_{i_k}, a_{j_l} in $CA(\mathcal{S})$ exists with $a_{i_k} <_{CA(\mathcal{S})} a_{j_l}$.* □

In contrast to the traditional serialization graph where edges are only inserted but never removed (except for the case when nodes are removed from the serialization graph), PSG considers both the removal of single edges and of nodes. The process serialization graph can be exploited in order to characterize process-serializability:

Theorem 5.1 (Process Serialization Graph and P-SR) *A process schedule $\mathcal{S}$ is P-SR if and only if its process serialization graph $PSG(\mathcal{S})$ is acyclic.* □

Proof (Theorem 5.1)

If: *Let $PSG(\mathcal{S})$ be an acyclic process serialization graph of process schedule $\mathcal{S}$ and let $\mathcal{S}'$ be a process schedule defined over the same set of processes than the committed and active projection $CA(\mathcal{S})$ of $\mathcal{S}$ ($\mathcal{P}_{CA(\mathcal{S})} = \mathcal{P}_{\mathcal{S}'}$), containing the same set of activities as $CA(\mathcal{S})$, and encompassing a total order on all processes that is compatible with the orders induced by the edges of $PSG(\mathcal{S})$. Process schedule $\mathcal{S}'$ can be derived from $\mathcal{S}$ by applying a topological sort. Since all pairs of conflicting activities appear in the same order in $CA(\mathcal{S})$ and $\mathcal{S}'$ (thus, both process schedules are conflict equivalent) and since $\mathcal{S}'$ is a serial process schedule, $\mathcal{S}$ is P-SR.*

Only if: *Let $\mathcal{S}$ be a P-SR process schedule. Hence, a serial process schedule $\mathcal{S}'$ exists which is conflict equivalent to $CA(\mathcal{S})$. Assume that the process serialization graph $PSG(\mathcal{S})$ of $\mathcal{S}$ contains a cycle $P_i \rightarrow P_{i+1} \rightarrow \ldots \rightarrow P_{i+n} \rightarrow P_i$. Since $PSG(\mathcal{S})$ does only contain edges induced by activities of the committed and active projection of $\mathcal{S}$, all these conflicts have to be present in $\mathcal{S}'$. Therefore, in the serial process schedule $\mathcal{S}'$, P_i has to precede P_{i+1} which, in turn, has to precede P_i. This obviously leads to a contradiction of the initial assumption that $\mathcal{S}$ is a P-SR process schedule.* □

For convenience, process-serializability can be tested using the standard serialization graph $SG(\mathcal{S})$, introduced in Definition 3.5, extended to the committed and active projection of a process schedule, i.e., $SG(\mathcal{S})$ contains a node for each active and committed process and an edge for each conflict between two of these processes. In contrast to the process serialization graph, however, $SG(\mathcal{S})$ additionally contains all edges induced by activities of aborted or aborting subprocesses of active or committed processes. Therefore, the process serialization graph $PSG(\mathcal{S})$ of a process schedule $\mathcal{S}$ can be considered as the serialization graph, restricted to the committed and active projection $CA(\mathcal{S})$ of $\mathcal{S}$, that is, $PSG(\mathcal{S}) = SG(CA(\mathcal{S}))$.

Theorem 5.2 (Serialization Graph and P-SR) *A process schedule $\mathcal{S}$ is P-SR if its serialization graph $SG(\mathcal{S})$ is acyclic.* □

Proof (Theorem 5.2) *Let $SG(\mathcal{S})$ be an acyclic serialization graph of process schedule $\mathcal{S}$. The committed and active projection, $CA(\mathcal{S})$, of $\mathcal{S}$ is obtained from $\mathcal{S}$ by dropping all activities of aborted and aborting subprocesses of completing processes. Therefore, the serialization graph of $CA(\mathcal{S})$ is still acyclic. Since $SG(CA(\mathcal{S})) = PSG(\mathcal{S})$, the process serialization graph of $\mathcal{S}$ is acyclic which, according to Theorem 5.1, implies that $\mathcal{S}$ is P-SR.* □

Note that —in contrast to the traditional transaction model— the converse of Theorem 5.2 does not hold. A process schedule may be P-SR albeit its serialization graph contains a cycle. This is the case since the serialization graph considers all active and committed processes and does not omit conflicts in which activities of aborted or aborting subprocesses are involved.

Although the acyclicity of $SG(\mathcal{S})$ is a stronger criterion than P-SR and allows a subset of all P-SR process schedules only, it can be used for dynamic scheduling since the abort of subprocesses does not require the examination of all edges of the graph and the deletion of those in which activities of these subprocesses are involved (which would, however, be the case for PSG). This subclass of P-SR which encompasses all process schedules whose serialization graphs are acyclic is called SG-P-SR. More formally,

Definition 5.6 (SG-Process-Serializability (SG-P-SR)) *A process schedule* $\mathcal{S} = (\mathcal{P}_{\mathcal{S}}, \mathcal{A}_{\mathcal{S}}, \prec_{\mathcal{S}}, <_{\mathcal{S}})$ *is* SG-process-serializable (SG-P-SR) *if its serialization graph* $SG(\mathcal{S})$ *is acyclic.* □

In contrast to $PSG(\mathcal{S})$, it is not possible to successfully terminate a set of processes in $\mathcal{S}$ (that is, to commit each of these processes) which induce a cycle in $SG(\mathcal{S})$, i.e., when $\mathcal{S}$ is not SG-P-SR, such that this cycle disappears after completion of all these processes. Therefore, a process manager has to guarantee that the serialization graph is at any point in time free of cycles. This leads to a further restriction of SG-P-SR, namely a prefix-closed variant, called P-SG-P-SR:

Definition 5.7 (Prefix-SG-Process-Serializability (P–SG–P–SR)) *A process schedule* $\mathcal{S}$ *is* prefix-SG-process-serializable (P-SG-P-SR) *if each prefix of* $\mathcal{S}$ *is SG-P-SR.* □

Note that SG-P-SR itself is not prefix-closed[1]: assume that a conflict cycle in the serialization graph $SG(\mathcal{S}')$ of some process schedule $\mathcal{S}'$ exists. Then, the abort of at least one process involved in this cycle makes the associated node disappear and may lead to a process schedule $\mathcal{S}$ with prefix $\mathcal{S}'$ that meets SG-P-SR.

Example 5.2 (Revisited) *As we have already seen, the process serialization graph of process schedule* $\mathcal{S}^2$ *contains, at time* t_1*, the cycle* $P_1 \leftrightarrows P_3$*, hence* $\mathcal{S}^2_{t_1}$ *is not P-SR. Therefore, this cycle also exists in* $SG(\mathcal{S}^2_{t_1})$ *such that* $\mathcal{S}^2_{t_1}$ *is also not SG-P-SR. However, the failure of* $a^p_{1_4}$ *leads to the abort of the subprocess including* $a^c_{1_3}$ *and* $a^p_{1_4}$ *which, in turn, leads to the deletion of the edge induced by* $a^c_{3_2} <_{\mathcal{S}^2} a^c_{1_3}$ *and removes the cycle in* $PSG(\mathcal{S}^2_{t_2})$*. Note that the abort of* P_1*'s subprocess does not make* P_1 *to completely disappear in* $PSG(\mathcal{S}^2_{t_2})$ *since* $a^p_{1_2}$*, the primary pivot, has already successfully committed such that* P_1 *is completing. While the abort of* $a^p_{1_4}$ *has made the edge corresponding to the conflict pair* $a^c_{3_2} <_{\mathcal{S}^2} a^c_{1_3}$ *disappear in* $PSG(\mathcal{S}^2_{t_2})$*, it is still present in* $SG(\mathcal{S}^2_{t_2})$ *such that* $\mathcal{S}^2_{t_2}$*, even though it is P-SR, does not meet the SG-P-SR criterion. Assume further that process* P_3 *is aborted for some reason after the execution of* $a^{-1}_{1_3}$*. Therefore, at time* t_3*,* P_3 *is aborting and activity* $a^{-1}_{3_2}$ *has been executed for recovery purposes. Thus,* P_3 *has disappeared from the committed and active projection of* $\mathcal{S}^2_{t_3}$ *and the corresponding node is removed from both PSG and SG. Hence,* $SG(\mathcal{S}^2_{t_3})$ *contains only one process, namely* P_1*, such that SG-P-SR trivially holds for* $\mathcal{S}^2_{t_3}$*. Since this is not the case for its prefix* $\mathcal{S}^2_{t_2}$*,* $\mathcal{S}^2_{t_3}$ *is not P-SG-P-SR.* □

[1] In the traditional transaction model where serializability is based on the notion of committed projection of a schedule, CPSR is prefix-closed: whenever a schedule is conflict-preserving serializable, so is also each prefix. The restriction to the committed projection of a schedule is possible in the traditional model since each active transaction can be aborted which is, however, not the case for active processes once they have committed a pivot.

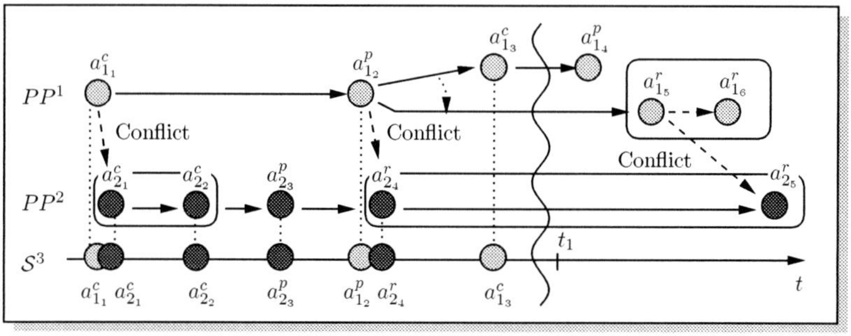

Figure 5.3: Correct P–SR Process Schedule $\mathcal{S}^3_{t_1}$ of Example 5.3

Example 5.3 *Consider again the two process programs PP^1 and PP^2, now executed concurrently by processes P_1 and P_2 in process schedule $\mathcal{S}^3$ as depicted in Figure 5.3. At time t_1, process schedule $\mathcal{S}^3_{t_1}$ is P-SR. Again, all conflicting activities do not belong to any aborted (sub-)process, yet they are contained in $CA(\mathcal{S}^3_{t_1})$, and must therefore be present in an equivalent serial schedule. The serial execution of all P_1 activities of $\mathcal{S}^3_{t_1}$ followed by all activities of P_2 would be conflict equivalent to the execution of process schedule $\mathcal{S}^3_{t_1}$.* □

While the required order of each process is given and has to be respected in a process schedule, the process manager (PM) is responsible for correctly ordering conflicting activities. By this, it is meant that the process manager has to guarantee process-serializability of process schedules, while taking into account all the information available to it. As already mentioned, the process manager has the possibility to impose a temporal order between conflicting activities or it can submit activities concurrently while at the same time specifying the order in which the associated transactions have to be serialized in the underlying subsystem. In both cases, commit-order serializability protocols implemented in the subsystems guarantee compliance with this order. Note that when activities do not correspond to transactions in the traditional sense (as we do assume here) but are implemented again by process programs, the notion of commit-order serializability needs to be extended. In this case, for each process in a subsystem, its commit and its pivot activities have to be treated the same way. Each pair of conflicting activities of any two subsystem processes then requires the next points-of-no-return of both processes (be it either a pivot or the process' commit) to follow the imposed serialization order.

The failure of retriable activities now may lead to a special treatment of other, concurrent activities. Suppose that two activities, $a^r_{i_k}$ and a_{j_l}, are executed concurrently within the same subsystem with a serialization order given by the process manager requiring $a^r_{i_k}$ to be serialized before a_{j_l}. If the local transaction T_{i_k} corresponding to $a^r_{i_k}$ fails after some operations of T_{i_k} have already been executed, then, in general, the local transaction T_{j_l} (which corresponds to activity a_{j_l}) running in parallel to T_{i_k} (with respect to the given weak order) has to be aborted. However, as this is not due to a failure of T_{j_l} (note that ACA is guaranteed by each subsystem such that the abort of T_{i_k} does not influence T_{j_l}), it must not cause an exception of P_j leading to another alternative. Therefore, after T_{i_k} is restarted, T_{j_l} also has to be restarted within the subsystem, hence guaranteeing compliance with the serialization order imposed by the process manager.

The above discussion has shown that a process manager extends a classical transaction scheduler in many ways. In particular, it considers additional information, i.e., about the structure of processes, which allows to provide more sophisticated correctness criteria that meet these additional constraints and thus reflect the higher-level semantics of processes. Hence, a process manager, compared to a classical transaction scheduler, can be characterized by the following three additional features:

i.) it exploits information about the properties of all activities (compensatable, pivot, or retriable) and thus, also about the different states of active processes (running or completing),

ii.) it considers, for each process P_i^k, all alternative subprocesses (which also include the assured termination trees) defined within the process program PP^k,

iii.) it respects the required order for each process as defined within the corresponding process program as well as its extensions to compensating activities and explicitly imposes appropriate weak orders between conflicting activities.

5.3 Process–Recoverability

Similar to concurrency control, also recovery in transactional process management has to take into account additional constraints imposed by the special structure and semantics of processes. Process-recoverability addresses the possibility to abort a subset of running processes correctly, even in the presence of concurrency. However, avoiding cascading aborts is too strong at the process level since —in the case of semantical rich activities where a distinction between read and write access to data is hardly possible— this would degenerate to strictness or even rigorousness. Yet, for each arbitrary set $R_{\mathcal{S}}$ of running processes of a process schedule $\mathcal{S}$, a superset $R^*_{\mathcal{S}}$, also of running processes, has to exist such that all processes of $R^*_{\mathcal{S}}$ together with all aborting processes can be aborted correctly without affecting other processes. Note that one cannot require that all partial processes can be aborted, since some of them may have already performed a pivot —an activity representing a point-of-no-return of the process— which leads to the restriction to running processes.

Thus, for $\mathcal{S}$ there must be a schedule $\mathcal{S}'$ which is defined over the same set of processes and in which all processes of $R^*_{\mathcal{S}}$ that are running in $\mathcal{S}$ and all aborting processes of $\mathcal{S}$ do not leave any effects. Furthermore, the return values of all other activities (not belonging to aborted processes in $\mathcal{S}$ or processes of $R^*_{\mathcal{S}}$) are the same in both process schedules. Since the return values of processes is a function on the return values of all its activities, the latter criterion guarantees the correspondence of the return values of all committed processes in both process schedules. The fact that the return values of all other activities, especially those of completing processes, are left unchanged is important because these processes must be able to commit successfully. Since the effects of all aborting processes and of all processes of $R^*_{\mathcal{S}}$ have to be eliminated, correspondence between the final states of $\mathcal{S}$ and $\mathcal{S}'$ is not required.

In the classical case, the abort of transactions can be performed by backward recovery. The ACA property guarantees that, if necessary, all running transactions can be aborted. However, it is not necessarily possible to consider a partial process as abortable since it may have already committed its primary pivot; this is why a distinction between the states running and completing is made. In the presence of concurrency, the constraints imposed by the special structure of process programs and the dependencies between concurrent processes may even preclude the possibility of aborting all running processes. Hence, process-recoverability has to cope with the different semantics of active processes and the dependencies that are imposed between them.

In the presence of concurrency, care is needed with situations where the execution of a sequence of activities of a process P_j is affected by the compensation of an activity a_{i_k} of another process P_i when the subprocess, in which a_{i_k} has been executed, is running and is now a candidate for being aborted. In here, two cases have to be differentiated: if P_j is running, then we can decide to abort it as well, i.e., when P_i is in $R^*_{\mathcal{S}}$, then so is P_j (note that we explicitly do not require the ACA property at the process manager level). However, in the second case, when P_j is completing (or has already committed), this is impossible. Note that once P_j has committed a primary pivot successfully, then it cannot be aborted such that the problem that P_i has to abort can no longer be solved by a joint abort of both processes. In fact, this reflects an unresolvable situation where execution may not progress correctly. Therefore, process-recoverability must encompass the restriction that no completing process must be dependent on a running process in the sense that the abort of a running process does imply also the abort of a completing process which, according to the state diagram depicted in Figure 4.4, is not possible.

To this end, we have to extend the notion of abort dependency [Bee00] to formally specify the situations possibly leading to a violation of process-recoverability. In short, there is an abort dependency between two processes P_i and P_j imposed by activities $a^c_{i_k}$ and a_{j_m} with $a^c_{i_k} <_{\mathcal{S}} a_{j_m}$ when the execution of a_{j_m} hinders the compensation of $a^c_{i_k}$.

Definition 5.8 (Abort Dependency) *An* abort dependency *between two processes P_i and P_j, imposed by activities $a_{i_k} \in P_i$ and $a_{j_m} \in P_j$, exists in a process schedule $\mathcal{S} = (\mathcal{P}_{\mathcal{S}}, \mathcal{A}_{\mathcal{S}}, \prec_{\mathcal{S}}, <_{\mathcal{S}})$ if the following properties hold:*

1. *a_{i_k} precedes a_{j_m} in $\mathcal{S}$, that is $a_{i_k} <_{\mathcal{S}} a_{j_m}$*
2. *a_{i_k} is compensatable*
3. *a_{j_m} is neither preceded in $\mathcal{S}$ by $a^{-1}_{i_k}$ nor by $a^*_{i_k}$, that is $a^{-1}_{i_k} \not<_{\mathcal{S}} a_{j_m}$ and $a^*_{i_k} \not<_{\mathcal{S}} a_{j_m}$, where $a^*_{i_k}$ is the next point-of-no-return of process P_i succeeding a_{i_k} (this can either be some pivot activity $a^p_{i_q}$ with $a_{i_k} \prec_{\mathcal{S}} a^p_{i_q}$ or the commit C_i of P_i)*
4. *In $\mathcal{S}$, an activity a_{j_l} of P_j exists which precedes a_{j_m} ($a_{j_l} \prec_{\mathcal{S}} a_{j_m}$), which conflicts with a_{i_k}, and which succeeds a_{i_k} in $\mathcal{S}$, that is $a_{i_k} <_{\mathcal{S}} a_{j_l}$*
5. *a_{j_m} conflicts with the inverse activity $a^{-1}_{i_k}$ of a_{i_k}.* □

Given the conditions of Definition 5.8, in a situation where the sequence $a_{i_k} <_{\mathcal{S}} a_{j_l} <_{\mathcal{S}} a_{j_m} <_{\mathcal{S}} a^{-1}_{i_k}$ appears in a process schedule $\mathcal{S}$, we cannot bring a_{i_k} and $a^{-1}_{i_k}$ together such that the latter one correctly undoes the effects of a_{i_k}. Note that, if commutativity is perfect, then we can take a_{j_l} and a_{j_m} to be the same. This is the case, for instance, in a read-from dependency: if a_{i_k} writes some data that a_{j_l} reads, then, $a^{-1}_{i_k}$ is also a write and a_{j_l} conflicts with both a_{i_k} and $a^{-1}_{i_k}$. However, due to the semantically rich nature of activities, a dependency may exist in other situations as well.

In the traditional model where each activity is compensatable, the requirement that all running transactions must be able to abort is captured by the notion of recoverability. As we have to deal with two different states of processes determining the way recovery has to be performed, we have to extend and to generalize the notion of recoverability in order to cope with the structure of transactional processes. This leads to the notion of *process-recoverability*. More formally,

Definition 5.9 (Process-Recoverability (P-RC)) *A process schedule $\mathcal{S} = (\mathcal{P_S}, \mathcal{A_S}, \prec_\mathcal{S}, <_\mathcal{S})$ is* process-recoverable (P-RC), *if for each pair of activities $a^c_{i_k}$ and a_{j_m} of $\mathcal{S}$ with $a^c_{i_k} <_\mathcal{S} a_{j_m}$ imposing an abort dependency between P_i and P_j, the following holds:*

1. *If activity a_{j_m} is compensatable ($a^c_{j_m}$) and when a^*_i is in $\mathcal{S}$, then the following ordering has to exist in $\mathcal{S}$: $a^*_i <_\mathcal{S} a^*_j$ where a^*_i is the next point-of-no-return succeeding $a^c_{i_k}$ with respect to P_i's required order $\prec_i$ (this may either be the commit C_i of P_i or a pivot; when P_i is running, then it will be the primary pivot of P_i, otherwise the pivot of one of P_i's subprocesses) and a^*_j is the next point-of-no-return succeeding $a^c_{j_m}$ with respect to $\prec_j$ (again, this may be C_j or a pivot of P_j).*
2. *If a_{j_m} is not compensatable, then the following order has to exist in $\mathcal{S}$: $a^*_i <_\mathcal{S} a_{j_m}$ where a^*_i is the next point-of-no-return succeeding $a^c_{i_k}$ with respect to $\prec_i$ (this may either be the commit C_i of P_i or a pivot; when P_i is running, then it will be the primary pivot of P_i, otherwise the pivot of one of P_i's subprocesses).* □

Note that, in analogy to the notion of abort dependency being a generalization of the read-from dependency which accounts for arbitrary conflicting activities, the traditional notion of recoverability is a special case of Definition 5.9. When no pivot activities exist as in the traditional case, then, according to Definition 5.9.1, only an order between C_i and C_j with $C_i <_\mathcal{S} C_j$ has to be imposed. But the semantics of "quasi commit" of pivot activities is also included in this definition since pivots are treated in the same way as the commit of a process. By successfully committing a pivot activity $a^p_{i_n}$, all preceding compensatable activities $a^c_{i_k}$ can no longer be compensated. Therefore, due to the ultimate absence of compensating activities $a^{-1}_{i_k}$, all abort dependencies imposed by pairs of activities $(a^c_{i_k}, a_{j_m})$ in which preceding activities of $a^p_{i_n}$ are involved can no longer lead to a violation of process-recoverability.

Obviously, the notion of process-recoverability is weaker than the ACA requirement which would require the total absence of abort dependencies in a process schedule. This absence would, in the case of perfect commutativity, for instance prevent to consecutively execute two conflicting compensatable activities $a^c_{i_k}$ and $a^c_{j_m}$ of two running processes P_i and P_j in a process schedule $\mathcal{S}$ since either $a^c_{i_k}$ would have to be compensated prior to $a^c_{j_m}$ or a^*_i would have to be executed prior to $a^c_{j_m}$ (where a^*_i is either C_i or a primary pivot of P_i). However, this is too strict (it would, in fact, correspond to the notion of rigorousness [BGRS91], applied to transactional processes) since in the case of $a^c_{i_k} <_\mathcal{S} a^c_{j_m}$, an abort of P_i would just require to abort P_j as well — which is possible when the requirements of P-RC are met in $\mathcal{S}$. On the other hand, even in the case where an abort dependency between two processes, P_i and P_j, imposed by some activities $a^c_{i_k} <_\mathcal{S} a^c_{j_m}$ exists in a process schedule $\mathcal{S}$, the abort of P_i does not necessarily require the joint abort of P_j. Assume that P_j is completing while the subprocess in which $a^c_{j_m}$ has been executed is running. Then, when P-RC is met, only the subprocess of P_j associated with $a^c_{j_m}$ to has to be aborted while P_j can still commit by executing another alternative.

In most practical applications, commutativity is perfect. This can be used to enforce P-RC since abort dependencies correspond to pairs of conflicting activities a_{i_k} and a_{j_m} where the first activity to execute is compensatable. In order to enforce P-RC for a process schedule $\mathcal{S}$, the serialization graph $SG(\mathcal{S})$ used for SG-P-SR and P-SG-P-SR can be exploited. Consider the nodes of this

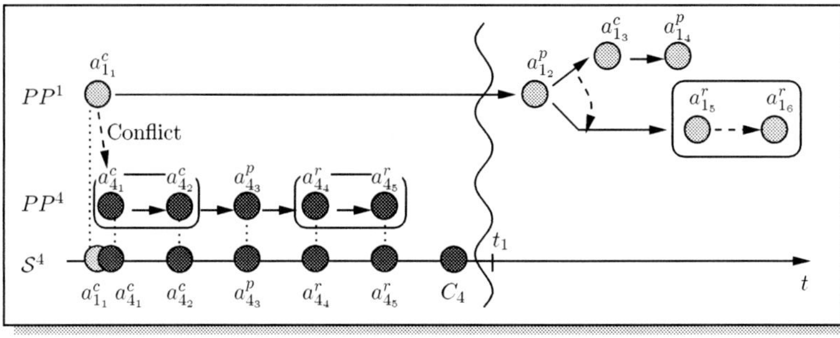

Figure 5.4: Non-P–RC Process Schedule $S^4_{t_1}$ of Example 5.4 (Commit-Dependency Violation)

graph to be colored, say red for running processes, blue for completing processes and green for committed processes. In terms of this colored graph, violations of P-RC may occur because of two reasons: firstly, by introducing an edge corresponding to an abort dependency and secondly, by a state change of a process, that is, by a change of the color of its corresponding node. The process manager may allow edges to be introduced in the colored serialization graph (due to a conflict $a_{i_k} <_S a_{j_m}$) between two red nodes as well as edges from a blue node to a red one (the first case is not critical since it can be resolved by a joint abort; the same is true in the second case when the completing, blue, process is in a running subprocess). However, edges from red to blue nodes are prohibited. Edges between two blue nodes may in some cases be allowed when a_{i_k} is itself a pivot or when it is succeeded by a pivot in S, but in general, this kind of edges has to be dealt with care. Furthermore, nodes may only change their color from red to blue or from red to green when the have no incoming edges originating from red edges (that is, they are not dependent on running processes). Incoming edges originating from blue nodes may be allowed but must also be dealt with care, especially in the case where the source node is in a running subprocess. Note that these mechanisms guarantee P-RC although they may rule out certain schedules that are correct with respect to P-RC. More details of a protocol dynamically providing P-RC and P-SG-P-SR are discussed in Chapter 6.

Example 5.4 *Consider process schedule S^4 depicted in Figure 5.4 reflecting the concurrent execution of two process programs, PP^1 and PP^4, by P^1_1 and P^4_4. Assume further that commutativity is perfect in this example. At t_1, process P_4 is committed while P_1 is running. An abort dependency exists between P_1 and P_4, imposed by $a^c_{1_1} <_{S^4} a^c_{4_1}$. According to Definition 5.9, the presence of this abort dependency requires the following order in S^4 for P-RC: $a^p_{1_2} <_{S^4} a^p_{4_3}$ and, due to $a^p_{4_3} \prec_{P_4} C_4$ also $a^p_{1_2} <_{S^4} C_4$ which, however, is violated in $S^4_{t_1}$. Therefore, in an execution where P_1 does not leave any effects (where activity $a^c_{1_1}$ does not appear), the return value of P_4 would not be the same as it is in $S^4_{t_1}$. In particular, when P_1 is aborted, this cannot be handled correctly by jointly aborting also P_4 since the latter one has already committed. Hence, $S^4_{t_1}$ is not P-RC.* □

Example 5.5 *Consider the execution of processes P_1 and P_2 in process schedule S^5 as depicted in Figure 5.5. At time t_2, P_1 is completing and P_2 is running. An abort dependency between P_2 and P_1 exists by $a^c_{2_1} <_{S^5} a^c_{1_1}$. At time t_1, when this dependency has been introduced, it was allowed (i.e., no violation of the dependencies imposed by P-RC was present) since both processes have*

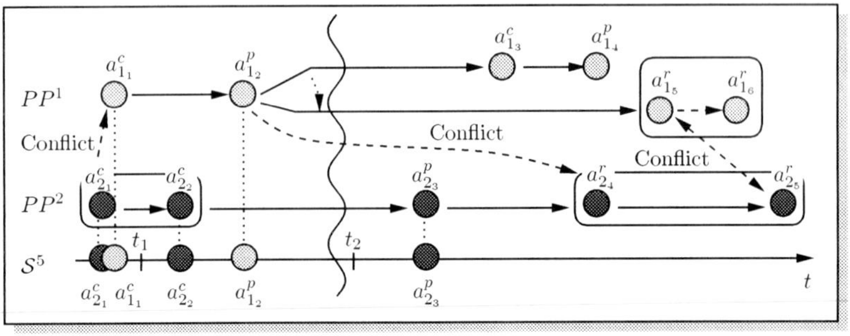

Figure 5.5: Non-P–RC Process Schedule $\mathcal{S}^5_{t_2}$ of Example 5.5 (State-Change-Dependency Violation)

been running. However, by executing the primary pivot $a^p_{1_2}$, P_1 changed its state to completing, thus making the abort dependency a disallowed one because of a violation of the order $a^p_{2_3} <_{\mathcal{S}^5} a^p_{1_2}$ required by P-RC. An abort of P_2 at time t_2 could no longer be treated correctly by a cascading abort including also P_1. Therefore, process schedule $\mathcal{S}^5_{t_2}$ is not P RC. □

The analysis of process-serializability has shown that although a given process schedule $\mathcal{S}$ may fulfill the P-SR property, there might exist a prefix $\mathcal{S}'$ of $\mathcal{S}$ that is not P-SR. This phenomenon cannot be found in process-recoverability which is subject of the following lemma:

Lemma 5.1 (P–RC & Prefixes) *Let $\mathcal{S}$ be a P-RC process schedule. Then, each prefix $\mathcal{S}'$ of $\mathcal{S}$ is also process-recoverable.* □

Proof (Lemma 5.1) *Let $\mathcal{S}$ be a P-RC process schedule and let $\mathcal{S}'$ be a prefix of $\mathcal{S}$ that is not P-RC. Since $\mathcal{S}'$ is not P-RC, there must exist at least one abort dependency between a pair of processes (P_i, P_j) whose constraints on the subsequent points-of-no-return are not met. Let (a_{i_k}, a_{j_m}) be the pair of activities imposing such an abort dependency in $\mathcal{S}'$ and let $a^*_{j_m}$ be the next point of no return succeeding a_{j_m} (in case a_{j_m} is not compensatable, then $a_{j_m} = a^*_{j_m}$). Therefore, the following orders have to exist in process schedule $\mathcal{S}'$: $a_{i_k} <_{\mathcal{S}'} a_{j_m} <_{\mathcal{S}'} a^*_{j_m}$ and $a^*_{i_k} \not<_{\mathcal{S}'} a^*_{j_m}$ where $a^*_{i_k}$ is the next point-of-no-return succeeding a_{i_k}. But this order must also be present in $\mathcal{S}$ which will then, in turn, also not be P-RC.* □

5.4 Process–Reducibility

So far, we have clarified the notions of serializability and recoverability in transactional processes by separately addressing isolation in multi-process executions without considering atomicity (P-SR), and the possibility to abort running processes (P-RC) in these concurrent executions. What is missing is a criterion to check whether the abort of (sub-)processes in the presence of concurrency is possible or not. This includes the property that no conflicting activity a_{j_m} must be executed between a regular activity a_{i_k} and its compensation $a^{-1}_{i_k}$ except for the case where the compensation $a^{-1}_{j_m}$ of a_{j_m} also appears between a_{i_k} and $a^{-1}_{i_k}$.

To this end, according to the unified theory of concurrency control and recovery, reduction techniques based on the permutation and cancellation of activities can be applied. Recalling the notion of commutativity, it is obvious that two consecutive activities of different processes can be permuted in a process schedule $\mathcal{S}$ if they do commute, hence this permutation does neither affect the final state reached by $\mathcal{S}$ nor the return values of any process. Additionally, also the elimination of two consecutive activities does neither influence any return value nor the final state when they together form an effect-free sequence. More formally,

Definition 5.10 (Reducible Process Schedule (P-RED)) *A process schedule* $\mathcal{S} = (\mathcal{P}_\mathcal{S}, \mathcal{A}_\mathcal{S}, \prec_\mathcal{S}, <_\mathcal{S})$ *is* reducible (P-RED) *if it can be transformed to a serial process schedule* $\underline{\mathcal{S}} = (\mathcal{P}_{\underline{\mathcal{S}}},\ \mathcal{A}_{\underline{\mathcal{S}}},\ \prec_{\underline{\mathcal{S}}},\ <_{\underline{\mathcal{S}}})$ *by applying the following two transformation rules finitely many times:*

1. **Commutativity Rule:** *The order* $(a_{i_k} <_\mathcal{S} a_{j_l})$ *of two activities* $a_{i_k}, a_{j_l} \in \mathcal{A}_\mathcal{S}$ *can be replaced by* $(a_{j_l} <_{\underline{\mathcal{S}}} a_{i_k})$ *if the following conditions hold:*

   (a) *Either* a_{i_k} *and* a_{j_l} *belong to different processes* $(i \neq j)$ *and they do commute, or they belong to the same process* $(i = j)$ *and are not ordered in* $\prec_\mathcal{S}$*, that is, the corresponding process program allows an unrestricted parallel execution of both activities.*

   (b) *There is no* $a_{q_t} \in \mathcal{A}_\mathcal{S}$ *with* $(a_{i_k} <_\mathcal{S} a_{q_t} <_\mathcal{S} a_{j_l})$.

2. **Compensation Rule:** *If two activities* $a_{i_k}, a_{i_k}^{-1} \in \mathcal{A}_\mathcal{S}$ *such that* $a_{i_k} <_\mathcal{S} a_{i_k}^{-1}$ *and there is no activity* $a_{q_t} \in \mathcal{A}_\mathcal{S}$ *with* $(a_{i_k} <_\mathcal{S} a_{q_t} <_\mathcal{S} a_{i_k}^{-1})$*, then* a_{i_k} *and* $a_{i_k}^{-1}$ *can both be removed from process schedule* $\underline{\mathcal{S}}$. □

The required order, $\prec_i$, of a process P_i is not required to be total. Therefore, two activities a_{i_k} and a_{i_n} of P_i, although appearing in an observed execution order in some process schedule $\mathcal{S}$, e.g., $a_{i_k} <_\mathcal{S} a_{i_n}$, may not be ordered in $\prec_\mathcal{S}$. The above definition of reducibility for process schedules captures this difference compared with reduction in the traditional unified theory, and, at the same time, extends this traditional notion in that it considers not only permutation for pairs of activities of different processes but also for activities of the same process, given that they are not required to be ordered by the associated process program.

Nevertheless, reducibility for process schedules is still similar to the reduction applied in the traditional unified theory of concurrency control and recovery except for one major difference. Prior to the application of reduction techniques, the unified theory requires the expansion of a schedule where each running transaction is treated as aborted. This expansion leads to a complete schedule where each transaction either has committed or aborted. In the latter case, all recovery-related operations are made explicit during expansion. Yet, reduction for process schedules does not require expansion, since the notion of process schedules already considers abort related activities and since process-recoverability does not require all active processes to abort.

P-RED is not prefix-closed (see, for instance, process schedule $\mathcal{S}^2$ of Example 5.2). A restriction of P-RED which requires that each prefix of a process schedule is P-RED leads to the notion of prefix-process-reducibility, P-P-RED. More formally:

Definition 5.11 (Prefix–Process–Reducibility (P-P-RED)) *A process schedule* $\mathcal{S}$ *is* prefix-process-reducible (P-P-RED) *if each prefix of* $\mathcal{S}$ *is P-RED.* □

5.5 Correct Termination

In addition to the previous ideas addressing non-complete process schedules, all completing processes must be able to commit correctly while all aborting processes must abort correctly such that they do not leave any effects. Thus, in order to extend the analysis of correct concurrency control and recovery for transactional processes by completely considering all activities of aborting and aborted (sub-)processes, and in analogy to reduction in the traditional unified theory which is only applied after a given schedule has been expanded, each process has to terminate. By this, it is ensured that all compensating activities are taken into account in the reduction phase.

Therefore, commutativity and compensation techniques (as indicated by the notion of process-reducibility) have to be applied to the completed process schedule, $\mathcal{C}(\mathcal{S})$, of a process schedule $\mathcal{S}$. This leads to the notion of *correct termination (CT)*. In the completed process schedule, all aborting processes of $\mathcal{S}$ and all running processes of $R^*_{\mathcal{S}}$, i.e., those for which an abort is requested, are aborted and all completing processes of $\mathcal{S}$ have committed. Since it is defined on completed process schedules, correct termination has to guarantee that it is possible to perform all aborts and all completions for partial process schedules correctly, even in the presence of concurrency. Moreover, and in order to allow CT to be provided dynamically, not only the completed process schedule has to be reducible but also all of its prefixes.

While guaranteed termination comprises the well-formed structure and inherent correctness of single processes, correct termination addresses the correctness of complete multi-process executions. The first step in formulating correct termination is that a given process schedule is completed:

Definition 5.12 (Completed Process Schedule $\mathcal{C}(\mathcal{S})$) *Let $\mathcal{S} = (\mathcal{P}_{\mathcal{S}}, \mathcal{A}_{\mathcal{S}}, \prec_{\mathcal{S}}, <_{\mathcal{S}})$ be a process schedule. The completed process schedule $\mathcal{C}(\mathcal{S}) = (\mathcal{P}_{\mathcal{C}(\mathcal{S})}, \mathcal{A}_{\mathcal{C}(\mathcal{S})}, \prec_{\mathcal{C}(\mathcal{S})}, <_{\mathcal{C}(\mathcal{S})})$ is a process schedule defined over the same set of processes ($\mathcal{P}_{\mathcal{S}} = \mathcal{P}_{\mathcal{C}(\mathcal{S})}$) with:*

1. *Each activity $a \in \mathcal{A}_{\mathcal{S}}$ is also in $\mathcal{A}_{\mathcal{C}(\mathcal{S})}$, that is $\mathcal{A}_{\mathcal{S}} \subseteq \mathcal{A}_{\mathcal{C}(\mathcal{S})}$.*

2. *$\mathcal{S}$ is a prefix of its completed process schedule $\mathcal{C}(\mathcal{S})$. That is, for each pair of activities a, a^* with $a \in \mathcal{A}_{\mathcal{S}}$ and $a^* \in \mathcal{A}_{\mathcal{C}(\mathcal{S})} \setminus \mathcal{A}_{\mathcal{S}}$, the following has to hold: $a <_{\mathcal{C}(\mathcal{S})} a^*$. Additionally, each pair of activities $a, a' \in \mathcal{A}_{\mathcal{S}}$ has to appear in the same execution order in both $\mathcal{S}$ and $\mathcal{C}(\mathcal{S})$, that is: $a <_{\mathcal{S}} a' \Rightarrow a <_{\mathcal{C}(\mathcal{S})} a'$.*

3. *$\mathcal{C}(\mathcal{S})$ is complete. That is, in $\mathcal{C}(\mathcal{S})$, all processes that are aborting in $\mathcal{S}$ are aborted and all completing processes of $\mathcal{S}$ are committed in $\mathcal{C}(\mathcal{S})$. Furthermore, for each arbitrary set of running processes $R_{\mathcal{S}}$ of $\mathcal{S}$, there must be a set $R^*_{\mathcal{S}}$ of running processes with $R_{\mathcal{S}} \subseteq R^*_{\mathcal{S}} \subseteq \mathcal{R}_{\mathcal{S}}$, $\mathcal{R}_{\mathcal{S}}$ being the set of all of $\mathcal{S}$'s running processes, where all processes of $R^*_{\mathcal{S}}$ are aborted in $\mathcal{C}(\mathcal{S})$ and all processes of $\mathcal{R}_{\mathcal{S}} \setminus R^*_{\mathcal{S}}$ are committed in $\mathcal{C}(\mathcal{S})$.* □

Note that the completion of a process schedule does not force all active processes P_i to follow their assured termination trees (as the completion of a single process does) but rather allows them to continue their regular execution with respect to the required order $\prec_i$.

Once a process schedule $\mathcal{S}$ is completed to $\mathcal{C}(\mathcal{S})$, correct termination requires the existence of a process schedule $\underline{\mathcal{C}(\mathcal{S})}$ that is serial on all processes and that is equivalent to $\mathcal{C}(\mathcal{S})$ with respect to the return values of all processes and the initial and final state. Note that this is more than just process-serializability of $\underline{\mathcal{C}(\mathcal{S})}$. In P-SR, only running, completing and committed processes are considered (in this case, since $\mathcal{C}(\mathcal{S})$ is complete, this would be only committed processes), but aborted processes are ignored (including aborted subprocesses of completing processes). However, an important aspect of correct termination is to address also the correct abort of processes, that is, the correct execution of compensating activities in the presence of concurrency, which requires $\mathcal{C}(\mathcal{S})$ to be serial on all processes. Correct termination therefore requires a completed process schedule and all its prefixes to be reducible. If this is the case, it is guaranteed that all aborted (sub-)processes do not leave any effect since all their regular activities together with the corresponding compensation activities will have disappeared.

Definition 5.13 (Correct Termination (CT)) *A complete process schedule $\mathcal{C}(\mathcal{S})$ has* correct termination (CT) *property if it is prefix-process-reducible (P-P-RED).* □

Example 5.6 *Consider the concurrent execution of the process programs PP^1 and PP^5 by processes P_1^1 and P_5^5, reflected in process schedule $\mathcal{S}^6$ as depicted in Figure 5.6. At time t_1, $\mathcal{S}_{t_1}^6$ is correct with respect to P-RC (P_5 is already completing, that is, $a_{5_1}^c$ will never be compensated) and P-P-RED (thus, also P-SR holds). However, the completion $\mathcal{C}(\mathcal{S}_{t_1}^6)$ of $\mathcal{S}_{t_1}^6$ does not have CT property. The execution of $a_{5_3}^r$, which is inevitably required to complete P_5, introduces cyclic dependencies. Since in the meanwhile also P_1 has changed to completing by committing its primary pivot $a_{1_2}^p$, this conflict cycle cannot be resolved (since no compensating activity is contained in $\mathcal{C}(\mathcal{S}_{t_1}^6)$, no compensation can be performed during reduction).* □

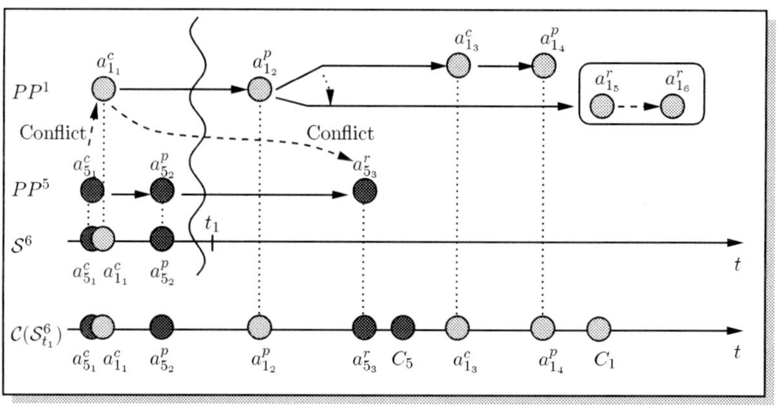

Figure 5.6: Non-CT Completion $\mathcal{C}(\mathcal{S}_{t_1}^6)$ of P–RED & P–RC Process Schedule $\mathcal{S}_{t_1}^6$ of Example 5.6

Example 5.6 (Revisited) *We have already shown that the commit of both P_1 and P_5 does not allow to correctly complete process schedule $\mathcal{S}_{t_1}^6$ with respect to CT. Since P_5 is already completing, the only possibility to successfully complete $\mathcal{S}_{t_1}^6$ correctly is to abort P_1 which imposes activity $a_{1_1}^{-1}$ to be executed. After the commit of $a_{1_1}^{-1}$ which leads to a state change of P_1 from aborting to aborted, P_5 is able to proceed forward by executing $a_{5_3}^r$ and to finally terminate correctly. This completion is reflected in the completed process schedule $\mathcal{C}'(\mathcal{S}_{t_1}^6)$ of $\mathcal{S}_{t_1}^6$ which is depicted in Figure 5.7. In*

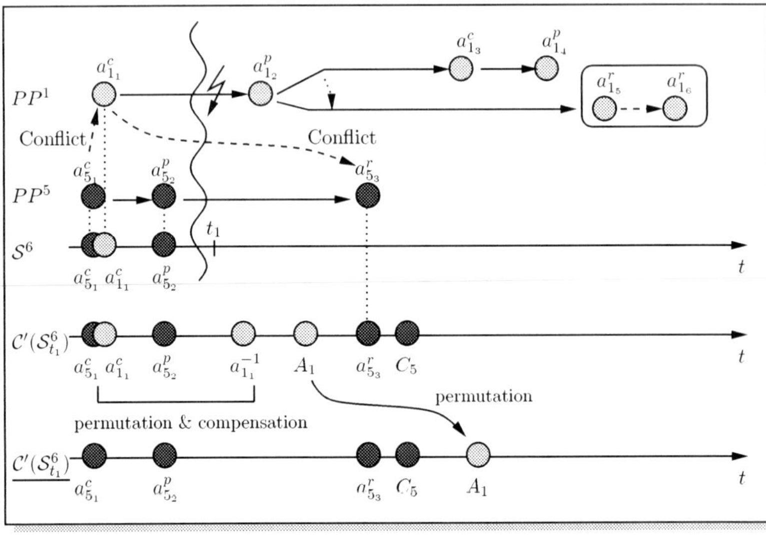

Figure 5.7: Correct CT Completion $\mathcal{C}'(\mathcal{S}^6_{t_1})$ of P–RED & P–RC Process Schedule $\mathcal{S}^6_{t_1}$ of Example 5.6

this completed process schedule, $a^c_{1_1}$ *and* $a^{-1}_{1_1}$ *can be eliminated by applying the commutativity and compensation rules such that the reduced process schedule* $\overline{\mathcal{C}'(\mathcal{S}^6_{t_1})}$ *of* $\mathcal{C}'(\mathcal{S}^6_{t_1})$ *is a serial one. Hence, since also each prefix of* $\mathcal{C}'(\mathcal{S}^6_{t_1})$ *can be reduced,* $\mathcal{C}'(\mathcal{S}^6_{t_1})$ *is CT.* □

Example 5.7 *A correct CT execution of process programs* PP^1 *and* PP^2 *is given by process schedule* $\mathcal{S}^7$ *depicted in Figure 5.8. At time* t_1, $\mathcal{S}^7_{t_1}$ *is both P-RED and P-RC (the constraints imposed by the only abort dependency* $a^c_{1_1} <_{\mathcal{S}^7} a^c_{2_1}$ *are met). Furthermore, although conflicts exist between the activities of the completion of both processes, the completed schedule* $\mathcal{C}(\mathcal{S}^7_{t_1})$ *is correct since it is conflict equivalent to a serial schedule where* P^1_1 *precedes* P^2_2. *Note that the completion of* $\mathcal{S}^7_{t_1}$ *does not require* P_2 *to abort although it is running in* $\mathcal{S}^7_{t_1}$. *However, once* P_2 *changes its state from running to completing, it must be ensured that it will commit correctly. In process schedule* $\mathcal{C}(\mathcal{S}^7_{t_1})$, *this is trivially the case since this state change —which is caused by the execution of* $a^p_{2_3}$, *the primary pivot of* P_2— *is performed after the commit of* P_1, $C_1 <_{\mathcal{C}(\mathcal{S}^7)} a^p_{2_3}$ *and since the serialization order in the reduced process schedule* $\overline{\mathcal{C}(\mathcal{S}^7_{t_1})}$ *is* $P_1 \rightarrow P_2$. *Note that* $\overline{\mathcal{C}(\mathcal{S}^7_{t_1})}$ *is defined over the same set of activities as the completed process schedule* $\mathcal{C}(\mathcal{S}^7_{t_1})$ *since the latter does not contain any compensating activity such that only the commutativity rule can be applied during reduction. Finally, it can be shown that* $\mathcal{C}(\mathcal{S}^7_{t_1})$ *as well as all its prefixes can be reduced.* □

Following the ideas of the unified theory of concurrency control and recovery [SWY93, AVA⁺94a, VHBS98], the notion of CT for process schedules addresses atomicity and isolation jointly. However, in the traditional unified theory, all active transactions have to be considered as aborted. The direct application of the unified theory to transactional processes implies that each running

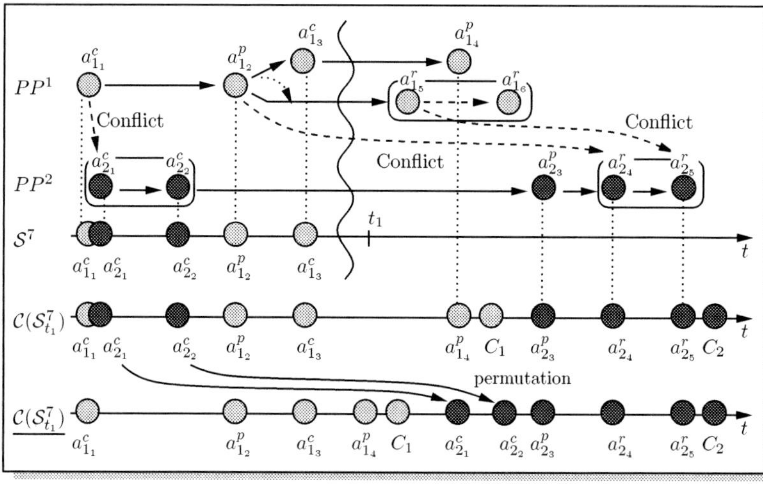

Figure 5.8: Correct CT Process Schedule $\mathcal{C}(\mathcal{S}^7_{t_1})$ of Example 5.7

process changes its state to aborting (such that it will be aborted in a complete process schedule), by introducing the corresponding compensating activities. In addition, each completing process is forced to follow its assured termination tree, that is, to execute its forward recovery path [SAS99]. Therefore, when the notion of expansion of a schedule is applied to transactional process management, an expanded process schedule $\tilde{\mathcal{S}}$ would only contain activities of the backward and/or forward recovery paths of all active processes, depending on their states. This is illustrated in Figure 5.9: when the expansion of a process schedule $\mathcal{S}$ is determined, which will result in a complete process schedule, each running process is aborted while each completing process would have first to execute compensating activities leading back to its most recent pivot activity and then to follow the assured termination tree succeeding this pivot. However, the notion of CT extends the direct application of the unified theory of concurrency control and recovery in three ways.

First, we do not require all running processes to abort when a process schedule is completed. This means that we allow cascading aborts for some running processes (i.e., for a subset $R^*_{\mathcal{S}}$ of all

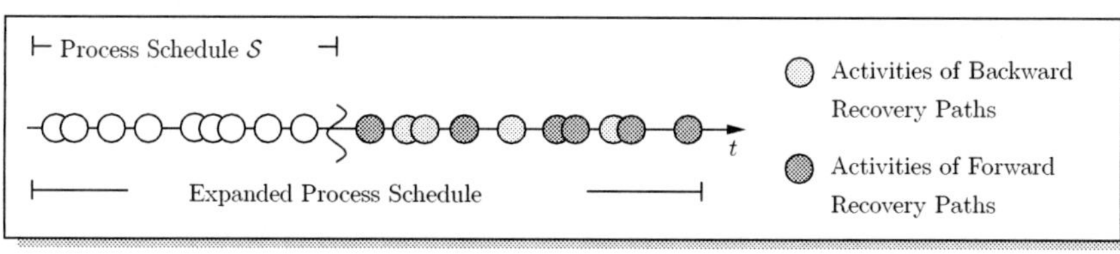

Figure 5.9: Expansion of the Unified Theory Applied to a Process Schedule $\mathcal{S}$ Would Add Only Activities of Backward and Forward Recovery Paths

running processes $\mathcal{R}_\mathcal{S}$) while, at the same time, we may even exclude other running processes from this possibility, that is, we explicitly avoid cascading aborts for $\mathcal{R}_\mathcal{S} \setminus R^*_\mathcal{S}$. In Chapter 7, a dynamic scheduling protocol is presented which provides the property of loosening ACA for certain processes.

Second, CT does not necessarily require completing processes to terminate via the retriable activities of their assured termination trees but rather allows to continue the execution of subprocesses according to the processes' preference order.

Third, the traditional unified theory does not consider recovery-related operations in a schedule until expansion. During this expansion phase, each abort operation in a schedule is replaced by all appropriate undo operations which are, by a set of rules, related both to all conflicting regular operations and to undo operations of concurrent transactions, thereby assuming that these rules are actually respected by the system. Following the notion of schedule proposed in [Bee00] which considers all operations as they appear (thus, jointly comprises regular and undo operations within the same framework), expansion is made obsolete. In the case of transactional process management where the scheduling of compensating activities is explicitly performed by the process manager rather than being encapsulated in a dedicated recovery service, this allows to view these activities in the actual context in which they are executed. However, despite of the differences in constructing completed schedules and by reducing the restrictions that have to be respected for this purpose, the correctness criteria induced by CT as well as the reduction rules for permutation and elimination of activities leading to these criteria still follow the original unified theory of concurrency control and recovery.

In the original unified theory, the criterion SOT (serializable with ordered termination) has been introduced in order to reason about correct concurrency control and recovery of a schedule S without considering its expanded schedule $\tilde{S}$ [AVA+94a]. However, a similar, SOT-like criterion does not exist in the case of transactional process management. The reason being is that in the traditional transaction model where each transaction can be aborted any time prior to its commit, all operations required for recovery purposes are known beforehand: for each regular operation, the associated inverse has to be considered. When, in addition, commutativity is perfect, then also the commutativity behavior of all recovery-related operations is known. In transactional process management and especially in the presence of completing processes, that is, when pivot activities exist, things become more complex. Then, the completion of a process schedule $\mathcal{S}$ introduces new activities which are not related to the ones that have already been committed. By this, additional pairs of conflicting activities may be present in $\mathcal{C}(\mathcal{S})$. Hence, relying only on information of a given process schedule $\mathcal{S}$ without analyzing the process programs associated to all active processes is not sufficient for reasoning about correct concurrency control and recovery in transactional process management.

According to Definition 5.13, CT for a process schedule $\mathcal{S}$ can be verified only over the completed process schedule $\mathcal{C}(\mathcal{S})$ — although it additionally requires process-reducibility of each prefix. However, completing a process schedule is not practical. Therefore, special considerations or even restrictions are required to guarantee that no violation of CT occurs during completion:

- A first approach is to require that all activities of all completing processes of $\mathcal{S}$ have to be known beforehand to analyze whether conflicting activities exist (transitively) or not and whether the joint completion of these processes may violate CT (even when conflicting activities exist, they may correspond to paths that are not effected). In the completed process schedule $\mathcal{C}(\mathcal{S}^6_{t_1})$ of Example 5.6, conflicts introduced by the completion have led to such a violation of CT since the additional conflict pair between P_1 and P_5, together with a pair of conflicting activities that was already present in $\mathcal{S}^6_{t_1}$, inevitably introduced cyclic conflicts such that the state change from running to completing of P_1 had to be prohibited. Although this variant may allow a high degree of concurrency, it necessitates, in turn, the complex analysis of the transitive closure of the commutativity behavior of all activities of all completing processes and thus, requires information about future process executions.

- Alternatively, the analysis can be restricted to the assured termination trees of all completing processes only. Then, it has to be ensured that at least one concurrent execution of all assured termination trees exists in which all completing processes successfully commit, that is, where P-SR is not violated. However, this would again be based on future activities and would, at the same time, restrict each completing process to its assured termination path.
- The previous variant could even be further restricted in that no pair of conflicting activities must exist in the assured termination trees of all completing processes which would trivially fulfill the requirement of CT (together with P-RED and P-RC of the given prefix $\mathcal{S}$ of $\mathcal{C}(\mathcal{S})$) since no new conflicts will be introduced during completion. Again, the drawback of this approach is that it requires information about future executions of process programs and it would also force each completing process to execute the assured termination trees while neglecting all other subprocesses with higher priority.
- Yet another approach could also be to allow only one completing process at a time. Although limiting concurrency, this variant does not restrict completion to the assured termination trees and does also not require information about the future behavior of process programs.

As a consequence of these various possibilities, the way a given process schedule has to be completed is left intentionally vague (c.f. Definition 5.13), and the problem is shifted to the design and implementation of concrete protocols.

5.6 Relationship Between Classes of Process Schedules

In the previous sections, we have reformulated the traditional notions of serializability and recoverability in the context of transactional processes and, in particular, we have introduced criteria that jointly consider isolation and atomicity in transactional process management. In this section, we recall the different criteria that have been introduced and we show how they are related.

To this end, we first consider the different levels of serializability for transactional processes:

Corollary 5.1 (P–SR ⊃ SG–P–SR ⊃ P–SG–P–SR) *The classes P-SR, SG-P-SR, and P-SG-P-SR are related in the following way:*

1. **P–SR ⊃ SG–P–SR:** *SG-P-SR is a proper subclass of P-SR.*
2. **SG–P–SR ⊃ P–SG–P–SR:** *P-SG-P-SR is a proper subclass of SG-P-SR.* □

Proof (Corollary 5.1)

1. **P–SR ⊃ SG–P–SR:** *A process schedule $\mathcal{S}$ is SG-P-SR when $SG(\mathcal{S})$ is acyclic. Since P-SR holds when $PSG(\mathcal{S})$ is acyclic and since $PSG(\mathcal{S})$ is obtained from $SG(\mathcal{S})$ by deleting edges,*

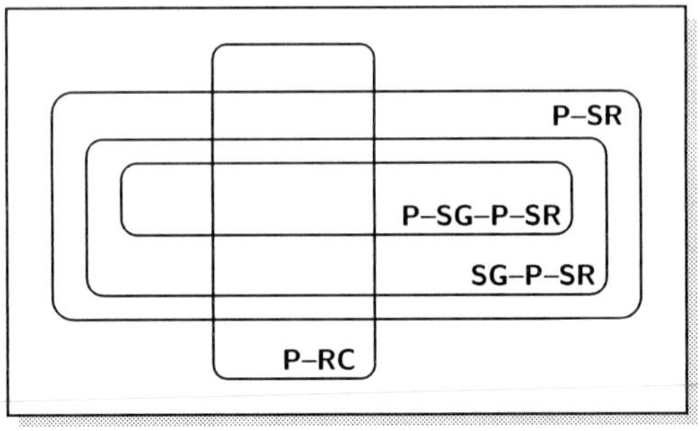

Figure 5.10: Relation Between P–RC, P–SR, SG–P–SR, and P–SG–P–SR

each SG-P-SR process schedule is also P-SR. Process schedule $\mathcal{S}^2_{t_2}$ *of Example 5.2 is P-SR but not SG-P-SR. Therefore, SG-P-SR is a proper subclass of P-SR.*

2. **SG–P–SR ⊃ P–SG–P–SR:** *When P-SG-P-SR holds for some process schedule* $\mathcal{S}$, *not only each prefix of* $\mathcal{S}$ *is SG-P-SR but also* $\mathcal{S}$ *itself. Process schedule* $\mathcal{S}^2_{t_3}$, *which is SG-P-SR (after* P^3_3 *changes its state to aborting, it does not appear in* $SG(\mathcal{S}^2)$ *at time* t_3*), with prefix* $\mathcal{S}^2_{t_2}$ *that is not SG-P-SR finally shows that P-SG-P-SR is a proper subclass of SG-P-SR.* □

The following discussion analyzes the relation between P-RC and P-SR as well as between P-RC and the two variants of serialization graph-based process serializability. This is also illustrated in Figure 5.10.

Theorem 5.3 (P–RC vs. P–SR) *P-SR, the class of process-serializable process schedules, and P-RC, the class of process-recoverable process schedules, are not comparable.* □

Proof (Theorem 5.3) *The relation between P-SR and P-RC is shown using the following examples:*

¬P-SR & P-RC: *Consider, for instance, process schedule* $\mathcal{S}^2_{t_1}$ *of Example 5.2. It has been shown that* $\mathcal{S}^2_{t_1}$ *is not P-SR. However, as no order imposed by abort dependencies is violated,* $\mathcal{S}^2_{t_1}$ *is P-RC.*

P-SR & ¬P-RC: *A process schedule that fulfills P-SR but that, at the same time, does not hold for P-RC can be found in* $\mathcal{S}^4_{t_1}$ *of Example 5.4.*

P-SR & P-RC: *The classes P-SR and P-RC are not disjoint. This is shown by process schedule* $\mathcal{S}^8_{t_1}$ *of Example 5.8 which accounts for both criteria.* □

Lemma 5.2 (P–RC vs. SG–P–SR) *P-RC and SG-P-SR are not comparable.* □

Proof (Lemma 5.2) *All examples used for the proof of Theorem 5.3 can also be applied here: process schedule* $\mathcal{S}^2_{t_1}$ *is P-RC but not SG-P-SR while* $\mathcal{S}^4_{t_1}$ *is SG-P-SR but it is not P-RC. Finally,* $\mathcal{S}^8_{t_1}$ *fulfills both criteria.* □

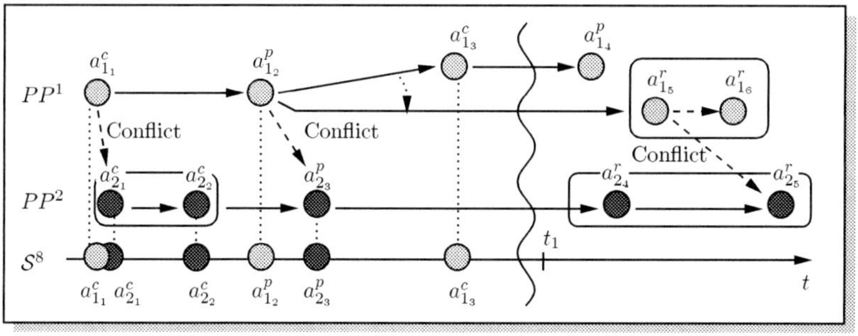

Figure 5.11: Correct P–SR & P–RC Process Schedule $\mathcal{S}^8_{t_1}$ of Example 5.8

Similar to Lemma 5.2, it can be shown that P–RC and P–SG–P–SR, the prefix-closed variant of SG–P–SR, are not comparable:

Lemma 5.3 (P–RC vs. P–SG–P–SR) *P-RC and P-SG-P-SR are not comparable.* □

Proof (Lemma 5.3) *Again, all examples used for the proof of Theorem 5.3 also clarify the relation between P-RC and P-SG-P-SR: process schedule $\mathcal{S}^2_{t_1}$ is P-RC but not P-SG-P-SR while $\mathcal{S}^4_{t_1}$ is P-SG-P-SR but it is not P-RC. Finally, $\mathcal{S}^8_{t_1}$ meets both criteria.* □

Example 5.8 *Consider again the concurrent execution of process programs PP^1 and PP^2, reflected in process schedule $\mathcal{S}^8$ depicted in Figure 5.11. At time t_1, $CA(\mathcal{S}^8_{t_1})$ is conflict equivalent to the serial execution of P_1 followed by P_2. As additionally also P-RC is met, $\mathcal{S}^8_{t_1}$ accounts for both criteria, namely P-SR and P-RC, simultaneously. Note that the pair of conflicting activities ($a^p_{1_2} <_{\mathcal{S}^8} a^p_{2_3}$) does not impose an abort dependency between P_1 and P_2 since $a^p_{1_2}$ is not compensatable.* □

Process-reducibility has been introduced as a criterion to account for both atomicity and isolation in transactional processes. In what follows, we compare P–RED and its prefix-closed variant, P–P–RED, to process-recoverability and to the different levels of serializability that have been identified for transactional processes.

Theorem 5.4 (P–SR ⊃ P–RED) *P-RED is a proper subclass of P-SR.* □

Proof (Theorem 5.4) *Let $\mathcal{S}$ be a P-RED process schedule and assume that $\mathcal{S}$ is not P-SR. Then, a cycle $P_i \rightarrow P_{i+1} \rightarrow \ldots \rightarrow P_{i+m} \rightarrow P_i$ has to exist in the committed and active projection $CA(\mathcal{S})$ of $\mathcal{S}$. Since neither aborting nor aborted (sub-)processes appear in $CA(\mathcal{S})$, all activities involved in the conflict cycle are regular ones and none of them is compensated in $\mathcal{S}$. Therefore, this cycle cannot be eliminated by any reduction rule which contradicts with the initial assumption of $\mathcal{S}$ being P-RED. Furthermore, P-RED is a proper subclass of P-SR. The latter considers only committed and active (sub-)processes. A conflict cycle imposed only by compensating activities will not affect P-SR but leads to a violation of P-RED as shown in Example 5.9.* □

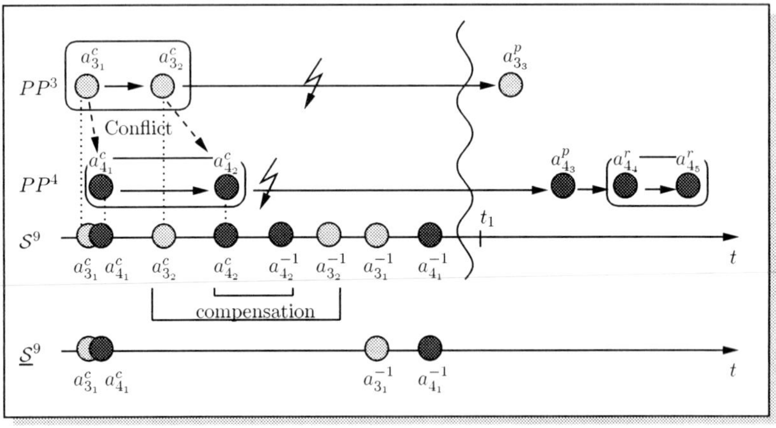

Figure 5.12: P–SR but Non-P-RED Process Schedule $\mathcal{S}^9_{t_1}$ of Example 5.9

Example 5.9 *Consider process schedule $\mathcal{S}^9$ reflecting the concurrent execution of process programs PP^3 and PP^4 illustrated in Figure 5.12. At time t_1, no active or committed process exists (both P_3 and P_4 are aborting). Therefore, P-SR trivially holds. However, although $a^c_{4_2}$ and $a^{-1}_{4_2}$ as well as $a^c_{3_2}$ and $a^{-1}_{3_2}$ can be cancelled by applying the compensation rule and thus do not appear in the reduced process schedule $\underline{\mathcal{S}}^9_{t_1}$, $\mathcal{S}^9_{t_1}$ is not P-RED. The pairs of conflicting activities $a^c_{3_1} <_{\underline{\mathcal{S}}^9_{t_1}} a^c_{4_1}$ and $a^{-1}_{3_1} <_{\underline{\mathcal{S}}^9_{t_1}} a^{-1}_{4_1}$ which are still present in $\underline{\mathcal{S}}^9_{t_1}$ lead to a case that cannot be resolved by reduction techniques.* □

Lemma 5.4 (P–RED vs. SG–P–SR) *P-RED and SG-P-SR are not comparable.* □

Proof (Lemma 5.4) *The following examples show the relation between P-RED and SG-P-SR:*

- **¬P-RED & SG-P-SR:** *Consider again process schedule $\mathcal{S}^9_{t_1}$ of Example 5.9. It has already been shown that $\mathcal{S}^9_{t_1}$ is P-SR. Since no active processes exist in $\mathcal{S}^9_{t_1}$, it is even SG-P-SR. However, due to the cyclic conflicts imposed by the compensating activities in the case of perfect commutativity, P-RED does not hold.*
- **P-RED & ¬SG-P-SR:** *Process schedule $\mathcal{S}^2_{t_2}$ of Example 5.2 is P-RED but it is not SG-P-SR.*
- **P-RED & SG-P-SR:** *Process schedule $\mathcal{S}^3_{t_1}$ of Example 5.3 shows that P-RED and SG-P-SR are not disjoint. Since no (sub-)process of $\mathcal{S}^3_{t_1}$ is aborted —thus it contains no compensating activity— and since $SG(\mathcal{S}^3_{t_1})$ is acyclic, both criteria hold simultaneously.* □

Lemma 5.5 (P–RED vs. P–SG–P–SR) *P-RED and P-SG-P-SR are not comparable.* □

Proof (Lemma 5.5) *In order to prove the non-comparability of P-RED and P-SG-P-SR, the process schedules used in the proof of Lemma 5.4 can be exploited as examples here: process schedule $\mathcal{S}^9_{t_1}$*

is not P-RED but it meets P-SG-P-SR. Conversely, $\mathcal{S}^2_{t_2}$ is P-RED but not P-SG-P-SR. Finally, by process schedule $\mathcal{S}^3_{t_1}$ of Example 5.3 which holds for both criteria, it can be shown that P-RED and P-SG-P-SR are not disjoint. □

We have previously shown that P–RED and P–SR are not comparable. The same is true when comparing the classes P–RED and P–RC:

Theorem 5.5 (P–RC vs. P–RED) *P-RC and P-RED are not comparable.* □

Proof (Theorem 5.5) *The relation between P-RC and P-RED is shown using the following three examples:*

- **¬P-RC & P-RED:** *It is possible that violations of constraints imposed by abort dependencies exist in a process schedule $\mathcal{S}$ albeit $\mathcal{S}$ is P-RED. This is the case when, for instance, the (sub-)processes involved in the abort dependency are not aborted (they may be running or even be aborting), that is, the compensating activity that would violate P-RED is not present in $\mathcal{S}$. Process schedule $\mathcal{S}^4_{t_1}$ of Example 5.4 represents such a case: $\mathcal{S}^4_{t_1}$ is not P-RC but it is P-RED; yet the compensation of a_{1_1} —which is not executed at t_1— would also violate P-RED.*

- **P-RC & ¬P-RED:** *Consider process schedule $\mathcal{S}^2_{t_1}$ of Example 5.2. Since no compensating activity exists, the compensation rule cannot be applied and the commutativity rule does not allow to transfer $\mathcal{S}^2_{t_1}$ to a serial schedule. Thus, it is not P-RED. However, it can be shown that $\mathcal{S}^2_{t_1}$ is P-RC since no constraints imposed by abort dependencies are violated.*

- **P-RC & P-RED:** *Process schedule $\mathcal{S}^8_{t_1}$ of Example 5.8 meets both P-RC and P-RED. The commutativity rule allows to rearrange all activities in order to transform $\mathcal{S}^8_{t_1}$ to a serial execution of P_1 succeeded by P_2. The compliance of $\mathcal{S}^8_{t_1}$ with P-RC has already been shown.* □

Process-reducibility not only guarantees process-serializability but it also addresses the correct execution of compensating activities, both from aborting processes and aborting subprocesses. However, P-RED does not provide both P-SR and P-RC jointly:

Lemma 5.6 (P–RED $\not\subseteq$ P–RC $\cap$ P–SR) *P-RED does not hold for P-RC and P-SR simultaneously.* □

Proof (Lemma 5.6) *Consider again process schedule $\mathcal{S}^4_{t_1}$ of Example 5.4. It has already been shown that $\mathcal{S}^4_{t_1}$ is P-RED. In addition, it has also been shown that it is not P-RC. Therefore, it does also not meet P-RC $\cap$ P-SR, i.e., it does not hold for both criteria simultaneously.* □

P-RED does not jointly hold for both P-RC and R-SR for two reasons. First, we do not require all active processes of a process schedule $\mathcal{S}$ to abort but only a subset $R^*_{\mathcal{S}}$ of all active processes. Therefore, violations of constraints imposed by abort dependencies do not affect P-RED when the corresponding processes will not be aborted. Second, P-RED does not require process schedules to be complete. Even if violations of P-RC exist and the associated (sub-)processes do not commit, they might be aborting and the compensating activity finally leading to a violation of P-RED might not yet be present in the process schedule. However, P-RED ensures that no aborted process

P_i is involved in an abort dependency with another process P_j that is not aborted. Let P-RC-A be the class of process schedules where P-RC, restricted to abort dependencies involving aborted processes, holds. Obviously, since the absence of abort dependencies imposed by pairs of activities (a_{i_k}, a_{j_m}) where P_i is aborted but not P_j is essential in a P-RED process schedule, it meets both P-SR and P-RC-A simultaneously, that is P-RED $\subset$ P-SR $\cap$ P-RC-A.

Corollary 5.2 (P-P-RED) *The following relationships can be identified between P-P-RED and P-RED, P-P-RED and SG-P-SR, P-P-RED and P-SG-P-SR, as well as between the classes P-P-RED and P-RC:*

1. **P-P-RED $\subset$ P-RED:** *P-P-RED is a proper subclass of P-RED.*
2. **P-P-RED vs. SG-P-SR:** *P-P-RED and SG-P-SR are not comparable*
3. **P-P-RED vs. P-SG-P-SR:** *P-P-RED and P-SG-P-SR are not comparable*
4. **P-P-RED vs. P-RC:** *P-P-RED and P-RC are not comparable* □

Proof (Corollary 5.2)

1. **P-P-RED $\subset$ P-RED:** *When each prefix of a process schedule $\mathcal{S}$ is P-RED, so is also $\mathcal{S}$. Moreover, P-P-RED is a proper subset of P-RED: process schedule $\mathcal{S}_{t_2}^2$ of Example 5.2, for instance, is P-RED although its prefix $\mathcal{S}_{t_1}^2$ is not P-RED.*
2. **P-P-RED vs. SG-P-SR:** *Process schedule $\mathcal{S}_{t_1}^9$ is not P-P-RED but it is SG-P-SR. Conversely, a process schedule $\mathcal{S}$ might be P-P-RED but not SG-P-SR when a conflict cycle is induced by two completing processes $a_{i_l}^c <_{\mathcal{S}} a_{j_m}^c <_{\mathcal{S}} a_{j_m}^{-1} <_{\mathcal{S}} a_{i_l}^{-1}$ with $a_{i_g}^p <_{\mathcal{S}} a_{i_l}^c$ and $a_{j_h}^p <_{\mathcal{S}} a_{j_m}^c$. In this case, since both P_i and P_j are completing, the conflicts of their aborted subprocesses are included in $SG(\mathcal{S})$ but by applying the commutativity and compensation rules, all activities of the conflict cycle can be cancelled. Finally, P-P-RED and SG-P-SR are not disjoint since, for instance, process schedule $\mathcal{S}_{t_1}^8$ meets both criteria.*
3. **P-P-RED vs. P-SG-P-SR:** *A process schedule $\mathcal{S}$ is P-SG-P-SR but not P-P-RED if it is, for instance, defined over two processes, say P_i and P_j, and if it contains a conflict cycle $a_{i_l}^c <_{\mathcal{S}} a_{j_m}^c <_{\mathcal{S}} a_{i_l}^{-1} <_{\mathcal{S}} a_{j_m}^{-1}$ where both processes are aborted or aborting and where no other pairs of conflicting activities exist. Although the cycle cannot be eliminated by the reduction rules, SG is, for $\mathcal{S}$ as well as for each prefix $\mathcal{S}'$ of $\mathcal{S}$, acyclic (since at least one process has been aborting when the conflict cycle was introduced). A process schedule $\mathcal{S}$ over two completing processes, P_i and P_j, is P-P-RED but not P-SG-P-SR when, for instance, a conflict cycle $a_{i_l}^c <_{\mathcal{S}} a_{j_m}^c <_{\mathcal{S}} a_{j_m}^{-1} <_{\mathcal{S}} a_{i_l}^{-1}$ with $a_{i_g}^p <_{\mathcal{S}} a_{i_l}^c$ and $a_{j_h}^p <_{\mathcal{S}} a_{j_m}^c$ exists. Although all activities of the conflict cycle can be eliminated by applying reduction rules, a cycle is present in $SG(\mathcal{S})$. Process schedule $\mathcal{S}_{t_1}^8$ of Example 5.8 accounts for both criteria such that P-SG-P-SR and P-P-RED are not comparable.*
4. **P-P-RED vs. P-RC:** *Process schedule $\mathcal{S}_{t_1}^4$ of Example 5.4 is P-P-RED but not P-RC. When a conflict cycle $a_{i_k}^p <_{\mathcal{S}} a_{j_m}^p <_{\mathcal{S}} a_{i_l}^p$ exists in a process schedule $\mathcal{S}$ formed only by pivot activities and when, in addition, $\mathcal{S}$ is free of abort dependencies, it is P-RC but not P-P-RED. Therefore, the classes P-P-RED and P-RC are not comparable.* □

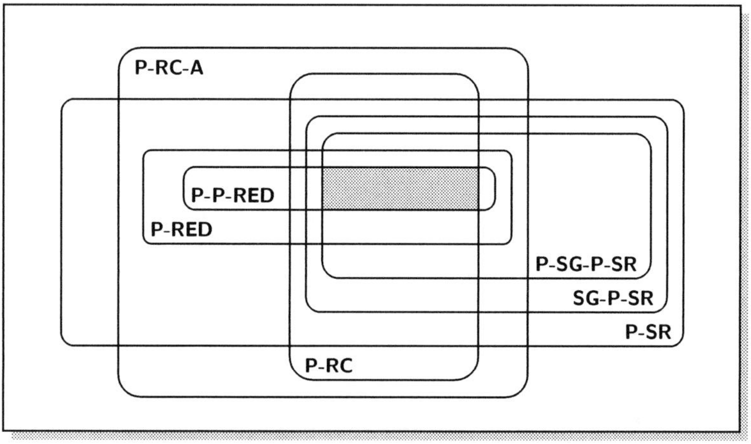

Figure 5.13: Relation Between P-SR, SG-P-SR, P-SG-P-SR, P-RC, P-RC-A, P-RED, and P-P-RED

In Lemma 5.6, we have proven that process-reducibility does not meet P-SR and P-RC jointly. In what follows, we show that the same is true for P-P-RED, the prefix-closed subclass of P-RED:

Lemma 5.7 (P–P–RED $\not\subseteq$ P–RC $\cap$ P–SR) *P-P-RED does not hold for P-RC and P-SR simultaneously.* □

Proof (Lemma 5.7) *In order to show the relation between P-P-RED and P-SR $\cap$ P-RC, again process schedule $\mathcal{S}_{t_1}^4$ can be analyzed. Since each prefix of $\mathcal{S}_{t_1}^4$ can be correctly reduced, it meets P-P-RED. However, since $\mathcal{S}_{t_1}^4$ is not P-RC, P-P-RED does not provide process-serializability and process-recoverability jointly.* □

The discussion of this section is summarized in Figure 5.13 where the relationships between the classes P-SR, SG-P-SR, P-SG-P-SR, P-RC, P-RC-A, P-RED, and P-P-RED (thus, also CT) are illustrated.

Since CT corresponds to P-P-RED for completed process schedules, it holds for both P-SR and P-RC-A. But since the process-recoverability requirement explicitly includes the possibility to chose, for each partial process schedule $\mathcal{S}$, an arbitrary set $R_{\mathcal{S}}$ of running processes and to abort all processes of its superset $R_{\mathcal{S}}^*$ correctly, P-RC-A is not sufficient. The reason being is that, in contrast to the traditional unified theory, we do not require all active processes to abort and that, when scheduling is performed dynamically, the subset of active processes that will finally be aborted in the completed process schedule is not known in advance. Therefore, a dynamic scheduling protocol for transactional processes has to provide P-RC and P-P-RED simultaneously. In addition, such a dynamic protocol has to guarantee that CT, the correct termination, is possible for each partial process schedule by implementing one of the four strategies for completion we have discussed in Section 5.5.

6 Process Locking: A Dynamic Scheduling Protocol for Transactional Processes

"≪Die Natur ist niemals korrekt!≫ dürfte man eher sagen. Korrektion setzt Regeln voraus, und zwar Regeln, die der Mensch selbst bestimmt, nach Gefühl, Erfahrung, Überzeugung und Wohlgefallen."

Johann Wolfgang von Goethe, Schriften zur Kunst

In Chapter 5, we have identified certain classes of process schedules which address correctness with respect to concurrency control and/or recovery. These classes respect the special semantics of transactional processes, and, at the same time, account for the additional constraints on the execution of concurrent processes that are imposed by the process structure. Moreover, as the discussion on the various strategies for enforcing CT for partial process schedules has shown, either considerably more information than provided by a partial process schedule is needed —namely information about the future activities required for completion— thus prohibiting dynamic scheduling, or, alternatively, additional restrictions have to introduced when scheduling is performed dynamically.

In this chapter, we present *process locking*, a dynamic scheduling protocol that guarantees CT process schedules and which, since scheduling is performed dynamically, also guarantees that each prefix of a complete process schedule is P-RED (as required by CT), and, at the same time, also SG-P-SR and P-RC. First, we introduce the basic ideas of process locking and the protocol in detail. Then, we prove the conformance of process locking with respect to P-P-RED, P-SG-P-SR, and P-RC, and we show that each partial process schedule can actually be completed correctly.

6.1 Introduction to Process Locking

Process locking aims at providing a dynamic scheduling protocol that supports P-P-RED & P-SG-P-SR & P-RC multi-process executions and which guarantees the correct termination (CT) of each partial process schedule. Hence, it allows a process manager (see Figure 4.1) to dynamically decide on the execution, deferment, and rejection of activities.

Such a process manager that relies on the process locking protocol has been implemented as part of the WISE system [AFH+99, AFL+99, LASS00] which, in turn, is based on the kernel of the process support engine OPERA [AHST97a, AHST97b, Hag99].

Process Locking makes use of some basic assumptions on the process programs to be executed as well as on the commutativity behavior of activities and the applicability of compensation. First of all, each process program to be executed has to be inherently correct: according to Axiom 5.1, it has to follow the guaranteed termination property (Definition 4.6). Additional assumptions address commutativity and compensation: the commutativity relation must be perfect (see Definition 3.20) and compensation must be state-independent.

Assumption 6.1 *Commutativity is* perfect. □

Assumption 6.2 *Compensation is* state-independent*: a compensating activity can be executed at any point in time (thus in any state) after the commit of its associated regular activity.* □

All these assumptions are not limiting the applicability of process locking but they rather reflect realistic conditions.

In the discussion of CT (Chapter 5.5), we have presented various strategies on how to guarantee correct termination for partial process schedules. Most of these solutions require information about the future execution, i.e., the completion, of partial processes. In general, since the (correct) structure of single process programs is known to the process manager, execution orders could be determined beforehand, especially in terms of the completed process schedule $\mathcal{C}(\mathcal{S})$ of some partial process schedule $\mathcal{S}$. However, process programs may contain execution paths that are not followed (e.g., due to some decision choosing one path but skipping others, or since alternative executions need not be executed when no failure occurs). Therefore, the a priori determination of multi-process executions would have to consider more activities than are actually executed and thus, would be very restrictive in nature. This is even the case when only the safe alternatives of completing processes, their assured termination trees, are considered for this purpose. Hence, protocols like altruistic locking [SGA87], designed for long lived transactions, do not provide a feasible solution since they require the access pattern of a process to be known beforehand (which would again include all possible execution paths). Moreover, the predetermination of execution paths would not only neglect the load on the subsystems and thus, the execution time of activities, it would also prevent the support for dynamic changes of processes and process programs [RD98]. This kind of modification, however, is highly important in certain application domains, such as, for instance, medical information systems [MR99].

Another, yet more restrictive strategy to avoid unresolvable deadlocks in which two or more completing processes are involved (note that this kind of deadlocks could not be resolved by the abort of any of these processes) is to allow at most one completing process at any point in time. This restriction goes along with the observation that completing processes are in general "old", i.e., long-running, having already executed a rather large number of activities and thus, having accessed a rather large number of resources compared to running processes. Therefore, since according to [Gra80] the deadlock probability increases linearly with the number of processes and to the power of four with the number of resources accessed (i.e., activities executed in subsystems), such unresolvable deadlocks are more likely to occur the more completing processes are allowed concurrently. Yet, a dynamic scheduling protocol following the restriction of only one completing process at a time needs only to consider the activities that are really executed in a process and does not have to cope with others of unconsidered paths. This distinguished completing process will have a special status and will be preferred against other processes, much like the "golden transaction" of the early System R database [GMB+81], the only transaction of the system that was allowed to perform undo operations at a time.

For all these reasons, the restriction on one completing process at a time is a key feature of the process locking protocol in order to allow a process manager to enforce CT dynamically.

6.2 Process Locking: The Core Protocol

In short, the process locking protocol is based on and extends ideas of locks with constrained sharing [AA90] and timestamp ordering [Tho79, BHG87]. In what follows, we will motivate the necessity of advanced mechanisms for supporting CT and present the protocol in detail. Since process locking considers the aforementioned restrictions in order to enforce CT, it does not only provide P-P-RED and P-RC but also P-SG-P-SR. The superclass P-P-RED & P-RC & P-SG-P-SR of all process schedules produced by process locking is highlighted in gray color in Figure 5.13 where the relations between all correctness classes of process schedules that have been introduced in Chapter 5 are illustrated.

6.2.1 Locks with Constrained Sharing

In most concurrency control protocols, locking techniques are applied to control concurrent access to shared resources. In the traditional read/write model, the semantics of data access is exploited which allows to share locks for read accesses —which do not change any database state— but requires exclusive access when data is written, that is when state changes are performed.

These locking techniques consider locks to be associated with single data objects. However, in the context of transactional process management where activities correspond to transactions which are executed in some subsystem, things become more complex. In general, these subsystem transactions and the objects accessed by them are not known to the process manager. Since their characteristics are completely hidden by the subsystem, these transactions and therefore also the corresponding activities rather appear as black boxes. For these reasons, conventional locking techniques at data level cannot be applied to transactional processes. Hence, despite of the black box characteristics of the actual implementation of activities, the process manager nevertheless exploits information on the activities' commutativity behavior, given by a commutativity relation as discussed in Chapter 5, which allows to dynamically identify pairs of activities that conflict. Yet, in contrast to traditional approaches, process locking associates locks with activity types to indicate whether or not an activity can be invoked in the context of a given process schedule.

But, activities of transactional processes cannot be qualified as read or write. They are, in general, located at a semantical higher level of abstraction. As a result, the difference between shared access and exclusive access blurs and locks on activities would inevitably have to be exclusive. When combined with two phase locking or even strict two phase locking [EGLT76], this would unnecessarily reduce the degree of concurrency (since each activity corresponds to a transaction in a subsystem, its execution and, consequently, the execution of the whole process may be very long). Furthermore, it does not prevent two different processes to be completing which could, in the worst case, lead to deadlocks that cannot be resolved.

In order to avoid (nearly) serial executions of processes when conflicting activities exist, sharing of locks should nevertheless be allowed. To this end, the ideas of locks with constrained sharing [AA90], that have been introduced in the context of the traditional locking scheme, i.e., locks on data objects, can be applied to process activities. Basically, this approach has introduced, in addition to shared and exclusive locks, a third category, namely *ordered shared locks (OSL)*. Starting from the standard lock compatibility table (where two read locks may be shared while all other combinations of locks have to be exclusive), various relaxations are proposed, the most permissive of them being the case where only shared locks (for concurrent read access to data objects) and

held \ acqu.	C Lock	P Lock
C Lock	$\Rightarrow$	$\not\Leftrightarrow$
P Lock	$\Rightarrow$	$\not\Leftrightarrow$

Table 6.1: Compatibility Matrix of C and P Locks ($\Rightarrow$: Ordered Shared; $\not\Leftrightarrow$: Exclusive)

ordered shared locks (for all other concurrent accesses) are exploited. According to [AA90], locks can be shared between different transactions under certain constraints: with each sharing, an order is associated which has to be respected not only for the execution of the respective operations but also when acquiring further locks and when locks are relinquished. A lock l_i of a transaction T_i is said to be *on hold* if l_i was acquired after another transaction T_j has acquired a lock l_j on the same data object but before l_j has been released. The lock *relinquish rule* then guarantees that all locks are shared with the same order in that a transaction may not release a lock as long as any of its locks is on hold. In process locking, the ideas of ordered shared locks are now combined with the special semantics that can be found in processes in that locks on activities can be ordered shared.

The prerequisite for the application of locking techniques at activity level is that a complete commutativity relation is available to the process manager. A possibility to implement this relation is to exploit an $(n \times n)$ matrix CON, with n being the number of all activities in $\mathcal{A}^*$, where $CON(a_i, a_j) = TRUE$ when a_i and a_j conflict, and $CON(a_i, a_j) = FALSE$ otherwise. Due to the assumption of perfect commutativity (c.f. Assumption 6.1), the specification of CON is facilitated since only the commutativity behavior for the m regular activities of $\mathcal{A}^*$ (with $m \leq n$) is required, leading to an $(m \times m)$ matrix which can be automatically extended to the complete commutativity matrix CON. This matrix indicates conflicts on a rather coarse granularity, on the level of activity types, i.e., for different transaction programs that can be executed in the underlying subsystems, but does not consider parameters associated with these invocations. However, this is the most general possibility that accounts for the black box semantics of activities which, due the lack of detailed information about their implementation and their structure, does in certain cases not allow to consider conflicts on a more fine-grained level.

In Chapter 5, we have seen that the allowed (as well as the disallowed) interleavings of processes are governed by the conflict behavior of activities and their termination properties, i.e., whether or not they can be compensated. Hence, applied to process schedules and to the requirements imposed by transactional process management, ordered shared locks at activity level provide a straightforward means to map allowed interleavings of processes into a compatibility matrix of different lock types. For this purpose, and similar to the usage of the read/write characteristics of operations in traditional locking protocols, the semantics of activities with respect to their termination characteristics (compensatable or pivot) can be exploited.

Therefore, *C locks* for compensatable activities and *P locks* for pivot activities, respectively, are used. While two C locks for conflicting activities of different processes as well as a P lock followed by a C lock may be ordered shared, this is not the case for a C lock followed by a P lock. In the latter case, when the process having requested the C lock is running, this would correspond to an abort dependency which has to be prevented in order to guarantee P-RC. Therefore, a C lock followed by a P lock cannot be ordered shared but must be exclusive. Finally, the combination of two P locks has also to be dealt with care since this combination of locks implies that both associated processes are completing and may impose deadlocks that cannot be resolved. The lock compatibility matrix of the process locking protocol is depicted in Table 6.1 where $\Rightarrow$ denotes ordered shared mode and

$\not\Leftrightarrow$ stands for non-shared (exclusive) mode. This compatibility matrix corresponds to the algorithm deciding whether edges in the colored serialization graph are allowed or disallowed, as discussed in Chapter 5.3.

Note that, since two P locks are not compatible, process locking —as each protocol does— will rule out some process schedules that are considered as correct. This is even reinforced by the additional restriction of allowing at most one completing process at a time. Therefore, process locking allows only a subclass of P-P-RED & P-SG-P-SR & P-RC process schedules, highlighted in Figure 5.13.

6.2.2 Timestamp Ordering

The original OSL protocol proposed by Agrawal and El Abbadi [AA90] generalizes standard two phase locking by bringing it together with the constrained sharing of locks. This protocol has an optimistic character since the compliance of orders is not checked until the first lock is to be released (due to the lock relinquish rule) which may not be performed until no further lock has to be acquired. But since preclaiming does not appear to be the ultimate solution in the case of transactional processes (all possible paths would have to be considered although eventually only few of them are effected), the validation would more or less coincide with the commit of a process. This, in turn, means that violations of the order constraints associated with shared locks are detected at a very late stage and even worse, may occur in situations where appropriate corrective strategies, i.e., the abort of the processes involved, are not possible since these processes are completing, not running.

To circumvent this drawback, we impose early verification of the correct order of shared locks that immediately takes place whenever locks are acquired. To do this, we adopt and apply ideas borrowed from timestamp ordering (TO) protocols [Tho79, BHG87]. We use the same mechanisms to control the order in which ordered shared locks are acquired than the original TO protocol does for an a priori determination of the serialization order and thus, the order in which shared data objects are accessed. The only prerequisite is that each process is assigned a unique timestamp taken from a strictly monotonically increasing series.

6.2.3 Process Locking: Combining OSL & TO for Processes

Following the previous discussion, the application of ordered shared locks and timestamp ordering in the context of transactional processes requires that for each activity, i.e., for each transaction program that can be invoked by the process manager, additional information in the form of an ordered list is maintained which comprises the locks held for all invocations of that activity. Each lock, in turn, refers to the process by which the lock has been acquired (and by which the corresponding activity is invoked), thereby implicitly associating each lock with a process timestamp. Finally, for each activity a_i, the set of activities a_j with $CON(a_i, a_j) = TRUE$, taken from the commutativity matrix, has to be available.

Even when combining the extended OSL protocol based on P and C locks with timestamp ordered lock requests, special treatment is necessary for pivot activities. The previous discussions made the dual character of pivot activities obvious: on the one hand, they are "normal" activities; on the other hand, they have a commit-like semantics ("quasi commit") since they make compensation unavailable for all preceding activities and lead to state changes (of the process itself or of sub-processes) which have to be dealt with care. Due to this dualism, a pivot activity can neither be treated like the commit of a process nor like a normal activity. Although, for instance violations of constraints imposed by abort dependencies between processes P_i and P_j, caused by pairs of activities $(a^c_{i_k}, a_{j_m})$ are no longer possible once a pivot of P_i succeeding $a^c_{i_k}$ is executed, locks on these compensatable activities must not be released (as would be the case for a commit). Otherwise, P-SR could no longer be guaranteed. When pivot activities $a^p_{i_k}$ are considered just as regular activities, only abort dependencies could be detected in which the pivot itself is involved, but no others, i.e., abort dependencies in which activities preceding the pivot with respect to $\prec_i$ are involved. Reconsider the P-RC algorithm based on the colored serialization graph where also certain state changes of a process (e.g., by executing a primary pivot) were subject to special considerations and led to the verification of all existing dependencies of this process. This verification is captured in process locking by the requirement of converting all preceding C locks held for compensatable activities to P locks once a pivot activity is to be executed such that also all abort dependencies between activities $(a^c_{i_h}, a_{j_l})$ with some $a^c_{i_h}$ preceding $a^p_{i_k}$ with respect to $\prec_i$ will be considered.

Aborting processes executing compensating activities require special treatment because it has to be guaranteed that aborting processes themselves are not aborted. Additionally, once a process is completing, it will be favored in that it may override timestamp orders for lock requests.

Process locking can be briefly summarized as follows: When instantiated, a process P_i is assigned a unique timestamp $ts(P_i)$. Before an activity a_{i_k} is to be executed, a lock must be acquired which has to meet a_{i_k}'s termination property (either a C lock or a P lock). This lock then corresponds to an entry in the lock list of the activity. However, prior to the permission of a lock, all conflicting activities, and in particular all locks held for these activities have to be analyzed so as to decide whether or not the lock for a_{i_k} can be granted. The following six rules specify the acquisition and the release of locks, respectively, and define process locking in detail:

1. **Comp–Rule: Execution of a Compensatable Activity $a^c_{i_k}$**

   For the execution of a compensatable activity, a C lock is required. Depending on the process timestamp of P_i and the timestamps of potential other processes holding locks for conflicting activities, a C lock request can either be granted immediately, requires the abort of concurrent processes, or has to be deferred.

   Granting C Locks: A C lock for some activity $a^c_{i_k}$ of a running process can be granted when either no other process holds a lock for a conflicting activity, or when all locks held for conflicting activities (either C or P locks) are from older processes with respect to the process timestamp. Once the C lock has been successfully acquired, $a^c_{i_k}$ can be executed.

   Aborting Concurrent Processes: If a process P_j with a younger timestamp, $ts(P_j) > ts(P_i)$, holds a C lock for a conflicting activity a_{j_l}, then P_j will be aborted. If P_j is already aborting, then P_i has to wait until P_j is aborted (aborting processes cannot be aborted). Once P_j is aborted correctly, its locks are released, the C lock required for the execution of $a^c_{i_k}$ can be acquired, and $a^c_{i_k}$ can be executed. After completing the abort of P_j, it is resubmitted with the same timestamp in order to avoid its starvation. This is possible since P_i is able to execute $a^c_{i_k}$ in the meanwhile such that, when P_j redoes the execution of a_{j_l}, the constraints imposed by the process timestamps on the sharing of locks and thus, on the associated C locks, are met.

   Additionally, the request of a C lock by a completing process leads to the abort of older processes already holding a C lock for a conflicting activity since completing processes are treated as "first-class processes" and are favored compared to running processes.

Deferment of C Lock Requests: If a younger process P_k, $ts(P_k) > ts(P_i)$, exists which already holds a P lock for a conflicting activity, then $a^c_{i_k}$ has to be deferred (since P_k cannot be aborted) until the commit of P_k. Special treatment is also applied if a completing process P_k with a younger timestamp holds a C lock (this is possible since we allow a pivot activity of a process program to be recursively followed by process programs). Then, P_i has also to be deferred until the commit of the completing process P_k. The latter ones are the only cases where the lock sharing order (and thus, the serialization order) and the timestamp order do not coincide.

2. **Piv–Rule: Execution of a Pivot Activity $a^p_{i_k}$**

   When a_{i_k} is a pivot activity, then P_i has to acquire a P lock before it can be executed. However, prior to the P lock request for $a^p_{i_k}$, all C locks of P_i held for activities a_{i_h} preceding $a^p_{i_k}$ have first to be converted to P locks. The reason being is the dual character of pivots. There can be C locks ordered shared with older processes which are still running or are in a running subprocess. The execution of the pivot $a^p_{i_k}$, which additionally corresponds to a state change from running to completing in the case it is a primary pivot, could violate constraints imposed by potentially existing abort dependencies which, in turn, would correspond to a violation of P-RC. Again, a distinction on whether the P lock can be granted immediately after lock conversion, whether it requires the abort of concurrent processes, or whether it has to be deferred is possible.

Granting P Locks: A P lock is granted, after lock conversion, if no other process holds a lock for a conflicting activity.

Aborting Concurrent Processes: In case younger processes P_j, $ts(P_j) > ts(P_i)$, hold C locks for conflicting activities, all these P_j have to be aborted if they are running, otherwise, if they are already aborting, P_i has to wait until they are aborted. After A_j, they are resubmitted with the same timestamp so as to avoid starvation.

Deferment of P Lock Requests: If older processes hold C locks or if any other process holds a P lock, then the request has to be deferred until the end of these processes. This is the case since, according to the lock compatibility matrix, a newly acquired P lock may not be shared with any other lock already held (and since at most one completing process at a time is allowed).

3. **Comp→Piv–Rule: Conversion of C Locks to P Locks**

   This conversion is required for all C locks of a process P_i as prerequisite for the execution of a pivot activity $a^p_{i_k}$. Since the conversion of a C lock to a P lock is similar to the acquisition of a P lock, the same conditions hold: C→P lock conversion succeeds when either no other process holds a lock for a conflicting activity or if all existing locks are C locks held by younger processes P_j, $ts(P_j) > ts(P_i)$, which then have to be aborted (and which are resubmitted with the same process timestamp). In case older processes hold C locks or if any other process holds a P lock, then C→P lock conversion has to be deferred until the end of these processes.

4. **C^{-1}–Rule: Execution of a Compensating Activity $a^{-1}_{i_k}$**

   When a process P_i is aborting, it must be able to correctly undo all its activities. Eventually, there are processes P_j with younger timestamps than P_i, $ts(P_i) < ts(P_j)$, that have executed an activity a_{j_l} which conflicts with $a^c_{i_k}$ and which appears after $a^c_{i_k}$ with respect to the observed order $<_{\mathcal{S}}$ in a process schedule $\mathcal{S}$. According to the Comp–Rule, this case is allowed, at least when all these processes P_j are running. To correctly undo $a_{i_k}^c$, again a C lock has to be acquired by $a_{i_k}^{-1}$. This leads to the abort of all such processes P_j which have common locks with P_i but younger timestamps. Yet, the abort of a process P_i may induce cascading aborts, conforming with notion of P-RC. In the case of cascading aborts, all aborted processes are resubmitted in timestamp order, thereby keeping their original timestamp. All older processes P_k having locks in common with P_i are not affected by the C lock request induced by $a_{i_k}^{-1}$ and thus, by the abort of P_i.

5. **Abort–Rule: Abort $\mathbf{A_i}$ of a Process $\mathbf{P_i}$**

   The abort A_i of a process P_i leads to the release of all locks held by P_i.

6. **Commit–Rule: Commit $\mathbf{C_i}$ of a Process $\mathbf{P_i}$**

   In accordance with the lock relinquish rule of the original OSL protocol, a process P_i is finally allowed to commit if all its locks are shared in the correct order. Applied to transactional processes and to the criterion of P-RC, a process must not commit if it has common locks (which correspond to abort dependencies) shared with older processes P_j, $ts(P_j) < ts(P_i)$. In this case, C_i must be deferred until all these P_j have committed. Note that all common locks shared with older processes may only be C locks. Otherwise, if no common locks with older processes exist, P_i is allowed to commit and to release all its locks; therefore, process locking follows the strict two phase locking (S2PL) paradigm [EGLT76].

Note that, although compensating activities are themselves required to be pivot, i.e., compensation cannot be compensated, we do not demand them to acquire P locks since this would, due to the Piv–Rule, require C→P lock conversion for all C locks of aborting processes. Essentially, this would not be possible if older processes exist holding ordered shared C locks. Yet, it is sufficient for guaranteeing CT to abort only processes which have been executed conflicting activities between a regular and a compensating activity — which is already captured by requiring C locks for compensation (as part of the special treatment being part of the acquisition rules for C and P locks).

Obviously, by allowing to share locks in timestamp order, a process may induce cascading aborts. Avoiding cascading aborts would be far too restrictive since it would, in the case of semantically rich activities where a distinction between read and write access to data is impossible, degenerate to rigorousness [BGRS91]. However, due to the exclusive treatment of certain combinations of locks, it is ensured that cascading aborts are restricted to running processes, not to completing ones. After the cascading abort of some process P_j is completed, it is resubmitted with the same timestamp in order to avoid starvation. Additionally, process locking makes use of timestamp-based deadlock prevention strategies [RSL78, BHG87]. In particular, the deferment or abort of processes is based on process timestamps and on the termination properties of single activities (i.e., the type of lock to be acquired), and exploits the restriction to at most one completing process at a time. Hence, the ideas of Wound–Wait and Wait–Die strategies [RSL78] are applied to transactional processes such that process locking guarantees the absence of deadlocks imposed by cyclic wait-for dependencies.

Example 6.1 *Consider again the CIM scenario introduced in Example 2.1 with the two process programs, construction and production, being executed in parallel. Assume that all activities of the process program PP^C (construction) are compensatable while activity "produce" of PP^P, i.e., the production, is pivot (yet, for reasons of guaranteed termination, "transfer to stock" has to*

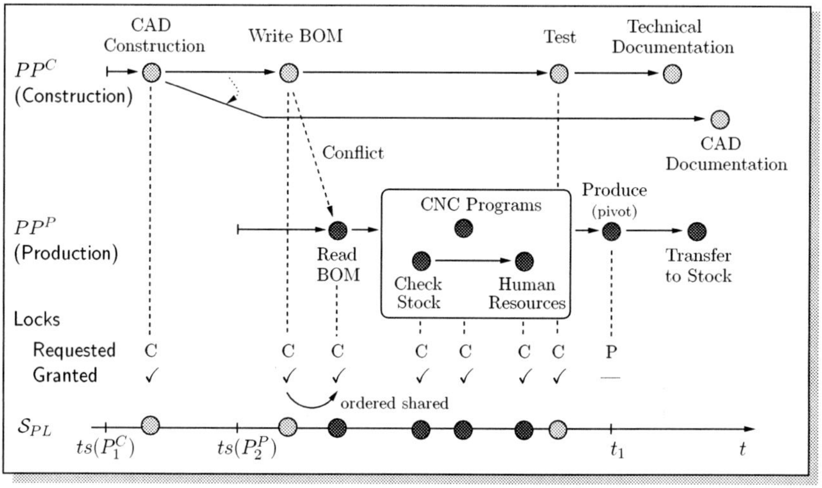

Figure 6.1: Process Locking Applied to CIM Processes of Example 6.1

be retriable). In Figure 6.1, the concurrent execution of both process programs by P_1^C *and* P_2^P, *respectively, reflected in process schedule* S_{PL} *is depicted. For the timestamps of both processes, the following holds:* $ts(P_1^C) < ts(P_2^P)$. *Since the first two activities of* P_1^C, *namely "CAD construction" and "write BOM", are compensatable, they have to request C locks which can be granted immediately according to the Comp–Rule. The lock request for activity "read BOM" of* P_2^P *can also be granted and the corresponding C lock is shared in timestamp order with the C lock held for the conflicting activity "write BOM" of* P_1^C *(Comp–Rule). Moreover, also the locks for all activities of* P_2^P *being defined in* PP^P*'s multi-activity node as well as the lock for activity "test" of* P_1^C *can be granted and the activities can be executed. At time* t_1, *a P lock request is issued for activity "produce" of* P_2^P. *According to the Piv–Rule, this first requires the conversion of all C locks of* P_2^P. *But, the Comp→Piv–Rule prohibits the C lock held for activity "read BOM" to be converted since it is shared with process* P_1^C *(since the latter process has an older timestamp). Hence, activity "produce" of* P_2^P *has to be deferred. In the meanwhile, process* P_1^C *can terminate correctly and release all locks at commit time (none of these locks is on hold). Since, at* t_2, *none of the locks of* P_2^P *is shared with other processes, C→P lock conversion can be performed successfully and the P lock for activity "produce" can be acquired (see Figure 6.2). Process schedule* S_{PL}, *generated by process locking, now reflects the correct concurrent execution of* PP^C *and* PP^P. □

6.3 Process Locking: Correctness

In what follows, we prove the correctness of process locking, i.e., we show that it produces P-P-RED & P-SG-P-SR & P-RC process schedules and that it allows each partial process schedule to be completed correctly (CT).

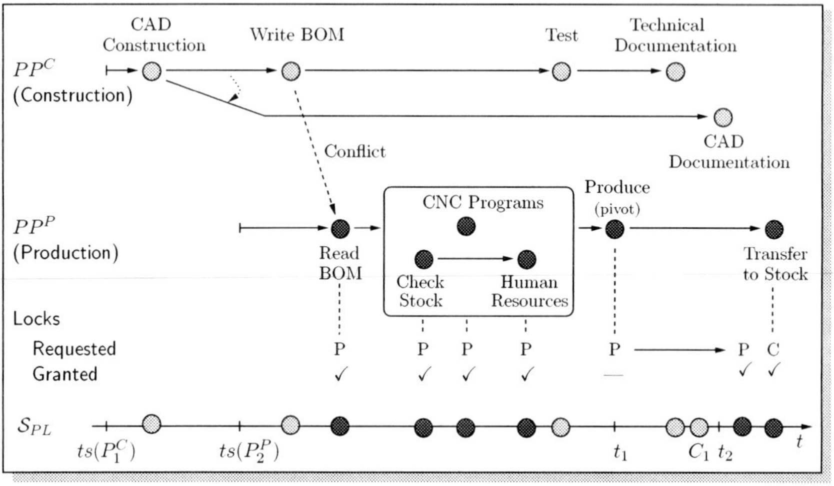

Figure 6.2: Process Locking Applied to CIM Processes of Example 6.1 (continued)

6.3.1 Process Locking and P-SG-P-SR

Each process schedule $\mathcal{S}$ produced by the process locking protocol satisfies P-SG-P-SR, the prefix-closed subclass of P-SR which requires that the serialization graph of each prefix $\mathcal{S}'$ of $\mathcal{S}$ is acyclic.

Lemma 6.1 (Process Locking and P-SG-P-SR) *Process locking guarantees P-SG-P-SR.* □

Proof (Lemma 6.1)

Assume that a process schedule generated by process locking is not P-SG-P-SR, that is that a cycle $P_i \rightarrow P_{i+1} \rightarrow \ldots \rightarrow P_{i+k} \rightarrow P_i$ in the serialization graph $SG(\mathcal{S}')$ of a prefix $\mathcal{S}'$ of a process schedule $\mathcal{S}$ exists. Consider the first edge, $P_i \rightarrow P_{i+1}$, of this cycle which has to correspond to a pair of conflicting activities $(a_{i_k}, a_{(i+1)_l})$. The execution order of conflicting activities coincides with the order in which the corresponding locks are applied; therefore, there must be a successful lock request issued by P_{i+1} preceded by a lock that has been granted to P_i. Since only two kinds of locks exist, the following four combinations have to be considered. By analyzing all possible cases, we show that no such conflict cycle can exist in $SG(\mathcal{S}')$:

1. *Assume that the locks acquired by P_i and by P_{i+1} are both P locks. Since at any point in time only one completing process is allowed, P_i must have committed before the P lock of P_{i+1} has been granted. However, this contradicts with the edge $P_{i+k} \rightarrow P_i$ in the serialization graph which can occur in two cases: It would either require that some activity a_{i_n} of P_i succeeds C_i, or it requires that a pair of conflicting activities $(a_{(i+k)_q}, a_{i_h})$ with $a_{i_h} \prec_i a_{i_k}$ exists. Then, P_{i+k} must be older than P_i such that a_{i_k} has to be deferred until C_{i+k}. But P_{i+k} has locks on hold which means that C_{i+k} is deferred until C_{i+k-1} which, in turn has also to be deferred leading*

transitively to a deferred commit dependency with C_{i+1}. Yet, this would imply the following orders on the commits of P_i and P_{i+1}: $C_i <_{S'} C_{i+1}$ and, at the same time, $C_{i+1} <_{S'} C_i$.

2. *Assume that the lock acquired by P_i is a C lock while process P_{i+1} has successfully requested a P lock. According to the lock acquisition rules, the following possibilities exist:*

   (a) *P_i is younger than P_{i+1}, $ts(P_i) > ts(P_{i+1})$, and P_i is still running when P_{i+1} requested its P lock. Then, in order to grant the P lock to P_{i+1}, P_i must have been aborted and its effects undone. In this case, P_i cannot appear in the serialization graph and thus, also not in the conflict cycle.*

   (b) *P_i is younger than P_{i+1}, $ts(P_i) > ts(P_{i+1})$, and P_i is completing when P_{i+1} requested its P lock. In this case, $a_{(i+1)_l}$ would have to be deferred until C_i (leading to a serialization order that does not coincide with the timestamp order). However, the edge $P_{i+k} \rightarrow P_i$ in the serialization graph would, similar to case 1, either require the execution of an activity a_{i_n} of P_i after its commit or it would impose cyclic dependencies on the commits of P_i and P_{i+1} with $C_i <_{S'} C_{i+1}$ and $C_{i+1} <_{S'} C_i$.*

   (c) *P_i is older than P_{i+1}, $ts(P_{i+1}) > ts(P_i)$, and $a^p_{(i+1)_l}$ is the primary pivot of P_{i+1}. Due to the lock compatibility matrix disallowing the sharing of a C lock followed by a P lock, P_i must have been committed by C_i prior to the P lock acquisition of P_{i+1}. However, the additional edge $P_{i+k} \rightarrow P_i$ that appears in the conflict cycle after the execution of $a^p_{(i+1)_l}$ again implies that another activity a_{i_n} of P_i would have been executed after its commit, or that cyclic dependencies between C_i and C_{i+1} exist.*

   (d) *P_i is older than P_{i+1}, $ts(P_{i+1}) > ts(P_i)$, and P_{i+1} is already completing when $a_{(i+1)_l}$ is to be executed. In this case, the special treatment of completing processes leads to the abort of P_i such that the edge $P_i \rightarrow P_{i+1}$ would not occur in the serialization graph.*

3. *Assume that P_i has acquired a P lock while P_{i+1} has acquired a C lock subsequently. This can occur in one of the following cases:*

   (a) *Process P_i has committed prior to the lock request of P_{i+1}. Then, independently of the process timestamps of both processes, the P lock for P_{i+1} can be granted. However, in order to add the edge $P_{i+k} \rightarrow P_i$ to the serialization graph, either an activity a_{i_n} of P_i would have to be executed after the commit C_i, or a conflict must have been occurred between P_{i+k} and P_i prior to the execution of P_i's primary pivot. The latter case is only possible when P_{i+k} is older than P_i such that the primary pivot of P_i has to be deferred until C_{i+k}. Since P_{i+k} has locks on hold, C_{i+k} is deferred until C_{i+k-1}. The same is true for all P_j with $j \in \{i+2, \ldots, i+k\}$ whose commits C_j have to be deferred until C_{j-1}. Therefore, the following orders on the commits of P_i and P_{i+1} would have to hold: $C_i <_{S'} C_{i+1}$ and, at the same time, $C_{i+1} <_{S'} C_i$.*

   (b) *Process P_i is completing when the C lock is successfully granted to P_{i+1} which is running. In order to allow this kind of shared locks, P_i has to be older than P_{i+1}, that is $ts(P_{i+1}) > ts(P_i)$. Since the C lock of P_{i+1} is on hold, the commit C_{i+1} has to be deferred until the termination of P_i. The same holds for all other processes involved in the conflict cycle: P_i is the only completing process and all other processes are only allowed to execute compensatable activities (in state running), thus to request C locks. In order to correctly acquire these C locks, each edge in the conflict cycle has to coincide with the timestamp order of the associated processes. Thus, all these locks of processes*

$P_{i+2}, \ldots, P_{i+k}$ are on hold and the commits of all associated processes have to be deferred. Since P_{i+k} is younger than P_i, the execution of a_{i_n} which is in conflict with some $a_{(i+k)_q}$, and which would not only cause the edge $P_{i+k} \rightarrow P_i$ to appear in the serialization graph but would also complete the conflict cycle, leads to the abort of P_{i+k}. Therefore, the last edge $P_{i+k} \rightarrow P_i$ cannot exist in the serialization graph such that no cycle of the previously assumed kind is possible.

(c) *Process P_i is completing when the C lock is successfully granted to P_{i+1} which is also completing. This leads, however, to a violation of the strategy of process locking which allows at any point in time at most one completing process.*

4. *Assume finally that both P_i and P_{i+1} are holding C locks.*

   (a) *Assume that both processes, P_i and P_{i+1}, are completing when they issue a C lock request. Since only one completing process is allowed at any point in time, P_i must have committed prior to the C lock request of P_{i+1} and thus, $C_i <_{S'} a_{(i+1)_l}$ has to hold. However, the edge $P_{i+k} \rightarrow P_i$ would either require another activity a_{i_n} to be executed after the commit of P_i or it would, due to the Commit–Rule in the presence of locks on hold, induce cyclic dependencies on the commits of P_i and P_{i+1} such that this case cannot happen.*

   (b) *Assume that P_i is running while P_{i+1} is completing when the C lock request is issued. Due to the Comp-Rule for the acquisition of C locks, P_i must have committed prior to the C lock request of P_{i+1} (otherwise, P_i would have been aborted and would therefore not appear in the serialization graph). But when $C_i <_{S'} a_{(i+1)_l}$ holds, again an activity a_{i_n} would have to be executed by P_i after its commit or cyclic dependencies between C_i and C_{i+1} would exist.*

   (c) *Assume that P_i is completing (i.e., a_{i_k} succeeds a primary pivot of P_i) and P_{i+1} is running. Considering the process timestamps, the following two cases can be distinguished:*

      i.) *P_i is older than P_{i+1}, $ts(P_{i+1}) > ts(P_i)$: The sharing of C locks is then legal with respect to the Comp-Rule. When activity a_{i_n} introducing the edge $P_{i+k} \rightarrow P_i$ in the serialization graph is executed, none of the processes $P_{i+1}, \ldots, P_{i+k}$ may have committed (each process $P_j, j \in \{i+1, \ldots i+k\}$ has locks on hold). However, the successful execution of a_{i_n} requires the abort of P_{i+k} which then could not appear in the serialization graph such that the conflict cycle would not exist.*

      ii.) *P_i is younger than P_{i+1}, $ts(P_i) > ts(P_{i+1})$: Then, the lock sharing order and the timestamp order do not coincide since $a_{(i+1)_l}$ would have to be deferred until P_i is committed. Therefore, the edge $P_{i+k} \rightarrow P_i$ of the serialization graph cannot occur.*

   (d) *Assume that both P_i and P_{i+1} are running. Then, with respect to the process timestamps, the following two possible scenarios can be identified:*

      i.) *P_i is older than P_{i+1}, $ts(P_i) < ts(P_{i+1})$: The sharing of C locks is then legal with respect to the Comp-Rule. Assume further that all activities involved in the conflict cycle are compensatable and that their associated processes are running. The execution of activity a_{i_n} introducing the edge $P_{i+k} \rightarrow P_i$ in the serialization graph would require the following relation of process timestamps: $ts(P_i) < ts(P_{i+1}) < \ldots < ts(P_{i+k}) < ts(P_i)$ which, however, contradicts with the monotonicity requirement of process timestamps.*
      Otherwise, at least one process $P_j \in \{P_{i+2}, \ldots, P_{i+k}\}$ is completing. If some activity a_{j_m} leading to an edge in the serialization graph is pivot, P_j must be younger than

P_{j-1}, the process preceding P_j in the serialization graph. Then, however, a_{j_m} would have to be deferred until C_{j-1}. Since all processes preceding P_j have locks on hold, they have to be deferred until C_i such that the edge $P_{i+k} \rightarrow P_i$ could not exist. If P_j is older than P_{j-1}, the latter one is aborted and does not appear in the serialization graph. If activity a_{j_m} leading to an edge in the serialization graph precedes the primary pivot $a^p_{j_p}$ of P_j, a lock conversion has to be performed prior to the execution of $a^p_{j_p}$. According to the Comp→Piv–Rule, this case induces the acquisition of a P lock even for a_{j_m}.

If, finally, activity a_{j_m} leading to an edge in the serialization graph is compensatable and succeeds P_j's primary pivot, only a C lock is required. Independently of process timestamps, the C lock request of P_j for activity a_{j_m} would lead to an abort of P_{j-1}, the process immediately preceding P_j in the serialization graph (due to conflicting activities of P_{j-1} and P_j). Yet, this abort would prevent a conflict cycle to occur.

ii.) P_i is younger than P_{i+1}, $ts(P_i) > ts(P_{i+1})$: In order to allow the execution of $a_{(i+1)_l}$, it must succeed the commit C_i of P_i. However, this is not possible because either another activity a_{i_n} of P_i would have to be executed after C_i in order to introduce the edge $P_{i+k} \rightarrow P_i$ in the conflict cycle or, due to the Commit-Rule in the presence of locks on hold, cyclic dependencies between the commits of P_i and P_{i+1} would exist.

All possible cases which could lead to the assumed cycle in the serialization graph of $\mathcal{S}'$, a prefix of process schedule $\mathcal{S}$, do not correspond to legal executions with respect to process locking. Hence, no such cycle exists and each process schedule that is emerged by process locking is P-SG-P-SR. □

6.3.2 Process Locking and P-RC

Process recoverability, P-RC, is based on the presence of certain orders of conflicting activities (defined via the notion of abort dependency) for which it imposes constraints on state changes of the associated processes. In order to provide P-RC, process locking both maps "problematic" orders of conflicting activities to non-compatible locks which prevents certain abort dependencies to occur and it prevents forbidden state changes —in the presence of allowed abort dependencies— by the Comp→Piv–Rule for lock conversion and the verification which is part of the Commit-Rule, respectively.

According to Definition 5.8 and given the basic assumption that commutativity is perfect (Assumption 6.1), an abort dependency exists between two conflicting activities $a_{i_k} \in P_i$ and $a_{j_l} \in P_j$ if a_{i_k} is compensatable, if a_{i_k} precedes a_{j_l} in $\mathcal{S}$ ($a_{i_k} <_{\mathcal{S}} a_{j_l}$), and when $a^{-1}_{i_k}$ does not precede a_{j_l} in $\mathcal{S}$.

Lemma 6.2 (Process Locking and P-RC) *Process locking guarantees P-RC.* □

Proof (Lemma 6.2) *Assume that a process schedule $\mathcal{S}$ generated by process locking is not P-RC. According to Definition 5.9, a violation of the constraints imposed by an abort dependency between P_i and P_j, caused by a pair of conflicting activities $a^c_{i_k}$ and a_{j_l}, must exist. In order to analyze all possibilities, the following two cases depending on the termination property of a_{j_l} have to be considered:*

1. *Assume that a_{j_l} is compensatable, thus its execution necessitates a C lock to be granted to P_j. The observed order $a^c_{i_k} <_{\mathcal{S}} a^c_{j_l}$ requires shared C locks between P_i and P_j which is only possible if P_i is older than P_j, that is if $ts(P_i) < ts(P_j)$, and if additionally P_j is running.*

In case process P_j wants to commit, then, due to the Commit-Rule, C_j has to be deferred until the commit C_i of P_i since P_j has a lock on hold. Therefore, process locking enforces the order $C_i <_{\mathcal{S}} C_j$.

In case P_j wants to execute a pivot activity $a^p_{j_p}$ succeeding $a^c_{j_l}$, i.e., $a^c_{j_l} \prec_j a^p_{j_p}$, then, according to the Comp→Piv–Rule for lock conversion, all C locks of P_j would have to be converted to P locks. Since P_i is older than P_j, this lock conversion for $a^c_{j_l}$ would have to be deferred until the C lock held by P_i is released which will take place at commit time. Therefore, $C_i <_{\mathcal{S}} a^p_{j_p}$ will hold such that P-RC is preserved.

2. *Assume that a_{j_l} is pivot, thus its execution necessitates a P lock to be granted to P_j. Since $a^c_{i_k}$ and $a^p_{j_l}$ are in conflict, this P lock request of P_j would not be reconcilable with the C lock already held by P_i. Due to the Piv-Rule, P_j's lock request would have to be deferred until P_i has released its locks which, according to the strict 2PL property of process locking, coincides with C_i. Therefore, the order $C_i <_{\mathcal{S}} a^p_{j_l}$ will be observed which is compliant to the P-RC requirements.*

Both cases are treated correctly by process locking which therefore guarantees process-recoverability for each process schedule $\mathcal{S}$. □

6.3.3 Process Locking and P-P-RED

After having shown that process locking ensures both P-SG-P-SR and P-RC, we have additionally to show that abort-related activities are executed correctly, even in the presence of concurrency. This is the case when each prefix of a process schedule $\mathcal{S}$ is also reducible (P-P-RED). The difference to P-SG-P-SR is that P-P-RED also considers activities of aborted and aborting processes. Given the initial assumption of perfect commutativity, violations of P-P-RED arise for P-SG-P-SR and P-RC process schedules $\mathcal{S}$ due to conflict cycles of the form $P_i \rightarrow P_j \rightarrow P_i$ in a prefix $\mathcal{S}'$ of $\mathcal{S}$, i.e., by conflicting activities $a^c_{i_k}$ and a_{j_l} with $a^c_{i_k} <_{\mathcal{S}'} a_{j_l} <_{\mathcal{S}'} a^{-1}_{i_k}$.

Lemma 6.3 (Process Locking and P-P-RED) *Process locking guarantees P-P-RED.* □

Proof (Lemma 6.3) *Violations of P-P-RED, given a process schedule $\mathcal{S}$ is already P-SG-P-SR, are possible by the execution of a compensating activity $a^{-1}_{i_k}$ of an aborting process leading to cyclic conflicts of the form $a^c_{i_k} <_{\mathcal{S}'} a_{j_l} <_{\mathcal{S}'} a^{-1}_{i_k}$ with $a^{-1}_{j_l} \not<_{\mathcal{S}'} a^{-1}_{i_k}$ in a prefix $\mathcal{S}'$ of $\mathcal{S}$. Hence, this conflict cycle is also present in $\mathcal{S}$. All possible cases can be addressed by analyzing the different termination properties of a_{j_l}:*

1. *Assume that a_{j_l} is compensatable. In order to allow the execution of $a^c_{j_l}$ after $a^c_{i_k}$, one of the following orders of process timestamps of P_i and P_j has to hold:*

   (a) *P_i is older than P_j, $ts(P_i) < ts(P_j)$: The sharing of C locks for the execution of $a^c_{j_l}$ is allowed. When $a^{-1}_{i_k}$ is to be executed, P_j may be in one of the following states:*

      i.) *P_j is running. In this case, according to the Comp-Rule, the execution of $a^{-1}_{i_k}$ requires a C lock and thus, leads to the abort of P_j. Additionally, $a^{-1}_{i_k}$ has to be deferred until all abort-related activities of P_j have successfully terminated, that is, until P_j*

is aborted. Then, however, also $a_{j_l}^{-1}$ *is present in* S' *which contains the following cycle:* $a_{i_k}^c <_{S'} a_{j_l}^c <_{S'} a_{j_l}^{-1} <_{S'} a_{i_k}^{-1}$. *Yet, both pairs of do/undo activities can be eliminated by applying the compensation rule.*

ii.) P_j *is completing. Then, either* $a_{j_l}^c$ *precedes* P_j*'s primary pivot, or such a primary pivot* $a_{j_p}^p$ *has been executed prior to* $a_{j_l}^c$. *If* $a_{j_l}^c$ *precedes a primary pivot, a P lock would be required for* $a_{j_l}^c$ *when* $a_{j_p}^p$ *is to be executed, due to the Comp→Piv–Rule. Since* P_i *is older and still running, this P lock could only be granted after the termination of* P_i *which would lead, in the case* $a_{i_k}^{-1}$ *is present in* S', *to the following observed execution order:* $a_{i_k}^c <_{S'} a_{i_k}^{-1} <_{S'} a_{j_l}^c$. *If* $a_{j_l}^c$ *succeeds a pivot* $a_{j_p}^p$, *the special treatment of completing processes would first cause an abort of* P_i *and would lead to the following order of the considered activities:* $a_{i_k}^c <_{S'} a_{i_k}^{-1} <_{S'} a_{j_l}^c$.

iii.) P_j *is aborting. When* $a_{i_k}^{-1}$ *is to be executed while* P_j *is aborting, it will be deferred until* A_j *is completed, leading to:* $a_{i_k}^c <_{S'} a_{j_l}^c <_{S'} a_{j_l}^{-1} <_{S'} a_{i_k}^{-1}$.

iv.) P_j *is committed. Since* P_i *is running and at least one lock of* P_j *is on hold, this case is not allowed according to the Commit-Rule.*

(b) P_i *is younger than* P_j, $ts(P_i) > ts(P_j)$: *In this case, the order in which the C locks are shared would contradict the timestamp order. Therefore, prior to the execution of* $a_{j_l}^c$, P_i *would be aborted which leads to the observed order* $a_{i_k}^c <_{S'} a_{i_k}^{-1} <_{S'} a_{j_l}^c$.

2. *Assume that* a_{j_l} *is pivot.*

(a) *If* P_i *is older than* P_j, $ts(P_i) < ts(P_j)$, *activity* $a_{j_l}^p$ *would have to be deferred until* P_i *is terminated.*

(b) *If* P_i *is younger than* P_j, $ts(P_i) > ts(P_j)$, *the execution of* $a_{j_l}^p$ *would first induce an abort of* P_i *and would lead to the observed execution order* $a_{i_k}^c <_{S'} a_{i_k}^{-1} <_{S'} a_{j_l}^p$.

All possible cases do not allow conflict cycles to be introduced by compensating activities since process locking considers special treatment for aborting processes and since the distinguished completing processes are treated as "first-class-processes". □

6.3.4 Process Locking and CT

Finally, each completed process schedule has to be correct in that no unresolvable deadlocks between completing processes may exist and in that all abort-related activities are performed correctly.

Lemma 6.4 (Process Locking and CT) *Process locking guarantees CT.* □

Proof (Lemma 6.4) *In Lemma 6.3, we have already shown that process locking enforces P-P-RED. Since CT and P-P-RED, applied to complete process schedules, coincide, each complete process schedule* S *produced by process locking meets CT.* □

In here, the restriction that only one completing process at a time is allowed is essential in order to ensure that no situation occurs in which a pivot activity is to be executed that would impose cyclic conflicts between pivot activities, such that none of them could be compensated to break or avoid this cycle.

7 Cost–Based Process Scheduling

"For which of you, intending to build a tower, sitteth not down first, and counteth the cost, whether he have sufficient to finish it?"

Lukas 14, 28

In the previous chapter, we have introduced process locking, a dynamic scheduling protocol that supports the correctness criteria for transactional processes, and especially the criterion of correct termination (CT) we have introduced in Chapter 5. Although the process locking protocol substantially relies on the rather coarse distinction between compensatable and pivot activities which, in turn, is based on the availability of distinguished transactions in the same subsystem, namely compensating activities, it nevertheless seamlessly integrates and accounts for the special semantics of processes.

By making additional information available to the process manager, the discrete classification of compensatable and non-compensatable activities can be relaxed. This, in turn, allows to extend the core process locking protocol so as to refine the degree of concurrency the process manager allows on a per-process basis, relying on information about execution costs and failure probabilities of single activities. In particular, this avoids that all compensatable activities are treated in the same way, independent of their cost and of the complexity of their compensating activity. However and most importantly, these extensions leading to *cost-based process scheduling* are seamlessly integrated into the core process locking protocol and also support the correctness criteria that jointly account for concurrency control and recovery of transactional processes.

In this chapter, we motivate the need for exploiting additional information, especially on the cost of activities, for dynamic scheduling. Then, we show how the basic classes of activities we have identified in Chapter 4 can be specified by cost information and failure probabilities and how this information can be exploited to validate the guaranteed termination property of single processes. Finally, this additional information is exploited for cost-based process scheduling, an extension of the core process locking protocol.

7.1 Exploiting Cost Information for Process Scheduling

When analyzing process locking with respect to the different reasons leading to an abort of a process P_i, three cases can be identified. In some of these cases, the aforementioned distinction between compensatable and pivot activities is implicitly present.

i.) The failure of the primary pivot of P_i or the failure of any activity preceding this primary pivot leads to the compensation of all previously committed activities of P_i.

ii.) When abort dependencies between some process P_j and P_i exist, then the abort of P_j may require to cascadingly abort also P_i. In terms of process locking, this means that there are ordered shared locks between both processes where the C locks acquired by P_j precede those of P_i.

iii.) The violation of timestamp orders may lead to the abort of a process P_i when an older, conflicting process P_j issues some lock request. Analogously, independent of timestamp orders, a process P_i may be aborted if it is in conflict with a completing process P_j.

The first case is inherent to the guaranteed termination property of single processes which requires that the failure of any activity of a process P_i must always be handled correctly such that P_i nevertheless leads to a well-defined state. The second case is based on the presence of cascading aborts which is in accordance with P-RC. Finally, the third case stems from the optimistic character of process locking that allows certain locks to be shared in an order induced by the timestamps of the associated processes and from the special treatment of completing, "first-class" processes.

While the first reason for aborting a process is an axiomatic property of transactional processes, the other two may be subject to a more detailed analysis. In terms of ACA, it has previously been discussed that the total absence of cascading aborts would impose too strict limitations on the degree of concurrency in a process manager. But one may question whether the protocol could be tightened for certain, distinguished processes such that cascading aborts could not affect them although they are running while the possibility of cascading aborts would still exist for other processes for which this is rather tolerable. Consider, for instance, a process P_i that contains an activity a_{i_k} which intensively binds or consumes resources and which has an associated compensating activity $a_{i_k}^{-1}$, although the latter may also be very costly. However, due to the presence of this compensation, a_{i_k} would be treated just like any other compensatable activity and may be subject to compensation due to the abort of some other process. The transaction program associated with the "produce" activity of our initial CIM scenario discussed in Example 2.1 could illustrate such a case. We have initially classified this activity as pivot but one may argue that production could be trivially undone by throwing the newly generated parts away and thus, classify this activity as compensatable. Yet, executions as sketched in Example 2.1 leading to the compensation of "produce" would suddenly be legal. Hence, an extension of process locking could consider such valuable activities like pivots (pseudo pivots), thus apply special treatment to their associated processes although they might be running, not completing, and prevent their compensation due to cascading aborts.

Moreover, consider as additional example some long-running, complex process P_k whose process program does not contain any pivot activity such that P_k will never reach the state completing. Then, although the timestamp-based process locking rules cause that the longer P_k is running, i.e., the more activities it has successfully executed, the less is the probability of falling into conflict with some even older process P_l. But the special treatment of completing processes may nevertheless and independent of process timestamps lead to an abort of P_k, effecting the compensation of a potentially considerable amount of work that has been invested in P_k. Again, some additional information about the value of P_k could be exploited in order to prevent this kind of aborts and to apply special treatment to P_k.

Finally, process locking, in general, optimistically allows locks between two conflicting activities $a_{i_k}, a_{j_l}^c$ to be ordered shared — unless some special rule of process locking prevents these shared locks. However, given a reasonable high failure probability of activity a_{i_k} (for instance due to the limited availability of its associated subsystem), then process P_j is very likely to be aborted due to cascading aborts. When information about the failure probability of activity a_{i_k} is available to a process scheduler, it may decide to restrict the sharing of locks in this special case in order to avoid that P_j is subject to a cascading abort with fairly high likelihood while it can nevertheless allow the sharing of locks for all other compensatable activities (with lower failure probability) of other processes with respect to the lock compatibility matrix of Table 6.1.

In order to cope with the above discussed limitations, we introduce an extension of process locking that allows a process manager to exploit information about the execution cost associated with each activity as well as about its failure probability. This extension, however, still goes along with the basic process program model which requires each process program to meet the guaranteed termination criterion. Even more, the extension we add to the activity specification will provide a neat means for the correctness validation of single processes. Finally, all these extensions do not impose a redefinition of process locking but they can be embedded into the core protocol in a seamless way.

7.2 Activity Specification

In order to extend the transaction programs model while, at the same time, keeping the basic differentiation between compensatable and pivot activities, we associate both execution cost $c(a_{i_k})$ and failure probability $p_f(a_{i_k})$ with each activity a_{i_k}. The specification of these values is required for each activity $a_{i_k} \in \mathcal{A}^*$, independently whether it is a regular, thus forward activity, or a compensating activity. More formally:

Definition 7.1 (Cost Function c) *A function c with $c : \mathcal{A}^* \mapsto \mathbb{R}_0^+$ assigning the expected execution cost to each activity of $\mathcal{A}^*$ is called* cost function. □

Definition 7.2 (Failure Probability Function p_f) *A function p_f with $p_f : \mathcal{A}^* \mapsto [0, 1)$ assigning the estimated failure probability to each activity of $\mathcal{A}^*$ is called* failure probability function. □

In terms of the failure probability, we disregard unsatisfiable activities in that we restrict the failure probability to $p_f(a_{i_k}) < 1$ for all $a_{i_k} \in \mathcal{A}^*$.

For the purpose of process program specification, it is convenient not to define both functions totally but rather to assign the appropriate cost information and failure probabilities to each single activity of a process and to the associated compensating activities, for instance by capturing special knowledge about the subsystems and the subsystem transactions associated to activities, and/or by estimation, using some heuristics. By considering the cost of each activity, a differentiation between execution cost (for regular execution) and compensation cost (i.e., the execution cost of the associated compensating activity) is possible.

Since the goal of this activity specification is to keep guaranteed termination as requirement for the inherent correctness of single processes, it must provide the possibility to express the basic termination properties of activities in terms of execution costs and failure probabilities:

Compensatable Activity $a^c_{i_k}$ According to Definition 4.1, compensatable activities are characterized by the existence of a compensating activity:

Execution Cost:	$0 < c(a^c_{i_k}) < \infty$
Failure Probability:	$0 \leq p_f(a^c_{i_k}) < 1$
Compensation Cost:	$0 \leq c(a^{-1}_{i_k}) < \infty$

In some cases, when an activity does not perform any state change in the underlying subsystem, compensation may be superfluous, thus correspond to the null activity λ, similar to the inverse of a read operation in the traditional read/write model. Therefore, the cost of compensation $c(a^{-1}_{i_k})$ of a compensatable activity $a^c_{i_k}$, i.e., the execution cost of its compensating activity, may equal zero.

Pivot Activity $a^p_{i_k}$ Pivot activities are characterized by the non-existence of appropriate compensating activities (Definition 4.2). This can be modeled by assigning infinite costs to the compensation $a^{-1}_{i_k}$ of some pivot activity $a^p_{i_k}$:

Execution Cost:	$0 < c(a^p_{i_k}) < \infty$
Failure Probability:	$0 \leq p_f(a^p_{i_k}) < 1$
Compensation Cost:	$c(a^{-1}_{i_k}) = \infty$

Retriable Activity $a^r_{i_k}$ In general, retriability is orthogonal to the availability or unavailability of compensation. The special property of a retriable activity $a^r_{i_k}$, i.e., that it is guaranteed to succeed after a finite number of invocations, is reflected in its failure probability, independent of its cost and the cost of its compensation:

Execution Cost:	$0 < c(a^c_{i_k}) < \infty$
Failure Probability:	$p_f(a^r_{i_k}) = 0$

Retriable activities may have to be invoked repeatedly until they finally succeed. Therefore, the cost associated with a retriable activity provides a straightforward means to account for these additional efforts.

Compensating Activity $a^{-1}_{i_k}$ Compensating activities must be retriable, thus guaranteed to succeed. Moreover, they are themselves not compensatable:

Execution Cost:	$0 \leq c(a^{-1}_{i_k}) < \infty$
Failure Probability:	$p_f(a^{-1}_{i_k}) = 0$
Compensation Cost:	$c((a^{-1}_{i_k})^{-1}) = \infty$

This advanced activity specification now allows for a more fine-grained consideration of the complexity of activities, thereby exceeding the classification of activities as either compensatable or pivot that may appear to be rather rough in certain applications. For instance, it may serve as a means to classify activities that can be performed automatically, without user interactions (and which therefore can be easily re-executed in the case of cascading aborts) as "cheap" and activities that involve human interaction as "expensive". Hence, this activity specification facilitates several extensions of process locking.

7.3 Validation of Guaranteed Termination

The advanced activity specification addresses only the properties of single activities. In terms of process programs where activities are grouped into nodes, the respective characteristics of nodes have to be derived from the specification of the activities they contain. While this is obvious for singleton nodes which inherit the specification (failure probability, execution cost, and compensation cost) of their associated activity, additional analysis is required for multi-activity nodes. Let n_i be a node in a process program containing $k \geq 1$ activities, that is $card(\mathcal{A}_{n_i}) = k$, with given cost information $c(a_{i_j})$ and $c(a_{i_j}^{-1})$, and failure probability $p_f(a_{i_j})$ for each $a_{i_j} \in \mathcal{A}_{n_i}$.

Execution Cost of Node $\mathbf{n_i}$ The execution cost of a node n_i in a process program is the sum of all execution costs of its activities (note that n_i succeeds if and only if all its activities succeed):

$$c(n_i) = \sum_{a_{i_j} \in \mathcal{A}_{n_i}} c(a_{i_j}) \tag{7.1}$$

Compensation Cost of Node $\mathbf{n_i}$ In analogy to the execution cost, the cost for compensating all activities of a node n_i, once this node has successfully and completely been executed, is the sum of the costs of all compensating activities associated with the regular activities of n_i:

$$c(n_i^{-1}) = \sum_{a_{i_j} \in \mathcal{A}_{n_i}} c(a_{i_j}^{-1}) \tag{7.2}$$

Failure Probability of Node $\mathbf{n_i}$ A node n_i is executed correctly if all its activities are committed, thus when none of these activities fail. Conversely, n_i fails if at least one of its activities fails. Let the set $\mathcal{A}_{n_i}$ containing the k activities of n_i be ordered, i.e., $\mathcal{A}_{n_i} = \{a_{i_1}, a_{i_2}, \ldots, a_{i_k}\}$. Then, n_i fails if either a_{i_1} fails, or if a_{i_1} succeeds but a_{i_2} fails, and so on. Therefore, the failure probability $p_f(n_i)$ of a node n_i evaluates to:

$$p_f(n_i) = \sum_{j=1}^{k} \left(p_f(a_{i_j}) \prod_{m=1}^{j-1} (\, 1 - p_f(a_{i_m})) \right) \tag{7.3}$$

According to (7.3), the failure probability of a node n_i is derived by applying the addition rule of probability theory to the events "activity a_{i_m} fails". That is, the failure probability of n_i is independent of the intra-node orders, $\ll_i$ and $<_i$. In particular, a node n_i is considered to be retriable if all activities of $\mathcal{A}_{n_i}$ are retriable. This is then also reflected in the failure probability $p_f(n_i)$ of n_i which evaluates, according to (7.3), to $p_f(n_i) = 0$.

In terms of the execution of process programs, the failure probability $p_f(n_i)$ associated with each node is also an indicator for the probability of a state change which goes along with the successful execution of n_i (by $1 - p_f(n_i)$), leading to the execution of a child node. Hence, the failure probability of nodes is related to the probabilities for state changes in Stochastic Petri Nets [ABC+95, Cia95, BK96], or discrete-time processes [Nel95], such as Markov chains [Der70, Tij94].

While all cost information and failure probabilities for both singleton and multi-activity nodes can be directly derived from the encompassed activities, an approximation is present in the above discussion by considering each multi-activity node n_i as atomic, thereby neglecting the compensation costs for all already committed activities in case an activity of n_i fails.

Once the execution costs and failure probabilities of all nodes of a process program tree are given, we can start analyzing this tree in order to verify whether the associated process program meets the guaranteed termination property. To this end, we first have to derive, for each node n_i, the probability that it is compensated as well as the probability for executing alternative j succeeding node n_i. Based on these information, the expected cost of a process program PP can recursively be determined; this cost will then serve as an indicator for the inherent correctness of PP.

Compensation Probability $\mathbf{p_c}$ A node n_i has to be compensated when i.) n_i has been executed correctly and when ii.) either all children of n_i fail or if they succeed but have to be compensated afterwards. Hence, the compensation probability $p_c(n_i)$ of a node n_i encompasses the probability that n_i succeeds as well as the failure probability and the compensation probability of its children. If n_i is a leaf node, then $p_c(n_i) = 0$, i.e., n_i will never be compensated; once a leaf node succeeds, its process commits. If n_i is a non-leaf node and has m children, $n_{k_1}, \ldots n_{k_m}$, then the following holds for $p_c(n_i)$:

$$p_c(n_i) \;=\; (1 - p_f(n_i)) \prod_{j=1}^{m} \left(\, p_f(n_{k_j}) + p_c(n_{k_j}) - p_f(n_{k_j}) p_c(n_{k_j}) \, \right) \tag{7.4}$$

Hence, according to (7.4), the compensation probability is recursively calculated bottom-up, starting from the leaf nodes of a process program.

Probability of Alternative Execution $\mathbf{p_{alt_j}}$ If a non-leaf node n_i has m children, $n_{k_1}, \ldots n_{k_m}$, that are totally ordered by $\lhd$ such that $n_{k_p} \lhd n_{k_q}$ if $p < q$, then node n_{k_j} (corresponding to alternative j) with $1 \leq j \leq m$ is executed when the execution of node n_i succeeds and when all preceding alternatives n_{k_l} with $l < j$ either fail or when they succeed but have to be compensated. Therefore, the probability for executing alternative j of n_i, $p_{\text{alt}_j}(n_i)$, evaluates to:

$$p_{\text{alt}_j}(n_i) \;=\; (1 - p_f(n_i)) \prod_{l=1}^{j-1} \left(\, p_f(n_{k_l}) + p_c(n_{k_l}) - p_f(n_{k_l}) p_c(n_{k_l}) \, \right) \tag{7.5}$$

In particular, and according to (7.5), the execution probability $p_{\text{alt}_1}(n_i)$ of the first alternative, node n_{k_1}, which is executed immediately after n_i is terminated correctly, evaluates to $p_{\text{alt}_1}(n_i) = 1 - p_f(n_i)$.

Expected Cost Ec The expected cost $Ec(n_i)$ of a node n_i estimates the cost that arises when a process program is executed, starting from n_i. Therefore, aside of the execution cost and compensation cost of n_i, the expected costs of all possible execution paths starting from n_i have to be considered, weighted by their execution probability $p_{\text{alt}_j}(n_i)$. In addition, $Ec(n_i)$ also considers the cost of compensation back to n_i when all alternatives fail. Hence, the expected cost denotes an estimation of the cost that incurs when node n_i is executed, rather than an actual cost (similar to the expected cost associated with a certain system state in finite state Markovian decision processes [Der70, Tij94]). Let $n_{k_1}, \ldots n_{k_m}$ be the children of n_i and assume a total order, $\lhd$, on them such that $n_{k_p} \lhd n_{k_q}$ if $p < q$. The expected cost $Ec(n_i)$ of n_i evaluates to:

$$Ec(n_i) \;=\; (1 - p_f(n_i))\; c(n_i) + \sum_{j=1}^{m} \Big(\, p_{\text{alt}_j}(n_i)\; Ec(n_{k_j}) \Big) \; + \; p_c(n_i)\; c(n_i^{-1}) \tag{7.6}$$

For leaf nodes n_i which, according to (7.4) have compensation probability $p_c(n_i) = 0$, the expected cost yields to $Ec(n_i) = (1 - p_f(n_i))c(n_i)$. The expected cost $Ec(PP)$ of a process program PP coincides with the expected cost of its root node n. Thus, given the expected costs of all leaf nodes, the expected cost of a process program PP (and that of all inner nodes of PP) can be calculated recursively bottom-up, starting from the leaf nodes of PP. Thereby, we will exploit the convention for (7.6) that $0 \cdot \infty = \infty \cdot 0 = 0$, i.e., an infinite compensation cost of a node will not be considered if this compensation will not be effected, due to a compensation probability that equals zero. The latter may occur in the presence of retriable alternatives — assured termination trees which, per definition, will not fail.

According to Definition 4.6, a process program PP is compliant to the guaranteed termination property if i.) all pivot activities are contained in singleton nodes, ii.) the preference order $\lhd$ is total on the children of each node containing a pivot activity and iii.) the last child (with respect to $\lhd$) of each singleton node encompassing a pivot activity is an assured termination tree, thus consists only of retriable activities, and each other child is the root of a subprocess program with guaranteed termination.

The first requirement can be easily checked based on the compensation cost of each node n_i in the process program tree: if $c(n_i^{-1}) = \infty$, then $card(\mathcal{A}_{n_i}) = 1$. That is, whenever the compensation cost of a node is infinite, it must be a singleton node which guarantees that no pivot activity is contained in a multi-activity node. For this property, it is sufficient to consider the compensation costs of all nodes only since the execution costs of all activities, and thus of all nodes, have per definition finite values. The compensation cost is also the basis for the verification of the second requirement since the order on the alternatives must be total for all nodes n_i with $c(n_i^{-1}) = \infty$.

The verification of the third criterion, however, is more challenging since it recursively addresses the structure of a process program with correct termination. But, the expected cost $Ec(PP)$ of a process program can be exploited to analyze the correct structure of PP. More formally,

Lemma 7.1 (Expected Cost and Guaranteed Termination) *Let PP be a process program for which holds: $\forall n_i \in N_{PP}: \; c(n_i^{-1}) = \infty \; \Rightarrow card(\mathcal{A}_{n_i}) = 1$ and for which the order on the children of each node n_i with $c(n_i^{-1}) = \infty$ is total. Then, PP has guaranteed termination property if its expected cost $Ec(PP)$ is finite, that is $Ec(PP) < \infty$.* □

Proof (Lemma 7.1) *For a process program PP that groups all pivot activities in singleton nodes and that contains a total order on the children of each singleton node containing a pivot activity, only the requirement on its structure has to be analyzed in order to determine whether PP meets the guaranteed termination property. According to this structural requirement, each child of a pivot activity must be the root of a process program with guaranteed termination except for the last one (with respect to $\lhd$) which has to be an assured termination tree. Assume that a process program PP with finite expected cost does not meet this requirement. When $Ec(PP)$ yields in a finite value,* *then each addend has to be finite. In particular, since $Ec(PP)$ is defined recursively, the expected cost of each node of PP has to be finite. In here, two different cases can be differentiated:*

i.) *Process program PP does not contain any pivot activity. Then, all execution costs as well as all compensation costs of all nodes have finite values such that also $Ec(PP)$ yields in a finite value. But then, a failure can always be handled correctly by compensating all already committed activities. Hence, this violates the initial assumption since PP trivially follows the guaranteed termination property.*

ii.) *In the presence of singleton nodes n_p encompassing pivot activities, the analysis of their children is necessary. Assume that a pivot node n_p does not have a child being the root of an assured termination tree. Then, n_p may be subject to compensation, yet its compensation probability evaluates to $p_c(n_p) > 0$. Since the activity of n_p is not compensatable, its compensation cost $c(n_p^{-1}) = \infty$ such that the addend $p_c(n_p)c(n_p^{-1})$ would induce infinite expected costs, thus leading to infinite expected cost $Ec(PP)$ of PP and to a violation of the initial assumption of $Ec(PP)$ having a finite value. The expected cost of PP is defined recursively. Therefore, the existence of an assured termination tree following a singleton node containing a pivot activity is not only ensured for the primary pivot of PP but for all pivot activities. Hence, each subtree being the child of a pivot node and preceding the assured termination tree with respect to the preference order $\lhd$ is a process program with guaranteed termination.* □

While a finite value for the expected cost of a process program guarantees that each node n_p containing a pivot activity has a child n_r being the root of an assured termination tree, it is not necessarily true that n_r is the last alternative with respect to $\lhd$. In general, there might be other alternatives succeeding n_r. But, due to the retriability property of n_r, for the execution probability p_{alt_j} of these additional alternatives n_j of n_p with $j > r$ holds: $p_{\text{alt}_j}(n_p) = 0$. Thus, these alternatives will never be executed. Although this induces potential redundancy in PP, it does not harm the property of guaranteed termination.

We have seen that two of the three requirements imposed by the guaranteed termination property can be easily verified based on the cost information derived for all nodes and for the process program, respectively (namely that all multi-activity nodes have finite compensation costs and that the expected cost of the process program yields a finite value), while the verification of the additional requirement —which demands a total order on the children of each singleton node containing a pivot activity— is not supported so far by the information provided by the advanced activity specification. However, the information on the expected cost of each node may allow to completely abandon the requirement of explicitly specifying the preference order. Instead, all children of each node n_i can be ordered according to their expected cost in a cheapest-first manner. That is, two children n_{j_k} and n_{j_l} of a node n_i are ordered by $n_{j_k} \lhd n_{j_l}$ if $EC(n_{j_k}) < EC(n_{j_l})$ holds. The ascending order of these nodes with respect to their expected cost then allows to minimize the actual execution cost of a process program. Yet, this induces a total order on the children of each node (as indicated in the original requirement of guaranteed termination) but does not necessitate any explicit specification aside of the basic information on execution cost and failure probability that have to be provided anyway for each activity. Again, the finite value of $Ec(PP)$ still guarantees the compliance with guaranteed termination although the cost-based order of alternatives does not prevent the assured termination tree to precede other alternatives. Since the expected cost $Ec(PP)$ of a process program is calculated recursively from the leaf nodes to the root of PP, the order between alternatives of a node n_i can immediately be determined once their expected costs are given, and it will then serve as input for the calculation of $Ec(n_i)$.

In Chapter 4, an extension of the core process program model has been discussed that allows branching decisions for processes based on conditions that are attached to edges in a process program tree, thereby restricting the execution of the subsequent nodes. This extension, however, can be seamlessly integrated in the correctness verification algorithm presented above. In the presence of branching conditions, only an assumption on the distribution of different conditions on the children of a node is required. Then, for each node, the children with the same condition have to be grouped and a total order on the nodes of each group has to be imposed, based on their expected costs. The calculation of the compensation probability of a node n_i, (7.4), then has to be extended in order to consider all possible groups of child nodes (weighted by the probability of the associated condition to be satisfied). Analogously, this extension is also required for the calculation of the expected cost, (7.6), which has to consider all possible groups of child nodes. However, once these extensions have been effected, the verification procedure of guaranteed termination does not change: when the value of $Ec(PP)$ is finite and when no multi-activity node has infinite compensation costs, process program PP is correct.

7.4 Pseudo Pivot Activities

The execution cost of individual activities that is part of the advanced activity specification now allows not only to apply special treatment to pivot activities in a process schedule $\mathcal{S}$ and thus, to completing processes, but also to single activities which are themselves considered to be costly or whose compensation is taken to be expensive, as well as to long-running processes. The exploitation of this additional information, that leads to an extension of process locking, is called *cost-based process scheduling*.

In short, the basic idea of cost-based process scheduling is to assign a cost threshold to each process program PP^j, to accumulate the cost actually effected by a process P_i^j in a process schedule $\mathcal{S}$, and to apply special treatment to P_i^j —similar to the privileges deployed for completing processes in the process locking protocol— once its accumulated cost exceeds the threshold specified for its process program.

To this end, the process manager has to perform some kind of bookkeeping for each active process P_i^j with respect to the cost it has accumulated in a process schedule $\mathcal{S}$. In order to account also for the cost of aborting P_i^j, this bookkeeping should not only consider the execution costs of regular activities but also those of the associated compensating activities, even if P_i^j is not aborting in $\mathcal{S}$, i.e., when none of these compensating activities is present in $\mathcal{S}$. The reason being is that these additional costs will incur in worst case when P_i^j is aborted, that is when a compensating activity is executed for each regular activity of P_i^j in $\mathcal{S}$. This leads to the notion of *worst-case cost* $Wcc(P_i^j, \mathcal{S})$ of a process P_i^j in a process schedule $\mathcal{S}$:

$$Wcc(P_i^j, \mathcal{S}) = \sum_{a_{i_k} \in \mathcal{A}_i^{\text{Reg}}} \Big(c(a_{i_k}) + c(a_{i_k}^{-1}) \Big) \tag{7.7}$$

where $\mathcal{A}_i^{\text{Reg}}$ encompasses all regular activities of P_i in a process schedule $\mathcal{S}$ while $\mathcal{A}_i^{\text{Comp}}$ is the projection of $\mathcal{A}_i$ on all compensating activities of P_i in $\mathcal{S}$ such that $\mathcal{A}_i \subseteq \mathcal{A}_i^{\text{Reg}} \cup \mathcal{A}_i^{\text{Comp}}$ (note that a process P_i may also contain one of the termination activities C_i or A_i, respectively, when it is terminated in $\mathcal{S}$ such that equivalence of $\mathcal{A}_i$ and $\mathcal{A}_i^{\text{Reg}} \cup \mathcal{A}_i^{\text{Comp}}$ not necessarily holds).

Obviously, the restriction to the regular activities of a process schedule $\mathcal{S}$ when accumulating the worst-case cost $Wcc(P_i^j, \mathcal{S})$ of some process P_i^j in $\mathcal{S}$ stems from the fact that the execution cost of the inverse $a_{i_k}^{-1}$ of each activity $a_{i_k} \in \mathcal{A}_i^{\text{Reg}}$ is already considered in (7.7). Thus, the notion of worst-case cost exceeds the actual cost that is currently caused by some process P_i^j but encompasses additionally the execution cost given that P_i^j would change its state to aborting and successfully execute all abort-related activities until it is finally aborted.

In addition to the worst-case cost of a process gathered dynamically at run-time, a finite cost threshold $Wcc^*(PP^j)$ has to be defined for each process program PP^j which then accounts for all associated processes P_i^j. To this end, the value of the expected cost $Ec(PP^j)$ that is calculated for all process programs for the purpose of correctness verification may support the specification of the cost threshold $Wcc^*(PP^j)$ since $Ec(PP^j)$ can be considered as an estimation of the cost that incurs when PP^j is executed.

When an activity a_{i_k} of P_i^j is to be executed, the worst-case cost of P_i^j has to be adapted first, that is, prior to the invocation of the corresponding transaction in the associated subsystem. Given that a_{i_k} is to be executed in a system state characterized by a process schedule $\mathcal{S}$, then the update of $Wcc(P_i^j, \mathcal{S})$ for a_{i_k} with $\mathcal{A}_{\mathcal{S}'} = (\mathcal{A}_{\mathcal{S}} \cup a_{i_k})$ evaluates to:

$$Wcc(P_i^j, \mathcal{S}') = Wcc(P_i^j, \mathcal{S}) + c(a_{i_k}) + c(a_{i_k}^{-1}) \tag{7.8}$$

The process manager can now decide on the treatment of activity a_{i_k} based on the value of $Wcc(P_i^j, \mathcal{S}')$. If the worst-case cost is below the cost threshold as defined in the process program, a_{i_k} can be treated as compensatable, thus deploying the Comp–Rule for lock acquisition. However, when $Wcc(P_i^j, \mathcal{S}')$ exceeds $Wcc^*(PP^j)$, the process manager will treat a_{i_k} as pivot, thereby enforcing that it is not compensated due to the failure of some other process. By applying the Piv–Rule for lock acquisition, it is additionally guaranteed that, due to C→P lock conversion, this also holds for all activities of P_i^j preceding a_{i_k} in $\mathcal{S}'$ (since a P lock will be acquired for a_{i_k} as well as for all its predecessors). The algorithm allowing cost-based process scheduling, thereby extending the process locking protocol, is presented in detail in Figure 7.1.

In order to provide correct process schedules, the cost-based extension of process locking has to recognize pivot activities by the worst-case cost of its corresponding process and thus, to apply special treatment for these pivots, according to the process locking protocol, in the form of the Piv–Rule for lock acquisition. To this end, the worst-case cost $Wcc(P_i^j, \mathcal{S})$ must, in any case, exceed the cost threshold defined in the associated process program whenever a process P_i^j changes its state from running to completing.

Lemma 7.2 (Worst-Case Cost and Pivot Activities) *The worst-case cost $Wcc(P_i^j, \mathcal{S}')$ of a process P_i^j, determined for the execution of a pivot activity a_{i_k} in a process schedule $\mathcal{S}'$, always exceeds the cost threshold of PP^j.* □

Proof (Lemma 7.2) *The advanced activity specification requires the cost of compensation for each pivot activity to be infinite. Therefore, when the worst-case cost $Wcc(P_i^j, \mathcal{S})$ of a process P_i^j is updated due to a pivot activity a_{i_k} to be executed, $Wcc(P_i^j, \mathcal{S}')$ with $\mathcal{A}'_{\mathcal{S}} = \mathcal{A}_{\mathcal{S}} \cup a_{i_k}$ will be infinite. The reason being is that $Wcc(P_i^j, \mathcal{S}')$ considers both a_{i_k}'s execution cost and those of its compensation, i.e., since $c(a_{i_k}^{-1}) = \infty$, $Wcc(P_i^j, \mathcal{S}') = Wcc(P_i^j, \mathcal{S}) + c(a_{i_k}) + c(a_{i_k}^{-1})$ contains at* *least one infinite addend. The cost threshold defined for a process program is, per definition, a finite value. Hence, the worst-case cost of a process in which a pivot activity is to be scheduled for execution, and in particular when a process changes its state from running to completing, always exceeds its cost threshold, independently of PP^j.* □

According to Lemma 7.2, the Piv–Rule for lock acquisition is applied to each pivot activity by the cost-based process scheduling algorithm. Moreover, there might be expensive activities whose execution exceeds the cost threshold; yet the Piv–Rule is also applied to them, leading to P locks, although these activities may themselves be compensatable. In particular, activities that are treated like pivots but are themselves compensatable and belong to a running process are called *pseudo pivots*. For pseudo pivot activities a_{i_k}, the following holds (with $\mathcal{A}'_\mathcal{S} = \mathcal{A}_\mathcal{S} \cup a_{i_k}$):

$$Wcc(P_i^j, \mathcal{S}) < Wcc^*(PP^j) \quad \wedge \quad Wcc(P_i^j, \mathcal{S}') \geq Wcc^*(PP^j) \quad \wedge \quad Wcc(P_i^j, \mathcal{S}') < \infty \qquad (7.9)$$

```
initiate_process(Process Proc, ProcessProgram PP)
begin
   Wcc(Proc) := 0;
   ts(Proc) := assign_timestamp();
   execute_process(Proc, PP);
end  /* initiate_process */


execute_activity(Activity act, Process Proc, ProcessProgram PP)
begin
   if ( act is a compensating activity ) then
     request_C_lock(act);                         /* apply C^-1-Rule              */
     invoke(act);
   else
     comp := get_compensating_activity(act);
     Wcc(Proc) := Wcc(Proc) + c(act) + c(comp);   /* update worst-case cost      */
     if ( Wcc(Proc) < Wcc_max(PP) )  then         /* act is compensatable        */
       request_C_lock(act);                       /* apply Comp-Rule             */
       invoke(act);
     else                                         /* treat act like a pivot      */
       foreach a in Proc do                       /* check all activities and */
         convert_C_to_P_lock(a);                  /* apply Comp→Piv-Rule         */
       od
       request_P_lock(act);                       /* apply Piv-Rule              */
       invoke(act);
     fi
   fi
end  /* execute_activity */
```

Figure 7.1: Algorithm for Dynamic Pivot Determination in Cost-Based Process Scheduling

Conversely to Lemma 7.2, a running process P_i^j can always be characterized by finite worst-case cost. In such running processes, a compensating activity exists for each regular activity. Thus, both execution costs for regular and compensating activities as they are considered in the worst-case cost of P_i^j have finite values. This leads to the third characterization of pseudo pivots which is present in (7.9), $Wcc(P_i^j, \mathcal{S}') < \infty$, that allows to distinguish a pseudo pivot from a primary pivot in a process.

In analogy to the notion of pseudo pivot, processes P_i^j exceeding the associated cost threshold but whose worst-case cost $Wcc(P_i^j, \mathcal{S})$ still yields a finite value in a process schedule $\mathcal{S}$ are called *pseudo completing*.

With this extension, it is possible to prevent the abort of a pseudo completing process P_i^j due to the abort of some other process, although P_i^j is actually running, without generally requiring the avoidance of cascading aborts for all processes. Unlike the core process locking protocol where only one completing process at a time is allowed, cost-based process scheduling may allow multiple processes with worst-case costs exceeding the cost threshold of their process programs, thus holding P locks for some activities. But, only one of these processes may be completing, thus encompass a "real" pivot activity which leads to infinite worst-case cost, while the rest of these processes must be pseudo completing. Then, although processes containing a pseudo pivot activity will not be subject to cascading aborts, still deadlocks may occur between these processes. Since only one completing process exists, deadlocks can nevertheless be resolved, although deadlock resolution may lead to the abort of a pseudo completing process. If, in addition, also the possibility of deadlocks between pseudo completing processes should be prevented, the strategy for cost-based process scheduling would have to be tightened in that only one process with worst-case costs exceeding the cost threshold (independently whether it is completing or pseudo completing) is allowed at a time. This, in turn, leads to a further limitation of the degree of concurrency compared to process locking since the number of candidates for the one and only distinguished process is increased and contains not only completing but also certain running processes.

Note that the cost-based approach may treat the successors of a primary pivot more restrictively than process locking does. While compensatable activities succeeding the primary pivot have to request a C lock in process locking, they are treated like a pivot in the cost-based protocol. The reason being is that the worst-case costs are accumulated during the execution of a process program and consider, for any activity to be executed, also the costs of all predecessors, that is, also those of the preceding primary pivot. Once the cost threshold is exceeded for some activity a_{i_k}, this will also be the case for all its successors.

Example 7.1 *Consider again transactional processes in CIM. Assume that process program PP^C (construction of final products) is executed in parallel to two instances of process program PP^{Part} addressing the construction of parts. These parts are then reused in the final CAD construction. Hence, activities "CAD part construction" of PP^{Part} and "CAD construction" of PP^C conflict. Assume further that the costs associated to all (regular and compensating) activities of PP^{Part} are considerably lower than the cost threshold $Wcc^*(PP^{Part})$ such that processes reflecting the execution of PP^{Part} never exceed $Wcc^*(PP^{Part})$, i.e., all activities are treated in cost-based process scheduling as compensatable. In contrast, activity "CAD construction" of PP^C is considered to be very complex and expensive (in contrast to the simple construction of parts). Thus, when this activity is executed, the cost threshold $Wcc^*(PP^C)$ will be exceeded and it will be treated as pivot. In Figure 7.2, the concurrent execution of P_1^{Part}, P_2^{Part}, and P_3^C, reflected in process schedule $\mathcal{S}_{CB}$ is depicted. Since the worst-case costs of P_1 and P_2 are lower than $Wcc^*(PP^{Part})$, both "CAD part construction" activities request C locks. However, activity "CAD construction" of P_3 is a pseudo pivot such that*

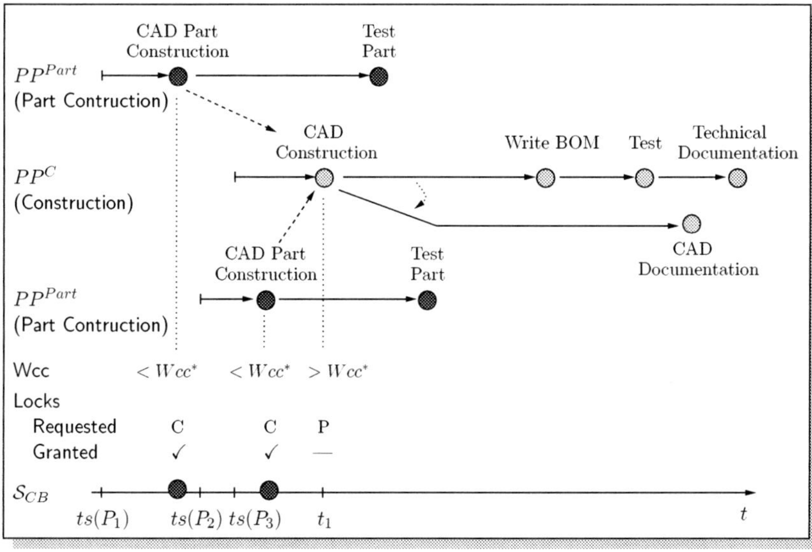

Figure 7.2: Application of Cost-based Process Scheduling (Example 7.1)

a P lock has to be requested at t_1. According to the Piv–Rule, this P lock cannot be granted (and "CAD construction" has to be deferred) since P_1 and P_2 already hold C locks for conflicting activities and since for the process timestamps holds: $ts(P_1) < ts(P_2) < ts(P_3)$. Regardless of P_3's deferment, P_1 and P_2 can proceed. Assume that "test part" of P_1 successfully completes (such that P_1 commits) while "test part" of P_2 fails. To this end, the preceding part construction is compensated and P_2 is aborted. At t_2, both P_1 and P_2 have released all locks and the P locks required for the activities of P_3 can be granted, hence P_3 can be executed correctly as illustrated in Figure 7.3. Note that due to the monotonicity of $Wcc(P_3, S_{CB})$, all activities of P_3 succeeding "CAD construction" also have to acquire P locks. When "CAD construction" would not have been treated as pivot, the abort of P_2 would have induced cascading aborts. In particular, this would have required the compensation of the complex "CAD construction" activity. Yet, the consideration of cost information has prohibited the cascading abort of this activity (although it is, in effect, compensatable). Current practice requires constructions to be released explicitly for synchronization purposes. However, by exploiting cost-based process scheduling, these release techniques are seamlessly provided without having to deal with synchronization problems explicitly (and manually). □

7.5 Fine-Grained, Dynamic Appliance of ACA

Cost-based scheduling applies special treatment to valuable activities and to their associated processes, thereby preventing them to be aborted due to the failure of other, concurrent processes. For all other activities, i.e., non-pivot and non-pseudo-pivot activities, still C locks have to be acquired

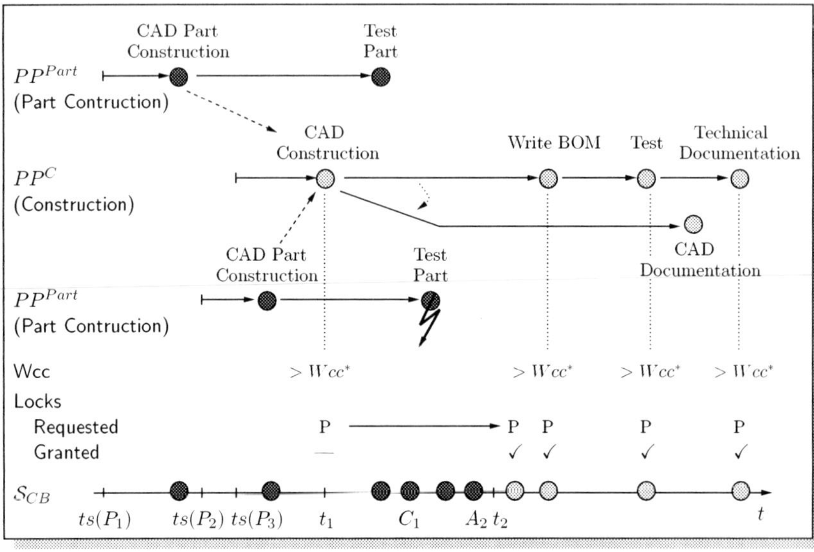

Figure 7.3: Application of Cost-based Process Scheduling (Example 7.1, continued)

prior to their execution. According to Table 6.1, any lock can be shared with a subsequent C lock in timestamp order without further restriction, but may lead to cascading aborts.

While the absence of ACA is reasonable in order to avoid unnecessary limitations on the degree of concurrency in a process manager, the sharing of locks, even in timestamp order, may in some cases be too liberal. Consider two conflicting activities, a_{j_l} and a_{i_k}, that both have to acquire C locks and assume that either the compensation probability of a_{j_l}, $p_f(a_{j_l})$, or the compensation probability $p_c(n_j)$ of the node n_j that encompasses a_{j_l} in the associated process program is sufficiently close to 1. When a_{j_l} now shares its C lock with a_{i_k} in the order $a_{j_l} \rightarrow a_{i_k}$, then the failure or compensation of a_{j_l} that is very likely to happen also affects a_{i_k} and yet leads to a cascading abort of P_i. This is also true when a_{j_l} shares a P lock with the C lock of a subsequent activity a_{i_k}.

In the basic process locking protocol where only information on the termination properties of single activities is available, this case cannot be prevented. The additional information provided by the advanced activity specification, however, which includes the failure probability of each activity and which allows, according to (7.4), the determination of the compensation probability of each node of a process program, can be exploited for scheduling purposes. By making this additional information available to the process manager, extensions of the basic process locking protocol are possible which allow, together with cost-based scheduling, the appliance of ACA on a per-process basis, namely for those processes encompassing valuable activities and for those conflicting with processes that are likely to be aborted.

To this end, a global threshold p^* for failure probabilities as well as for compensation probabilities has to be defined such that locks are only allowed to be shared for two activities a_{j_l} and a_{i_k}

where a_{j_l} precedes a_{i_k}, if both the failure probability of a_{j_l} and the compensation probability of its corresponding node n_j in the process program do not exceed p^*, that is: $p_f(a_{j_l}) < p^* \wedge p_c(n_j) < p^*$. When this constraint on a_{j_l}'s failure probability and its compensation probability is not satisfied, then the lock request of P_i has to be deferred until the termination of P_j, that is until C_j or A_j, respectively, when the locks held by P_j are relinquished.

When the above discussed mechanisms are implemented, the process manager first requires the specification of a global threshold p^*. The consideration of failure and compensation probabilities then causes an adaptation of the Comp–Rule of process locking, leading to the Comp*–Rule. All other rules of the process locking protocol are not concerned by this extension and can be applied unalteredly (in terms of the Piv–Rule, it has to be noted that a P lock cannot be shared with any lock already held such that no adaptation is required). Note that the consideration of failure and compensation probabilities for the sharing of locks does not affect cost-based scheduling but rather extends the process locking protocol on which cost-based scheduling relies.

Comp*–Rule for the Execution of Activity a_{i_k} A C lock for the execution of a_{i_k} can be granted to P_i when no lock on a conflicting activity is held by another process P_j. If some other process P_j holds a lock for a conflicting activity a_{j_l} (either a C lock or a P lock), then the C lock requested by P_i can be granted when

i.) P_j is older than P_i, i.e., $ts(P_j) < ts(p_i)$,

ii.) for the failure probability of a_{j_l} holds: $p_f(a_{j_l}) < p^*$, and

iii.) for the compensation probability of node n_j containing a_{j_l} holds: $p_c(n_j) < p^*$.

When i.) is not met, process P_j has to be aborted as governed in the original Comp–Rule. When either ii.) or iii.) do not hold, then a_{i_k} has to be deferred until the C lock of P_j held for a_{j_l} is released, that is, until P_j is terminated.

All other cases still coincide with the original Comp–Rule of process locking: if a younger process P_k holds a P lock for an activity that conflicts with a_{i_k}, then a_{i_k} (and thus also P_i) has to be deferred until P_k is terminated. Analogously, if a younger, albeit completing process P_k holds a C lock for an activity conflicting with a_{i_k}, then P_i has also to be deferred until P_k is terminated.

The Piv–Rule of process locking is originally designed for pivot activities but, due to the extensions imposed by cost-based process scheduling, it is also applied to pseudo pivot activities and to all activities succeeding a (pseudo) pivot in a process. Therefore, although the guaranteed termination property of process programs ensures that the compensation probability $p_c(n_i) = 0$ for all nodes n_i containing a pivot activity, restriction iii.) of the Comp*–Rule is even important when some older process holds a P lock for a conflicting activity. The reason being is that latter might be pseudo pivot, rather than pivot, such that its compensation probability exceeds zero, yet it might be compensated due to the failure of its children. Like the original Comp–Rule of process locking, the Comp*–Rule is also applied to compensatable activities only.

The basic process locking protocol is not intended to support ACA. However, the extensions imposed by cost-based process scheduling together with the exploitation of failure and compensation probabilities for restricting the sharing of locks according to the Comp*–Rule provide a generic framework in which a fine-grained, dynamic appliance of ACA on a per-process basis (for "special" processes) is possible while, at the same time, it does not affect the basic protocol that may still allow cascading aborts for all other, "normal" processes.

Therefore, this approach exceeds existing protocols which either provide ACA or renounce providing ACA but do not consider both options simultaneously within the same framework, or even within the same schedule. Even when ACA is loosened, this is done for certain cases only, but not in a general setting. The approach proposed by Badrinath and Ramamritham [BR92], for instance, aims at loosening ACA for one special scenario, namely for the case of non-perfect commutativity where pairs of operations (o_i, o_j) may exist such that o_i and o_j are in conflict while o_i^{-1} and o_j commute. Although a protocol is provided, tailored to this concrete semantics, that is more permissive than the traditional notion of ACA, cascading aborts are nevertheless avoided. But, this approach cannot be applied to more general cases and does also not allow different levels of restrictions with respect to recoverability within one schedule.

8 Transactional Coordination Agents

"Denn die einen sind im Dunkeln
Und die andern sind im Licht
Und man siehet die im Lichte
Die im Dunkeln sieht man nicht."

Bertolt Brecht, Dreigroschenoper

Transactional processes can be considered as higher level applications implementing semantically rich transactions in composite systems which are collections of distributed, heterogeneous, and autonomous software components, also called subsystems. In particular, as we have shown in Example 2.1, these higher level applications provide the possibility to enforce dependencies between components of composite systems by grouping related services into process programs. Hence, since service invocations within subsystems are mapped one to one to activities of process programs, the special characteristics of composite systems have to be considered when executing process programs. In order to guarantee correctness with respect to concurrency control and recovery at process manager level as discussed in Chapter 5, the possibility to connect all underlying subsystems to the process manager and to interact with these subsystems in the presence of distribution, heterogeneity, and autonomy is essential as well as basic transactional properties these subsystems and the services they offer have to provide.

The support for distribution is inherently present in the notion of transactional processes since each process encompasses a set of services independent of the subsystems they are to be invoked in (c.f. Figure 4.1), thereby implicitly integrating these subsystems into higher level applications. However, additional effort is, in general, required to overcome heterogeneity and autonomy of the diverse components of composite systems. In terms of heterogeneity, the non-uniformity of subsystems and in particular of their interfaces has to be taken into consideration. Although a crucial feature of a process manager is the possibility to invoke services in underlying subsystems, it cannot support all different interfaces that can be found in applications of composite systems. Rather, an additional software layer has to be introduced on top of the subsystems layer which provides a common interface towards the process manager and exploits, at the same time, the specific interfaces when interacting with the underlying application. This additional layer is formed by a set of individual components, called *transactional coordination agents (TCA)* [SST98, SSA99], one for each application of a composite system (see Figure 2.3). Although these auxiliary components are rather invisible from a global perspective where only the process manager and the underlying subsystems are beheld, transactional coordination agents play a very important role since the are inevitably required in order to transparently enhance the capabilities of the subsystems they are built for.

In terms of bridging heterogeneity, these transactional coordination agents behave like application agents as identified in the workflow reference model of the workflow management coalition [Hol95]. However, transactional coordination agents exceed the functionality of pure application wrappers in that they also have to provide support for the autonomy of applications. As a consequence of this autonomy, services may exist which are invoked locally by some user and which are not known to the process manager. While transactional processes aim at enforcing the consistency of composite systems at a global level, such local services may have converse effects. That is, they may violate inter-system dependencies and require the execution of appropriate processes to cope with these violations. Hence, aside of exploiting application-specific interfaces for the invocation of services, transactional coordination agents also have to monitor their underlying subsystem in order to be able to detect local operations violating global dependencies and to initiate the subsequent execution of process programs at process manager level.

In addition to distribution, heterogeneity, and autonomy, the individual characteristics of components of composite systems may affect or even hamper the execution of transactional processes. In particular, all these subsystems are required to be transactional in nature such that each service that can be invoked by the process manager provides key transactional functionality. Aside of the traditional all-or-nothing semantics of atomicity, we have identified in Chapter 4 further properties, namely conflict-preserving serializability (CPSR) and avoiding cascading aborts (ACA), as being mandatory for the enforcement of correct fault-tolerant and concurrent executions of process programs. In case this functionality is not provided by some subsystem, it has to be added by its transactional coordination agent such that each service appears from the point of view of the process manager as being in accordance with all the above discussed requirements. This functionality provided by a TCA exceeds those of application agents that have been proposed in the context of transactional workflows since the latter are mostly restricted to the provision of failure atomicity on top of arbitrary non-transactional applications [GHS95, RS95, AAA+96b, CHRW98]. Moreover, a further task of transactional coordination agents is the support for the special semantics imposed by the different termination properties of service invocations, i.e., the repeated invocation of retriable activities or the provision of compensating services for compensatable ones, in case this service is not directly provided by the respective subsystem.

In what follows, we first present the general architecture of a TCA and we then discuss in detail the requirements to be met by subsystems and their associated TCAs. To this end, we identify a minimal set of functionality the subsystems must provide and we also discuss how database functionality, if not available, can be added to them using transactional coordination agents so as to make these applications fit for participation in transactional process management. Finally, we discuss related work from application integration and from the field of autonomous agents. In particular, we present a detailed classification and overview of autonomous agents and relate TCAs to this classification.

8.1 Structure of Transactional Coordination Agents

According to the previous discussion, transactional coordination agents can be characterized by a set of tasks that have to be supported independent of the characteristics of the underlying subsystems and by additional features which strongly depend on the functionality of the subsystem a TCA is tailored to. This has also to be reflected in the general architecture of transactional coordination agents.

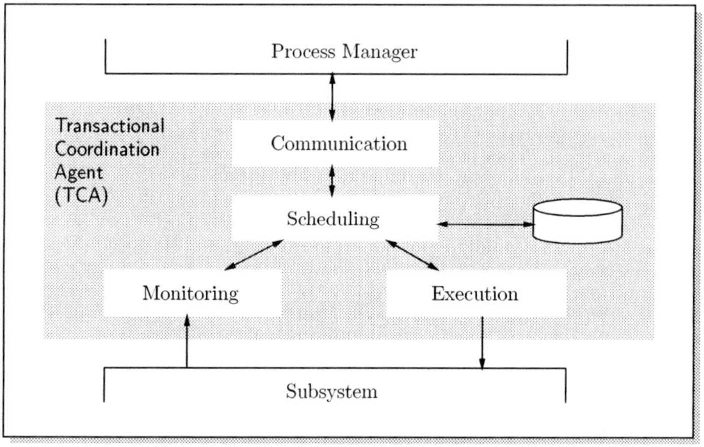

Figure 8.1: Structure of a Transactional Coordination Agent

In the context of subsystem coordination by applying open nested transactions [NSSW94a, Wun96], the functionality and the architecture of application agents has been discussed. While these application agents mainly focus on the interaction with their underlying subsystem rather than providing sophisticated transactional functionality exceeding those of failure-atomic service invocations and the provision of compensation-related information, their structure nevertheless coincides with those of transactional coordination agents as they are required for transactional process management. According to [Wun96], such agents can be characterized by four components: communication, scheduling, monitoring, and execution. These components and their interactions are illustrated in Figure 8.1.

Execution Activities of transactional processes have to be mapped to service calls within the underlying subsystem. To this end, a TCA has to exploit subsystem-specific interfaces. In addition, format conversions of parameters from the format supported by the process manager to the potentially proprietary format of the underlying application and vice versa is required. This is true for all kinds of process activities, i.e., both for regular ones and for compensating activities. Since the mapping of activities to local service calls is strongly dependent on the functionality and the interfaces provided by the underlying application, the *execution module* of a TCA has to be tailored and customized to its subsystem.

Monitoring The *monitoring module* has to perform the task of extracting information about local service invocations and local operations out of the underlying subsystem. In addition, this extraction must be accompanied with some filtering in order to determine whether information about local operations have to be forwarded to the process manager since they require subsequent coordination processes. Again, the functionality and the interfaces of the underlying subsystems determine the concrete implementation of this component which, therefore, has to be tailored to the underlying application.

Scheduling The *scheduling module* of a TCA comprises all necessary tasks required for the enrichment of subsystem services with respect to transactional functionality. This includes the preservation of orders between services imposed by the process manager, the provision of atomicity for service invocations, and the enforcement of serializable executions. Moreover, the availability of compensation has to be guaranteed for compensatable activities as well as support for retriability. For all these purposes, the TCA uses a database system for persistent logging of the services invoked within the subsystem together with the associated information about services and corresponding parameters for compensation purposes and the storage of necessary metadata. If the underlying subsystem is built on top of a database system which can be accessed by the TCA, its functionality can be exploited; otherwise, a separate database system has to be made available to the TCA for the management of metadata.

Communication A further task of a TCA is to hide the heterogeneity of the underlying subsystems. While the interaction with these systems takes place by exploiting their specific interfaces, a common interface has to be provided towards the process manager. The *communication module* implements this common interface such that all TCAs have the same appearance from the point of view of the process manager.

While the clear separation of TCA functionality in different modules introduced above provides a conceptual view rather then being present in each concrete TCA implementation which has to consider the particularities of subsystems, it nevertheless allows for a classification of the different TCA functionality. Obviously, the functionality of the communication module is independent of the underlying subsystem and can be provided in a generic way. In contrast, the generation of the execution and of the monitoring module can hardly be automated since subsystem-specific functionality has to be exploited. In terms of the scheduling module, i.e., the provision of transactional functionality, at least different classes of subsystems can be identified where each of these classes requires the same set of functionality to be added and provides similar support for this endeavor. This classification encompasses information on whether or not compensating services are already provided by the subsystem, whether or not subsystems are based on database systems which can be exploited by the TCA, etc. The common characteristics of subsystems belonging to the same class then allows to re-use concepts for the concrete implementation of the scheduling module of their respective TCA.

8.2 Interaction with Subsystems

A salient feature of composite systems is their inherent heterogeneity implied by the components they comprise. In particular, subsystems may differ in terms of the architectural paradigms they follow which may range from monolithic software systems (e.g., mainframe applications) to multi-tier client/server software systems [OHE99], eventually enriched by the use of sophisticated middleware technology [Ber96, Tre96]. As a consequence of these heterogeneous structures, subsystems also differ in the way they manage data. In general, the whole spectrum between subsystems exploiting the functionality of a fully-fledged (and potentially distributed) database management system on top of which they are built and applications that rather rely on flat files can be found.

This heterogeneity, induced by the different tiers that can be found in the architecture of subsystems, also implies different means for the interaction of a TCA with its underlying application. In general, two strategies can be distinguished. First, interaction can take place at application level via the APIs provided by the subsystem. Second, a TCA can also interact directly at data level with the database management system or the file system, respectively, depending on the way the underlying application manages application-specific data. In what follows, we analyze the different aspects of interactions between a TCA and its underlying application, namely the execution of process activities and the monitoring of local operations.

8.2.1 Execution of Process Activities

When a process manager schedules an activity for execution, it has to be guaranteed that the service that corresponds to this activity is actually effected in the underlying subsystem. This is not only true for regular activities that are explicitly specified in process programs but also for all compensating activities. However, since a process manager only supports a common protocol for the communication with subsystems and does not consider the particularities of each of these applications, the task of transforming the process manager's request into a format supported by the underlying subsystem for initiating and controlling the execution of services has to be provided by their transactional coordination agent such that heterogeneity is made transparent to the process manager.

As a consequence of the different architectural paradigms of subsystems, we have previously identified two basic strategies for the execution of services or of single operations related to these services: either by accessing data at the storage manager level or by exploiting interfaces provided at the application level. The interaction between a TCA and its subsystem at data level would require that data is directly shipped to the underlying storage manager, i.e., by inserting tuples into a database system or by appending data to the files the application uses for data management purposes. In any case, this approach totally ignores the specific semantics of the application since it lacks information on how services are mapped to interactions with the underlying storage manager. Consider, for instance, the enterprise resource planning (ERP) system SAP R/3 [SAP, Buc99]. Its underlying relational database consists, in a minimal configuration, of about 8700 tables (in version 3.1 H) from which a considerable number even comprises data that is not at all semantically related (but happens to follow the same schema). Most business objects are spread over several of these tables with foreign key relationships managed by the application. Thus, although access to the database of such applications may be physically possible, the various dependencies that exist are far too complex to be taken into account manually. In most cases, this is even reinforced by the fact that the application automatically tracks additional, application-specific metadata which would be violated by unknown side-effects when interacting directly at the lowermost level, thereby bringing a single application to an inconsistent state.

Hence, only the second possibility, the invocation of subsystem services at the application level provides the necessary semantics for the correct execution of process activities. In this case, the mapping of application objects to the underlying storage manager is transparently hidden and all application-specific constraints are automatically considered such that the drawbacks we have identified for the data level approach are avoided. Yet, an indispensable, minimal prerequisite is that all services that appear as activities in process programs are made available via the API of the application. However, in order to support the definition of new, even more comprehensive process programs, for instance to cover additional dependencies in composite systems that arise when new applications join, an ideal subsystem provides, via its API, exactly the same set of services that can be accessed via its GUI.

Finally, when bridging the heterogeneity of subsystems by providing a common interface towards the process manager, each TCA has to provide standard application wrapper functionality by transforming parameters associated with service invocations into a format that is understood by the underlying application. Reversely, it has to convert result parameters of services to the global data format supported by the process manager.

8.2.2 Monitoring of Local Operations

The autonomy of components of composite systems allows services to be invoked locally, without being under the control of the process manager. Since this may result in a violation of system-wide constraints which can only be tracked at global process manager level, these local operations may introduce severe inconsistencies. Hence, additional effort is required by the TCA of each subsystem in order to make information about local service invocations globally available such that appropriate processes can be executed to reestablish system-wide consistency. Again, the two possibilities induced by the architecture of subsystems, namely monitoring at data level and monitoring at application level, exist to support this endeavor. While the execution of service-related operations at data level has been proven to be infeasible, monitoring at data level may in certain cases be possible. However, exploiting APIs at application level, if available, is still the most appropriate solution. In addition to this differentiation, an orthogonal distinction can be made whether monitoring follows an active or a passive approach [SST98].

Active Monitoring The active monitoring approach shifts the burden of detecting globally relevant local operations partially to the underlying subsystem. It requires trigger mechanisms at application level or the possibility of plugging customer provided code to the application by customer exits or hooks provided by the subsystem. Then, based on appropriate trigger definitions or appropriate user-defined code, the subsystem can pass control to its TCA in the presence of certain local operations, thereby actively providing the full semantics of the latter. In general, these mechanisms can be applied to all local activities but then, the TCA has to filter the ones affecting global consistency. However, especially in the case of trigger mechanisms, it is also possible to publish only globally relevant local operations to the TCA such that the filtering can already be performed within the subsystem.

In certain cases, active monitoring can also be performed at data level by exploiting database triggers to notify the subsystem's TCA. But, this works only well for rather simple subsystems with known schemata where the service that has been invoked can be deduced from information about database operations.

Passive Monitoring When no active support for the monitoring task exists, a TCA has to periodically check whether operations have been executed locally in the underlying subsystem. In here, the subsystem plays a passive role since the TCA has to query its state by exploiting appropriate APIs. Alternatively, log files or traces at application level, in case they are generated by subsystems for bookkeeping purposes, are also well-suited to be exploited by TCAs to implement the monitoring task.

However, passive monitoring at data level is not appropriate for efficiently gathering information about local services. It would require that a TCA constantly keeps some recent version of the complete set of application data which would have to be compared periodically to a current snapshot.

The minimal requirement for subsystems to support the monitoring task is to provide APIs or log files at application level. Alternatively, also database triggers can be exploited for less sophisticated applications that are built on top of database management systems. In both cases, however, the TCA has to perform additional filtering to identify local services that are globally relevant. An ideal subsystem exceeds this functionality in that it supports user-defined code, e.g., in the form of triggers at application level, that can be added to the subsystem. This does not only allow monitoring to be done actively but also allows to extract information on important local services already inside the subsystem.

8.3 Requirements Imposed by Termination Properties

A characteristic feature of transactional processes is induced by the different termination properties of activities that are used in process programs. In particular, according to the discussion in Chapter 4, activities can be either compensatable or pivot. Optionally, the termination characteristics of single activities may be completed in an orthogonal way by retriability. Most importantly, this classification not only allows a fine-grained consideration of activities but also affects the scheduling of transactional processes (c.f. Chapter 6) and is the basis for the guaranteed termination property of single process programs.

Obviously, all these different termination characteristics have to be reflected in the services that correspond to process activities. This means that special services which semantically undo the effects of regular, compensatable activities along with the required parameters have to be made available. Additionally, appropriate support for retriability is required, i.e., by transparently re-invoking failed services. Both tasks, given they are not directly provided by the underlying subsystem, have to be added by its TCA.

8.3.1 Compensation of Process Activities

When an activity is specified as compensatable, the process manager assumes that the respective compensating activity is ubiquitously available as long as this activity, once it has been executed, can be compensated (which is the case either until the corresponding process commits or until a subsequent pivot activity is executed correctly). Aside of information on how a given activity has to be compensated, i.e., which services are to be invoked for this purpose, also the correct parameters for these services have to be stored persistently. In general, two approaches for the provision of compensation exist:

Registration When a subsystem is integrated into a composite system, it has to be extended by an appropriate TCA. In case a clear a priori assignment exists from regular services that are exported and that can be used as process activities to services for compensation purposes, this can be made explicit during the configuration of the TCA. In addition to the one-time registration of compensation services for each regular activity and to making this information persistent, only information about parameters associated with each invocation of regular services has to be stored by the TCA at run-time, that is, when a service is actually invoked. When later compensation is requested by the process manager, both parts, namely the static definition of the service to be invoked and the current parameters, have to be combined. However, this approach requires detailed knowledge about the underlying application which is needed for the manual registration effort. For the management of metadata and also for logging purposes, each TCA requires a database system. Ideally, the one of the underlying application can be exploited for this purpose. Otherwise, if the application relies on flat files or if such a database system cannot be accessed by the TCA, a separate private TCA database has to be provided.

Undo approach Not all applications provide the necessary information needed for the a priori assignment of compensation to regular services, especially when the concrete semantics of services and/or their structure is not completely available. However, given that subsystems provide some form of log file or trace file, respectively, where all operations executed as part of a service invocation are recorded, this information can be exploited for successively compensating the single operations performed within this activity by means of undo operations. It has to be noted that this gradual undo approach has to follow the same considerations we have presented in the context of the local execution of services corresponding to process activities. More precisely, this has to be performed at application level, by appropriate APIs rather than at data level.

Following the above classification of approaches, the production of log files that can be exploited for step-wise undoing the effects of services embodies the minimal requirement a subsystem has to provide to support the availability of compensation activities. Preferably, however, the subsystem allows compensation services to be registered with regular services such that the determination of the concrete operations for compensation purposes does not have to be repeatedly performed at run-time.

8.3.2 Retriability of Process Activities

In order to cope with non-compensatable activities that occur in process programs, appropriate alternatives are required by assured termination trees which have to consist only of retriable activities, i.e., activities that are guaranteed to commit but that eventually have to be invoked repeatedly, thereby succeeding exactly once. Again, for the provision of guaranteed termination, the process manager assumes that this property is enforced in the underlying subsystem. The need for the repeated invocation of services may stem from network problems, or the temporary non-availability of a subsystem. In all these cases, the TCA of an application system has to transparently hide these problems to the process manager.

In general, support for the retriability of activities is not directly provided by subsystems. However, they have at least to guarantee that the service associated with a retriable activity is able to be terminated successfully. Then, certain failures occurring during invocation can be intercepted by the TCA. The following approaches show how this task can be implemented by a TCA and how subsystems can support this endeavor.

Persistent Queues When subsystems support persistent queuing mechanisms [OHE99], it can be guaranteed that service invocations persist certain system crashes or non-availabilities both of the underlying subsystem (when the service is invoked) and of the associated TCA (which is important when the service returns). When network failures have to be considered, services must be repeatedly invoked by the TCA until they are successfully put in the application's persistent queue.

Exactly once guarantee In some cases, a TCA may be in doubt whether service calls have reached the underlying subsystem or whether the service is rendered correctly, especially in the presence of communication failures. However, when services are invoked repeatedly to overcome these problems, it has to be guaranteed that they are effected exactly once, not multiply. Given that subsystems support transactional remote procedure calls (TRPC) [GR93] which assign unique transaction identifiers to service invocations, a TCA can multiply invoke services —with the same TRPC identifier— and the subsystem guarantees that this does not lead to the repeated execution of this service.

Repeated execution When neither persistent queuing mechanisms nor exactly once guarantees are provided by the subsystem, the TCA has to invoke services in the presence of failures repeatedly, until they finally succeed. Yet, as a prerequisite for this approach, the TCA has to make sure that the effects of failed services are always undone before they are invoked for the next time, thus enforcing the atomicity of these failed service executions.

Aside of the basic requirement that services corresponding to retriable activities must not definitively fail, each service must be atomic, or the TCA must be able to remove the effects of failed service invocations such that they can be repeatedly invoked until they finally succeed. In the presence of exactly once guarantees or persistent queuing mechanisms, this endeavor is yet supported by the underlying subsystem.

8.4 Correctness Requirements

Aside of the support for the basic termination properties of single activities, each subsystem has to provide key transactional functionality that forms the basis for the correct concurrent and fault-tolerant execution of process programs by a process manager. In particular, each service that corresponds to an activity of a process program is required to be atomic in nature. Moreover, each subsystem has to guarantee that concurrent services are executed in a serializable manner, thereby even enforcing weak order constraints established by the process manager on the concurrent execution of conflicting activities. Finally, by the property of avoiding cascading aborts, services being executed in the same subsystem must be shielded from failures of other, concurrent services. These requirements are easily met in case all underlying subsystems are fully-fledged database management systems and the services that are invoked by the process manager are (conventional) database transactions. However, in the presence of arbitrary subsystems providing limited support for some or even all of these features, appropriate extensions by TCAs are required.

8.4.1 Atomicity of Services

In general, no subsystem is free of failures. Both site and application failures during the local execution of services may lead to undefined states where only some parts of a service (that corresponds to an activity of a transactional process) may have been executed. These undefined states, in turn, would induce severe inconsistencies and even impair the process manager's task of enforcing CT process schedules. Therefore, in order to avoid these undefined states, it has to be guaranteed that all services are executed atomically in the sense that they are either executed completely or not at all. Thus, failed services must not leave any side-effects.

Ideally, atomicity is directly provided by the respective subsystem. This is the case for database systems but also for applications supporting the notion of transactions or providing only atomic service invocations. For all these applications, no further work needs to be done by the corresponding TCA.

However, when a subsystem allows non-atomic services, two prerequisites have to be met in order to support its TCA in providing atomicity for activities executed by the process manager. The subsystem first has to provide the necessary information about what has actually been executed by a failed service until the failure occurred, and second, the required APIs to allow the TCA to undo all effects of such failed services have to be available. The latter requirement follows the previously discussed observation that interaction at data level for the execution of operations, and in particular the circumvention of the special semantics of applications, is far from being feasible. In terms of the first requirement, a subsystem must provide log or trace files at application level, as discussed in the undo approach of compensation. This information that has to be exploited by a TCA for step-wise undoing the effects of failed services then also supports the retriability property.

8.4.2 Conflict-Preserving Serializability and Order-Preservation in Subsystems

Allowing at any point in time only one single service to be processed in each subsystem would result in an unsatisfactorily humble degree of parallelism at the global process level. Hence, the ability to execute services concurrently is an essential feature of subsystems. Then, however, it has to be guaranteed that conflicting services whose order of execution matters, i.e., services that do not commute (c.f. Definition 3.18), are not interleaved in an inconsistent way. To this end, each subsystem has to provide conflict-preserving serializable (CPSR) service executions. Then, not only correct concurrency control for global services, i.e., services that correspond to activities of process programs, but also for global and local services (which, as a consequence of the autonomy of subsystems, are invoked locally without being under the control of the process manager) is enforced within subsystems.

Yet, the process manager already exploits information about conflicting activities and imposes appropriate orders such that consistent interactions between processes are enforced. This is done by establishing a weak order, which not only appears between conflicting activities of concurrent processes but also between activities of the same process (appearing in the same multi-activity node of a process program). Hence, in addition to guaranteeing CPSR, the weak order imposed by the process manager has to be respected in each subsystem which simply requires that the serialization order of two services does not contradict this imposed weak order.

An ideal subsystem directly supports the weakly ordered execution of conflicting services. A database system implementing, for instance, commit-order-serializability protocols [BBG89] is such an ideal subsystem. In this case, the TCA can directly pass the conflicting services to the subsystem with the commit order derived from the weak conflict order. If commit-order-serializability is not supported, the sequential execution of weakly ordered activities must be enforced. For all such subsystems, the associated TCA acts as a rather primitive scheduler which invokes conflicting services sequentially, hence transforms the weak order into a strong one. Although this transformation decreases the degree of parallelism achieved, it can be done with any application.

While the correct interleaving of global and local services is guaranteed by CPSR, indirect conflicts [BGS92] in subsystems may also affect the global level, e.g., in that the local serialization oder contradicts with a globally observed serial execution of activities. Although this case can be prevented by the application of strict two phase locking protocols [EGLT76] in subsystems, the coexistence of local and global services may nevertheless require special treatment, for instance by the approach proposed in [SWS91, Sch96a] where the commit of global services is deferred against all local services while, at the same time, isolation is given up against all other global services.

8.4.3 Avoiding Cascading Aborts in Subsystems

The previous discussion on the provision of atomicity for services has been caused by the observation that application failures in subsystems have to be coped with. Such failures not only necessitate mechanisms to undo the effects of erroneous services but also require that concurrent services are not affected. This follows the discussion of Chapter 4, where we have identified the property of avoiding cascading aborts (ACA) within subsystems as a crucial feature required by the process manager. More precisely, ACA within subsystems guarantees that no process is aborted by the failure of a service corresponding to an activity of another, concurrent process. This is particularly important for retriable activities that do not fail definitively but are rather re-invoked and thus, must not lead to the failure of concurrent activities (especially in case the latter are not retriable, this would lead to the abort of the associated process or subprocess, respectively). In contrast to ACA at the subsystem level, cascading aborts are not explicitly prohibited at process manager level. Yet, they are rather tolerated since the avoidance of cascading aborts at global level would imply the absence of abort dependencies and would induce severe restrictions on the degree of parallelism that can be achieved by a process manager.

An ideal subsystem shields concurrent services and provides the required ACA functionality. This is the case, for instance, for database systems providing strict schedules by implementing a strict two phase locking protocol. Analogously, it can even be supported by subsystems supporting appropriate locking functionality at application level (such as, for instance, check-in/check-out mechanisms).

However, if no support for ACA is present in a subsystem, its TCA has to prevent the concurrent execution of services and has to enforce sequential execution such that a service may only be invoked after the previous one has successfully returned. Although this may substantially decrease the degree of parallelism, it does not require any special prerequisites for subsystems.

8.5 Summary of Subsystem Requirements for TCA Support

The discussion of the previous sections on the functionality required by the process manager from subsystems and their TCA is summarized in the following two tables. We first compile a list of minimal requirements that subsystems must provide in order to allow their TCA to provide the required functionality (Table 8.1). Conversely, Table 8.2 summarizes the characteristics of an ideal subsystem, i.e., a subsystem that requires only minimal functionality to be added by its TCA.

The list of basic requirements of subsystems can be seen as a means to decide whether or not subsystems can be enhanced by TCAs with the functionality necessary for participating in transactional processes being executed on top of the components of composite systems. Among all requirements listed in Table 8.1, the support for atomicity and the execution of local services are the most important ones. In both cases, appropriate APIs have to exist to support this endeavor. Although all other features to be provided also require certain basic support of the underlying subsystem, these

	Basic Requirements
Execution	All services appearing as activities in process programs are available via the subsystem's API
Monitoring	APIs or log files at application level for passive monitoring, or database triggers for active monitoring at data level
Compensation	Subsystem provides log files; operations required for step-wise undoing services are available via API
Retriability	Services must not definitively fail; subsystem must support the atomicity of services to overcome temporary failures
Atomicity	Subsystem provides log files; appropriate undo operations available via API
Order Preservation	None; the weak order between services can be trivially but restrictively provided by sequential execution
Avoiding Cascading Aborts	None; a TCA can trivially enforce ACA by allowing only sequential executions in subsystems

Table 8.1: Summary of Basic Requirements of Subsystems

may, in certain cases, be even part of a composite system if this support is not present. When, for instance, compensation is neither provided by the subsystem nor can be added by its TCA, then each activity being executed in this subsystem would have to be treated as pivot. Similarly, the lack of support for retriability does not allow any activity of that subsystem to appear in an assured termination tree of a process program. Even when the basic requirements to support the monitoring task are not present, a subsystem can nevertheless participate in a composite system but only with the restriction that no local operations must exist. In this case, also the CPSR requirement can be relaxed given the appropriate TCA only allows serial executions (which is anyway required for the provision of ACA and for the preservation of weak conflict orders).

Although these very minimal properties do, in most cases, not impose unsatisfiable requirements, they may have severe impacts on the degree of concurrency not only within a single subsystem but also at the process manager level. Hence, applications providing more sophisticated support for participation in a composite system on top of which transactional processes are executed also allow more parallelism at process manager level. In Table 8.2, the characteristics of an ideal subsystem are listed. Such a subsystem minimizes the burden of a TCA since a considerable part of the functionality required from the point of view of the process manager is already present. In addition to basic support for monitoring, execution, and compensation, an ideal subsystem comprises sophisticated features like commit-order-serializability and strict two phase locking.

The discussion of TCA functionality and how this can be added to arbitrary non-transactional applications can be considered as guideline for supporting the task of coordination in composite systems, consisting of different, originally independent applications by means of processes. Actually, these concepts have been successfully applied for the concrete implementation of transactional coordination agents in the context of computer integrated manufacturing (c.f. Example 2.1). In particular, TCAs for different applications, such as the product data management system WorkManager [CoC96] or the enterprise resource planning system SAP R/3 [SAP, Buc99] have been built [SSAS99].

	Ideal Subsystem
Execution	Subsystem offers the same set of services via APIs than it does via its GUI
Monitoring	Possibility of plugging-in user-defined code for passing control to the TCA and for performing filtering within the subsystem
Compensation	Compensating services are provided via API and can be registered with regular services during configuration
Retriability	Subsystem provides persistent queuing functionality or exactly once guarantees; services must lead to success
Atomicity	Atomicity is provided for all services
Order Preservation	Support of commit-order-serializability
Avoiding Cascading Aborts	Support of strict two phase locking protocols

Table 8.2: Summary of the Properties of Ideal Subsystems

8.6 Classification of TCAs — From Application Integration to Process Enactment Agents

The paradigm of extending applications by transactional coordination agents has been intensively discussed in the previous sections. It has turned out that an essential feature of TCAs is to integrate subsystems into higher level applications and to add certain functionality to these subsystems. However, both aspects are not exclusively provided by TCAs but can be found, at least partially, in various commercial applications and research prototypes. In terms of integration, enormous efforts have been spent in the last couple of years in the area of enterprise application integration (EAI). This has led to comprehensive frameworks that not only allow to bridge the heterogeneity of applications but also provide the infrastructure to support applications that span multiple, independent systems. In this section, we discuss the common characteristics but also of the differences between these approaches and transactional coordination agents. Moreover, we compare related approaches from transactional workflows and federated database systems with our TCAs. Finally, we summarize related work in the area of autonomous agents and relate transactional coordination agents to these approaches.

8.6.1 Application Integration

In the field of (enterprise) application integration, various commercial tools are available that allow data to be extracted out of stand-alone applications and to be fed subsequently, possibly after certain transformation steps and based on dedicated middleware technologies, into other applications.

Adapters and Application Wrappers

Adapters (also called application wrappers) are key components in commercial enterprise application integration (EAI) frameworks since they are responsible for bridging the heterogeneity between systems. In most cases, two different types of adapters exist. First, each EAI framework comes with a set of prefabricated, ready-to-use adapters. Each of these adapters is tailored to a dedicated system, by exploiting the special interfaces of the latter. In general, the list of systems supported in an EAI framework comprises diverse ERP systems and database systems, but also distributed object platforms such as CORBA [OMG] or COM+ [Box98]. Second, this set of adapters is enriched by a tool which aims at simplifying the implementation of adapters for additional systems that are not supported a priori. These development kits make use of the fact that certain parts of adapters are generic (in the context of EAI, this is the interface towards the communication middleware used) while other parts, namely the exploitation of system-specific interfaces, have individually to be realized for each application to be integrated. Examples of such EAI systems comprising adapters and adapter toolkits are eLink Adapter [eLi00] of BEA's eLink framework, MQSeries Adapter of IBM [MQS00a], or TIB/Adapter of the TIB/Rendezvous framework [TIB] of TIBCO.

In addition, EAI frameworks have to cope with the different data formats that can be found in real systems. Since, in general, not all applications support the standardized data formats of their particular domain, i.e., STEP (standard for the exchange of product data), EDIF (electronic design interchange format), or EDIFACT (electronic data interchange for administration, commerce, and transport) [Abe90], dedicated components for data format conversion on top of adapters are required. These may be part of EAI frameworks, such as IBM's MQSeries Integrator [MQS00b], but there exist also stand-alone systems for this purpose. In medical domains, the diversity of data formats has led to special tools for format conversion, called communication servers (e.g., Cloverleaf [Clo00], or e*Gate [e*G00]).

A similar approach to overcome heterogeneity, yet from a global perspective, is followed by the Workflow Management Coalition (WfMC) [WfM]. As part of the workflow reference architecture [Hol95], the WfMC has defined an interface which specifies the interaction of a workflow engine with external applications [WfM98]. When these applications already support the common interface, they are called workflow-enabled; otherwise, applications have to be made available to a workflow engine by tool agents, i.e., appropriate wrappers. Concrete implementations of such application wrappers can be found in the context of workflow management systems and research prototypes, e.g., in MENTOR-lite [MWGW99] or in TransCoop [dBKV98]. Similarly, Vossen [Vos97], proposes application integration and, in particular, the coordination of distributed application systems by applying distributed object management techniques like CORBA [OMG] which requires that each application service has to be wrapped to appear as CORBA object.

In the field of database integration, special components, called mediators [Wie92], have been developed which provide a homogeneous view on top of distributed and heterogeneous data sources, thereby additionally combining and relating data stemming from these different sources. Mediators, in turn, have to be supported by appropriate wrappers which must be provided for each data source. Projects such as Garlic [CHS+95, CHN+95] or TSIMMIS [CGH+94, GPQ+97] have addressed wrapper technology for database systems but also for non-database repositories, although being restricted to a rather limited set of functionality (i.e., supporting queries in the underlying systems). Similar to commercial adapter development toolkits, TSIMMIS provides support for wrapper generation [PGGU95] by combining a generic wrapper part with tool support for the manual configuration of system-specific aspects.

Application Monitoring and Change Propagation

The problem of monitoring data sources as well as the subsequent propagation of changes has been intensively addressed in database research. In particular, the data warehousing architecture [CD97a] considers special monitors which observe changes in data sources and which are able to extract data. Similar to EAI adapters, most data warehousing solutions already provide monitors tailored to dedicated data sources. However, projects like WHIPS [WGL+96] also address the tool-supported generation of monitors [HGW+95]. In analogy to the observations that have governed the monitoring task of TCAs, two possibilities for extracting data for warehousing purposes exist: it can be done by periodically querying these data sources or comparing snapshots (which corresponds to the passive monitoring approach) or, alternatively, by exploiting active mechanisms of the underlying data source. In terms of monitor generation, it has been shown that this task can, in part, be automated (at least for the generic monitoring aspects) while system-specific functionality has to be added manually [HGW+95]. However, all these approaches consider the extraction of data at data level, by directly accessing databases or non-database repositories. Although this is appropriate for the problem of warehouse view maintenance which takes place at data level, these mechanisms can hardly be applied to support the monitoring task of TCAs.

In the context of EAI, adapters are part of comprehensive frameworks which additionally comprise dedicated middleware technologies for connecting systems. Hence, these frameworks not only support the extraction of information but also the subsequent propagation to other applications. Since the integration of applications is requested to be as loosely as possible, message-oriented middleware (MOM) [OHE99], i.e., asynchronous persistent queuing technologies, are considered to be better suited for this endeavor than synchronous, RPC-like communication [Lin99]. This goes along with the observation —coinciding with the one we have made in the context of the execution task of TCAs— that integration has to be performed at application level rather than connecting applications at data level [Lin00].

Most EAI frameworks deploy publish & subscribe techniques, e.g., TIB/Rendezvous [TIB99], or MQSeries Publish/Subscribe [MQS00c], to asynchronously connect senders and receivers of messages. All these systems provide similar functionality by allowing a sender to publish information encapsulated within messages without having to know which receivers have previously evinced interest, whether these receivers are currently available, and how temporary non-availabilities of receivers can be coped with. However, their architecture may feature substantial differences. Most publish & subscribe systems (e.g., MQSeries Publish/Subscribe) come with a centralized component, called broker, which is required to manage metadata indicating how subscribers are mapped to publishers. Messages are published, i.e., inserted into the broker's persistent queue, after senders have classified them by some topic. The broker is then responsible to forward these messages to all components that have previously subscribed for this particular topic. When messages are shipped, they are inserted into the client queues such that the applications at the back-end do not have to be alive when messages arrive. However, also completely decentralized publish & subscribe systems, like TIB/Rendezvous, exist. Message exchange in these systems is based on broadcast technologies over LANs rather than by imposing a dedicated message broker. Subscription is performed locally by filtering and forwarding only incoming messages of specific topics to the back-end application such that a sender again does not need any information about potential subscribers. Independent of the concrete realization, publish & subscribe systems provide key functionality for EAI frameworks. In addition, these mechanisms have also been proven to be of importance to allow TCAs in supporting the special termination properties of activities in transactional process management.

8.6.2 Databaseification

The vast majority of (transactional) workflow management approaches consider either only the integration of database systems, or, in case application integration is considered, lack support for "databaseification", i.e., for making applications —which were primarily designed for stand-alone usage— transactional [GHS95, RS95, AAA+96b]. Other approaches consider transactional support in a rather restricted sense in that they are either limited to atomicity and disregard concurrency control [CHRW98], or addresses the correct concurrent access to applications while neglecting the task of making application services atomic [KR96a].

In the CIM/Z project [NWM+94], tool agents for applications from the field of computer integrated manufacturing (e.g., revision control systems, or parts list managers) have been implemented [NW96, NW97]. In order to coordinate these systems by global transactions following the open nested transaction paradigm, each agent has to enrich the underlying application by providing support for atomicity and compensation [NSSW94a, NSSW94b]. Hence, these tool agents, although they do not address retriable service invocations or the support of weakly ordered service invocations, are closely related to the TCAs of transactional process management.

Aside of the databaseification of non-database components, certain agents also consider the extension of databases by adding features that are not natively provided. The 2PC agent method [WV90, VW92], for instance, allows to support two phase commit coordinated distributed transactions in federated database environments on top of component database systems that do not provide an XA interface. By establishing a prepared state and by allowing to recover locally after failures to this state, these agents add 2PC support but require that each component system provides strict schedules, i.e., by applying strict two phase locking mechanisms. While this approach has originally been limited to database systems, it can as well be applied to application systems following a strict two phase locking protocol at application level (e.g., the ERP system SAP R/3).

Although 2PC agents enhance components of federated database systems and allow to implement distributed transactions, the problems induced by the latter, namely that they may have blocking behavior and that they imply severe restrictions on the degree of concurrency, still persist. Yet, these problems can be avoided by applying open nested transactions. In this case, however, appropriate mechanisms have to be provided to prevent that local transactions violate global correctness when they are executed in parallel to global subtransactions. In [SS93, SSW95, Sch96a], specialized agents on top of component databases deal with the coexistence of local transactions and global subtransactions. By imposing a protocol where global subtransactions retain their locks against local transactions until the global commit while they immediately release their locks for other concurrent global subtransactions after they commit, these agents allow the problem to be solved without significantly restricting the degree of parallelism that can be achieved at global level [Sch96a].

8.6.3 Autonomous Agents

In the context of artificial intelligence (AI), and in particular in distributed artificial intelligence (DAI), agents and multiagent systems have been subject to intensive research for decades. However, despite of the vast variety of approaches, there is no commonly agreed clear and formal definition of the term agent yet. Rather, there is some implicit assumption on certain features associated with agents — although these features in general strongly vary in different application domains. In order to overcome this lack of clarity, we present a compilation of a definition for autonomous agents and provide a taxonomy that allows to differentiate the diverse kinds of agents. Then, we present one class of agents, namely agents for process management, and compare the characteristics of agent-based process management with our transactional process management approach.

Definition of Autonomous Agents

The term agent has been intensively used in the artificial intelligence community to denote independently acting computational components [HBS73]. With the advent of distributed artificial intelligence (DAI) [Mül93], the importance of agents as basic components for the formation of modular, complex systems (multiagent systems) has significantly increased. Aside of the traditional applications in the field of knowledge representation, these multiagent systems in DAI mostly focus on planning, distributed problem solving, and/or coalition forming (collaboration) [HS98a]. In addition, recent trends in distributed systems, object-oriented programming, and software engineering where the concept of agent is used as a proxy for some computation ("agent-oriented programming") also exploit the notion of agents as a paradigm to build complex systems. Most recently, induced by the proliferation of the Internet and the vast amount of information that is available there, software agents for extracting, filtering, and combining information, for instance in the form of sophisticated personal assistants, have also gained increasing importance.

However, when analyzing these various approaches, it becomes obvious that the notion of agent does not follow a common definition. In some cases, the term agent is used as an indicator for an architectural paradigm while in others, it denotes the capabilities and the particularity of individual components. Moreover, most approaches highlight individual features of agents that are of importance in the actual context but rather neglect others that are less relevant there. Yet, it may seem that there is rather an implicit consensus on the fact that, according to Russell and Norvig, "the notion of an agent is meant to be a tool for analyzing systems, not an absolute characterization that divides the world into agents and non-agents" [RN95].

Nevertheless, several attempts to define the notion of agent exist. However, most of these definitions were very general in nature and, in particular, they were lacking a clear demarcation that allows to distinguish agents from simple programs. Motivated by this Babylonian variety, Franklin and Graesser have compiled a definition for autonomous agents that aims at avoiding the imprecision and generality of existing definitions:

> *An* autonomous agent *is a system situated within and a part of an environment that senses that environment and acts on it, over time, in pursuit of its own agenda and so as to effect what it senses in the future [FG96].*

Obviously, autonomous agents are characterized by some key features which, as a whole, motivate why they are considered as being more sophisticated than conventional programs. The following properties summarize the above definition:

Autonomy An agent exercises control over its own functions. In particular, it must not depend on any other party (including humans or other agents).

Reactiveness An agent responds in a timely fashion to changes in the environment. This feature is in some cases also referred to as *sensing and acting.*

Goal-orientation An agent does not simply react in response to the environment, it is rather pro-active purposeful, i.e., it follows certain individual goals.

Temporal Continuity An agent is a continuously running process.

In addition to these inherent properties, autonomous agents may feature, in some cases, additional characteristics induced by the environment and by the kind of application they are developed for. While, in a considerable number of approaches, all agents are considered to be intelligent, mobile, and communicative (in [GK94], agents are even defined by the exploitation of agent communication languages), the definition of Franklin and Graesser intentionally only comprises the very basic characteristics and shifts additional features that can be found in concrete agent instances to further specializations. The most important of these features are:

Mobility Mobile agents are able to wander autonomously through networks in order to transport themselves from one machine to another so as to broaden their operational area.

Learning Capability Learning agents are able to change their behavior based on previous experience. This feature is also referred to as *intelligence*.

Communication Agents are able to communicate with other parties —including humans or other agents— by exploiting specific agent communication languages, i.e., KQML (knowledge query and manipulation language) [FFM94]. This feature is a basic requirement for the formation of multiagent systems.

Taxonomy

Aside of the formalization of the mandatory and the optional characteristics of autonomous agents, Franklin and Graesser have identified the need to classify the various agents and agent systems. To this end, they have elaborated on a detailed taxonomy of autonomous agents [FG96], depicted in Figure 8.2. The first distinction of this taxonomy considers the nature of agents which can either be robotic, biological, or computational. The latter, in turn, can additionally be classified whether they are software agents or artificial life agents. Software agents, finally, can be either entertainment agents, viruses, or task-specific agents. The latter ones, namely task-specific agents, are highlighted in Figure 8.2 since this class comprises all major areas, including the previously introduced agents from DAI, software engineering, information integration, etc. Hence, these task-specific agents are subject to the above mentioned refinements, both in terms of the optional characteristics, i.e. whether they are mobile, intelligent, and/or cooperative, and, orthogonally, in terms of the context they are used in and the concrete applications and domains they are tailored to.

As a result of the proliferation of the Internet and the vast amount of data that is made accessible by linking independent and distributed sources of information, a considerably large research community has emerged working on *information agents* [PLS92] which address problems induced by heterogeneity and distribution, in particular when semantically related information stemming from different sources has to be combined, filtered, and/or processed (e.g., [MEN98, MN00]). In addition, by generalizing the basic ideas of mediators [Wie92], these information agents may also be able to adapt and evolve to changing conditions, and/or to negotiate for and to purchase information, and they may even be capable of explaining the relevance, quality, and reliability of that information [Klu99].

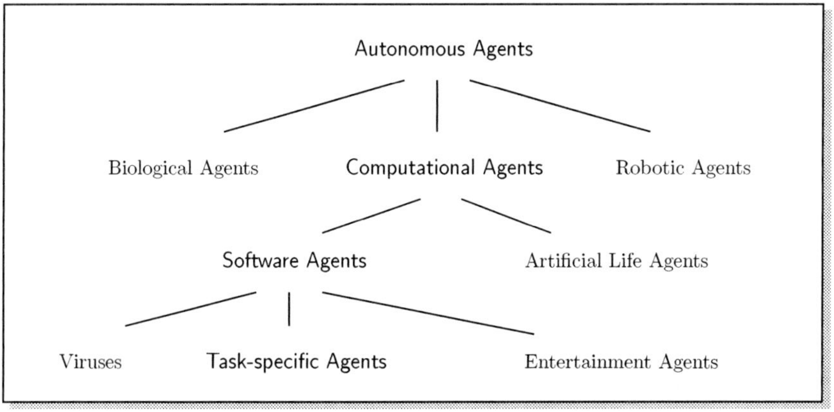

Figure 8.2: Taxonomy of Autonomous Agents (According to [FG96])

Despite of the variety of specializations —or even just because of this diversity— the information agent community, in contrast to most other areas in which work in agents is conducted, has come up with a detailed classification of approaches. To this end, the basic taxonomy of Franklin and Graesser has been extended [Klu96] and refined [Klu99], leading to the more detailed classification depicted in Figure 8.3. In this classification, which considers information agents as special instances of task-specific agents, a first distinction is made whether agents are cooperative or non cooperative. Orthogonal to the cooperation aspect, additional features of information agents are differentiated [Klu99], namely rationality (rational information agents are utilitarian in an economic sense in that they strive in increasing their own benefit; this kind of agents can be found, for instance, in the form of trading agents in electronic commerce), adaptiveness, and mobility.

This classification of information agents, although it comprises concepts that can be found in mediators and monitors, does not consider TCAs since the focus is primarily on information integration rather than on coordinating distributed, heterogeneous, and autonomous systems. Hence, a more detailed and extended classification of task-specific agents is required in order to reflect also the special aspects that can be found in coordination agents.

8.6.4 Integrating Coordination Agents into the Agent Taxonomy

We have previously seen how the basic agent taxonomy by Franklin and Graesser has been extended in order to classify the various approaches that can be found in the context of information agents. However, since all these approaches consider only information integration rather than the exchange of information for coordination purposes, this classification has to be extended so as to reflect also the various efforts that can be found in application integration, (transactional) workflow management, databaseification, and subsystem coordination.

To this end, we introduce the concept of *coordination agent* as an additional specialization of task-specific agents, at the same level than but independent of information agents. Coordination agents

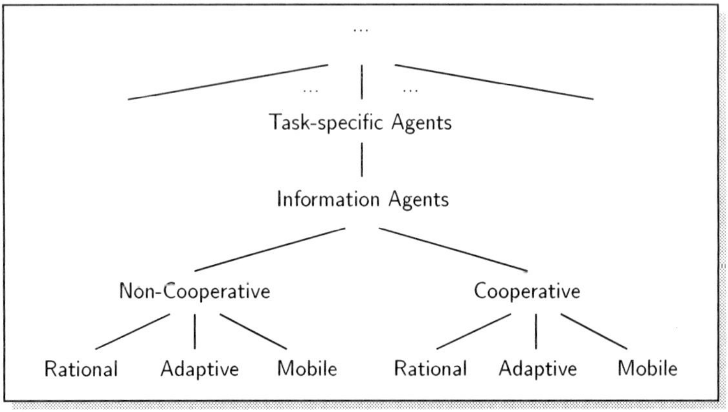

Figure 8.3: Taxonomy of Information Agents (According to [Klu99])

are considered as facilitators enabling the transfer of data between distributed, heterogeneous, and autonomous applications. Obviously, the property of supporting data transfer between systems is an important feature of coordination agents and induces more sophisticated interactions with systems than it is the case in information agents. Hence, this feature can be considered as a means to distinguish coordination agent functionality from those of information agents.

However, the notion of coordination agent is still quite generic and needs further refinement. A first and major differentiation can be made whether coordination agents are transactional or non-transactional. *Transactional coordination agents* are able to bring individual interactions with applications into a transactional context while this is not the case for *non-transactional coordination agents*. Orthogonal to the availability of transaction support, coordination agents may differ in the role they play in a coordination effort. In here, a distinction between cooperative and non-cooperative coordination agents is made. *Cooperative coordination agents* are components which actively enact processes, by controlling the transfer of data between applications by means of control flow dependencies. In contrast, *non-cooperative coordination agents* only provide the basic infrastructure that allows processes to be executed on top of applications. Hence, non-cooperative coordination agents do not interact among themselves, i.e., they only support processes rather than actively enacting them. In both cases, however, the notion of process is considered in a rather broad sense, leading from distributed transactions to sophisticated business processes. The so-extended taxonomy of autonomous agents is depicted in Table 8.4.

With this classification, the following assignment from the approaches we have introduced previously to the different concepts can be made:

Non-transactional non-cooperative coordination agents: This class of agents comprises all adapters and wrappers that allow to build distributed applications (processes) on top of the systems they are tailored to. Hence, the adapters that can be found in EAI frameworks as well as the tool agents specified by the workflow management coalition belong to this class.

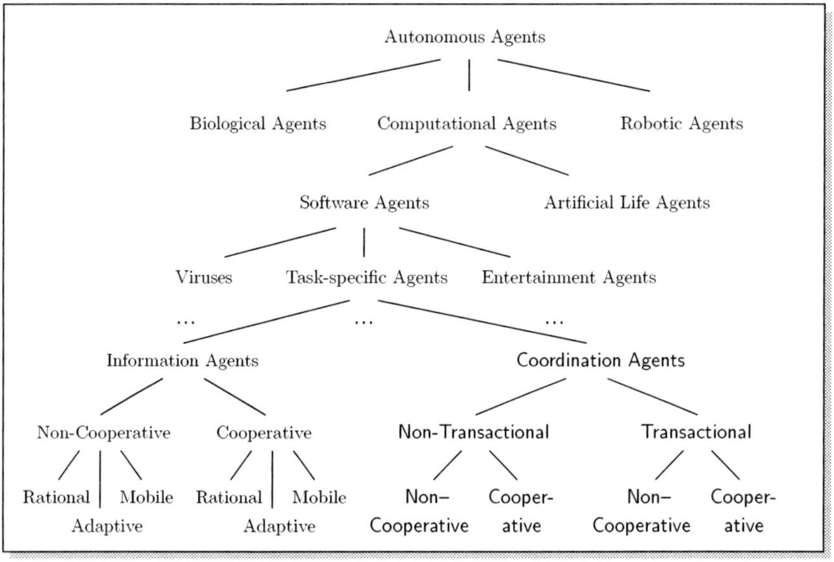

Figure 8.4: Agent Taxonomy Including Coordination Agents

In addition, it also comprises application wrappers that can be found in research projects like the program agents of TransCoop and the MENTOR-lite agents.

Non-transactional cooperative coordination agents: This class comprises all efforts in which processes are enacted by agents, yet without being enriched with transactional execution guarantees.

Transactional non-cooperative coordination agents: These agents bring the interaction with applications in a transactional context but do not control distributed applications or enact processes. The members of this category span a broad spectrum ranging from 2PC agents and agents in federated database systems over the application agents of CIM/Z to the TCAs of transactional process management. Yet, all agents of this class considerably differ in the degree of functionality they provide. While 2PC agents only support distributed transactions, the TCAs facilitate very sophisticated transactional processes, even including weakly ordered requests and support for different termination properties of service invocations.

Transactional cooperative coordination agents: This class is intended to encompass all agent-based approaches to process management which additionally enforce execution guarantees for processes with respect to concurrency control and recovery.

9 Discussion, Comparison, and Classification of Related Work

"Und indem wir nah oder fern verwandte Naturen betrachten, erheben wir uns über sie alle, um ihre Eigenschaften in einem idealen Bilde zu erblicken."

Johann Wolfgang von Goethe, Schriften zur Kunst

Transactional process management aims at combining the special semantics of process programs with transactional guarantees, namely correct concurrency control and recovery, for the execution of these process programs on top of distributed and heterogeneous databases and applications. Hence, transactional process management has much common ground with transactional workflows as well as with advanced transaction models. In both areas, considerable work has been done in the last decade. In terms of advanced transaction models, the main focus has been laid on relaxing certain transactional properties, especially in the context of multidatabases or federated databases, respectively. In terms of transactional workflows, some of these advanced transaction models have been extended in order to support the semantics that can be found in processes.

In this chapter, we provide a detailed introduction into related approaches from both fields. This is accompanied by a discussion of research prototypes and even of selected commercial workflow management systems, although the latter, in general, consider transactional execution guarantees in a rather restricted scope. In addition, we also discuss multiagent systems for process support. All these approaches are subject to a profound and detailed classification while, lastly, the chapter is concluded by a comparison of the characteristics of all these approaches with those of transactional process management.

9.1 Characterization of Related Work

The traditional transaction model and in particular the ACID paradigm of transactions cause several drawbacks when being applied to more general settings, especially in the presence of distribution, heterogeneity, and/or autonomy. To this end, various *advanced transaction models* [Elm92] have been proposed, extending ACID transactions in several directions. In here, work in the area of federated databases [SL90] and multidatabase systems [ERS99] has been a driving factor for the creation and refinement of advanced transaction models. These multidatabase and federated database systems require, for instance, the consideration of different levels of abstraction, i.e., global and local transactions. Moreover, since the ACID properties are considered as too restrictive, various advanced transaction models aim at relaxing certain transaction properties, while, at the same time, enforcing the remaining ones.

While multidatabase transactions and transactions in federated database systems both require the basic units of execution to be (local) database transactions, some extensions also consider the invocation of distributed, heterogeneous, and/or autonomous applications (although imposing strong requirements on the transactional characteristics of these applications). These extension have coined the notion of *transactional workflows* which have mainly evolved from advanced transaction models in multidatabase environments [LSV95] such that the special characteristics of the latter, for instance the relaxation of transactional properties, are also present in transactional workflows. Moreover, some approaches even attempt to decouple ACID properties, that is, to enforce them at different levels of abstraction or for different granularities, respectively (e.g., the scope within a transactional workflow in which isolation is to be enforced and the scope for atomicity guarantees may differ).

Before discussing related approaches in detail, we first point out the common characteristics as well as the differences between advanced transaction models and transactional workflows and we discuss efforts that aim at generalizing the concepts and ideas of both approaches (meta models). Moreover, we outline to what extent transactional properties are subject to reconsiderations and relaxations in both fields and we discuss to what extent multiagent systems are appropriate for the provision of transactional execution guarantees for processes.

9.1.1 Advanced Transaction Models vs. Transactional Workflows

Advanced transaction models have risen as a consequence of the effort of making transaction processing available to more general environments in which the applicability of the traditional transaction model, tailored to centralized database systems, is limited. Hence, when reasoning about advanced transaction models, they have always to be considered in the context of the environment and the kind of applications they are tailored to. Mostly, these advanced models consider the integration of multiple autonomous, heterogeneous, and distributed database systems, leading to the notion of multidatabase systems or federated database systems, depending on the degree of autonomy and the degree of coupling (loosely or strongly) of the participating component databases [LMR90].

Transactional workflows extend the idea of implementing cooperation and coordination on top of heterogeneous, distributed, and autonomous systems in that they allow the invocation of arbitrary applications while following the overall goal of providing transactional execution guarantees borrowed from or at least similar to those of advanced transaction models. Hence, advanced transaction models and transactional workflows are closely related [SR93, RS95, WS97], but the latter can rather be seen as a superset of advanced transaction models since transactional workflows have, in general, to deal with orders of magnitude more heterogeneity and distribution compared with multidatabase transactions or transactions in federated databases [AAA+96b]. Yet, the following list is commonly accepted as characterization of the extended features of transactional workflows:

i.) tasks, the basic units of execution —also called processing entities— in transactional workflows are not limited to refer to database transactions only (as it is the case in advanced transaction models which are restricted to subtransactions as units of execution) but can also be invocations of application services [SR93, RS95]. In here, arbitrary heterogeneous, autonomous, and distributed (HAD) applications can be considered [GHS95] which have, however, to be extended in case they do not provide the basic requirements needed to support transactional properties at global, i.e., workflow process, level.

ii.) transactional workflows consider the possibility to explicitly define sophisticated intertask dependencies (i.e., control flow) for regular execution but also for failure handling purposes [SR93, RS95, OHE99] leading to well-defined failure semantics and recovery features. In particular, these intertask dependencies also support conditions attached to the execution of activities, thus providing the possibility of branching decisions [AAA+96b]. Moreover, the specification of intertask dependencies can even be enriched about information where certain data elements have to be routed to (data flow).

Both multidatabase transactions and transactional workflows have to consider different levels of abstraction: at least a global level for the execution of global transactions (or workflow processes) on top of all component systems and the transactions or application services, respectively, that are provided by and executed within the component systems. Hence, each of these models has to support appropriate extensions such as nested transactions which have been discussed in Chapter 3.3. In terms of multidatabase transactions and transactions in federated databases, it has been shown that the possibility of blocking and locked resources imposed by two phase commit (2PC) protocols as they are used, for instance, by TP-monitors [GR93, BN97], has stringent drawbacks on to the degree of concurrency and even limits the degree of autonomy of the component systems [BGS92, BGS95]. Therefore, the open nested paradigm is applied in order to cope with these problems [WDSS93, SS93, DSW94, SSW95, Sch96a]. The necessity for open nested transactions is even more evident in the context of transactional workflows encompassing long-running, complex tasks [AS96a, AS96b].

Aside of addressing scheduling at multiple levels, the higher-level semantics of global transactions or processes must also be considered. Most approaches from the area of advanced transaction models and transactional workflows that will be discussed in detail in Section 9.2 follow the ideas of semantic transaction management [BDS+93, Dea95] which reflects the semantically rich nature of subtransactions and tasks to be executed. Semantic transaction management, in turn, follows the open nested paradigm in that tasks and subtransactions are allowed to commit as early as possible, thereby necessitating compensation for recovery purposes (semantic atomicity [GM83]). Moreover, the notion of semantic serializability has been introduced [BDS+93, Dea95] which comprises the consideration of commutativity at the level of global transactions and processes for concurrency control purposes. When taking a look at the most prominent advanced transaction models and transactional workflow models, there is obviously broad consensus, shared by most of these approaches, on the appropriateness of semantic transaction management, i.e., semantic atomicity and semantic serializability, for their purposes.

9.1.2 Meta Models

Most advanced transaction models are tailored to the requirements of a special application domain and extensions of the traditional transaction model are closely linked to concrete application semantics such that their re-use in different domains is often hindered. However, in order to avoid that models have to be invented repeatedly in different contexts and flavors, *meta models* aim at generalizing the concepts that can be found in advanced transaction models (and in transactional workflows) by providing an implementation- and application-independent toolkit-like set of primitives from which new transaction models can be generated and even be verified.

ACTA [CR90, CR91, CR94, RC96], the most prominent representative of these meta models, addresses the construction of advanced transaction models with respect to specific, custom-made notions of correctness. This specification relies on basic dependencies on termination states of transactions, similar to the dependencies that have been identified in [Kle91]. These dependencies formalize the interactions between transactions such that reasoning about the individual notion of correctness is facilitated. Aside of constructing new transaction models, ACTA supports the analysis of existing transaction models as well as the comparison of different models, once they have been expressed in this general framework.

While ACTA is a pure theoretical framework that facilitates reasoning about transaction models, a couple of approaches exist such as ASSET [BDG$^+$94], the reflective transaction framework [BP95], or the transaction specification and management environment (TSME) [GHM$^+$93, GHK93, GHKM94, GH94, GHM96], which more concretely provide the basic primitives of a meta model and allow for the implementation of new transaction models. In particular, TSME leads over from advanced transaction models to transactional workflows since it supports the integration of heterogeneous, autonomous, and distributed applications rather than requiring pure database systems like all other meta models do. Moreover, TSME supports various primitives that can be exploited for the specification of control flow dependencies and for the integration of failure handling mechanisms in the model and allows for various relaxed correctness criteria, e.g., for diverse intra- and inter-process serializability constraints.

9.1.3 Relaxation of Transactional Properties

The ACID paradigm has been commonly agreed to as a characterization of correct fault-tolerant and parallel transaction executions. But when transaction management is extended and applied to more general configurations as it is the case in advanced transaction models and transactional workflows, some of the ACID properties may impose severe restrictions. Hence, several approaches aim at relaxing the requirements and the restrictions imposed with some specific aspects of ACID while, at the same time, still respecting the remaining ones.

Atomicity originally comprises an "all-or-nothing" semantics which requires that either all operations of a transaction are executed completely and correctly or none of them, where, in the latter case, no effect is visible to the outside. The introduction of the open nested paradigm already led to a relaxation of this "all-or-nothing" semantics of atomicity: in order to cope with failures, semantical compensation has to be performed which may, in some cases, not completely undo the effects of the corresponding regular operations but rather lead to a state that is considered as equivalent from an application point of view (semantic atomicity [GM83]). Further relaxations of atomicity in the context of the open nested paradigm of advanced transaction models and transactional workflows do not exclusively rely on the requirement of performing compensation in the case of failures but also allow alternative executions. Thus, a transaction does not have one single final state that is considered as correct but may have multiple correct outcomes among which one is chosen during execution. These ideas can be found, for instance, in the flexible transaction model in the form of the preference order specifying alternative executions for failure handling purposes [ELLR90, RELL90, ZNBB94]; they are also present in the notion of guaranteed termination (see Definition 4.6), addressing the provable inherent correctness of process programs in transactional process management.

When subtransactions, according to the open nested transaction paradigm, are committed immediately rather than being deferred until the commit of the associated global transaction, obviously also the isolation property of transactions is affected. But, when the ideas of semantic serializability are applied in the context of the unified theory of concurrency control and recovery for semantically rich operations, the effects are still the same as if transactions were executed in isolation. However, isolation has been a heavily discussed issue in the area of multidatabase transactions. In general, when commutativity behavior is not known, artificial conflicts between all global subtransactions being executed at the same site have to be assumed in order to enforce correct concurrent executions (commonly by requiring the access of some hot-spot data items, called tickets [GRS91, GRS94]). This, in turn, notably decreases in the degree of parallelism. To this end, some proposals have come up which aim at completely abandoning isolation at a global level while only requiring serializability for each component system, even when the serialization orders of all systems may not coincide (local serializability [BGS92, BGS95]). Yet, it has to be noted that this approach only works correctly for so-called loosely coupled systems, i.e., multidatabase systems in which no constraints at global level exist.

The relaxation of the isolation property culminating in the total abandonment of isolation consequently also affects the consistency property of transactions. While, in the traditional model, a transaction —when started in some consistent state— will bring the system to another consistent state, this may no longer be the case in some advanced transaction models or transactional workflow models (cf. Section 9.2). Some approaches that relax or even abandon isolation have to consider special treatment for situations in which executions do not lead to outcomes that are considered as correct from an application point of view. In most cases, these problems have to be resolved by the simplest strategy (at least from the point of view of the transaction model), namely by manual intervention of some database or workflow system administrator.

The notion of durability, finally, captures the requirement that the effects of a transaction are made permanent once it is successfully committed. This requirement is not questioned in any of the most relevant advanced transaction models or transactional workflow models, respectively. However, in the context of transactional workflows, durability may be relaxed in that not necessarily all intermediate states of a process execution are made persistent [Alo97]. While this does not affect the persistence of the final state reached after the commit of a process, it can limit the availability of forward recovery after system crashes, that is, the possibility to resume some process execution. This relaxation reduces the administrative overhead during process execution, but it does not prevent the repeated execution of single tasks which are not compensated after the system crash —since the information required for this purpose is not available— but which are once again invoked after restart. Hence, this approach is limited to applications where the repeated execution of single tasks is not harmful to the overall correctness.

9.1.4 Spheres of Control — Decoupled Transactional Properties

The ACID paradigm originally requires all four aspects, namely atomicity, consistency, isolation, and durability, to hold simultaneously for each transaction. While this bundling is definitely appropriate in the conventional, centralized single-level transaction model, it may impose certain restrictions in the presence of distribution, heterogeneity, and/or autonomy. Hence, some advanced transaction models and especially certain transactional workflow models attempt in decoupling the (in some cases even relaxed) ACID guarantees and applying the single aspects for different granularities within a transaction or process. Note that this effort implies rather a counter movement compared to the unified theory of concurrency control and recovery which aims at addressing both problems jointly where the decoupling not only treats both problems independently but also at potentially different scopes.

For the purpose of decomposition, the metaphor of "spheres of control" which has been introduced by Davies in the general context of data processing [Dav78] is exploited to indicate the logical boundaries of the single concepts of transactional semantics when being applied independently. According to [Dav78], spheres may be nested, thereby allowing the appliance of certain guarantees at different levels simultaneously.

In the context of atomicity, spheres denote groups of subtransactions or tasks that have to be executed indivisibly, leading to the notion of *spheres of atomicity* [Alo97, AHST97b]. Commonly, a complete process or transaction is considered to be a sphere of atomicity. The nested character of spheres, however allows parts of processes to form nested spheres of atomicity (also called blocks [Alo97]). In terms of failure handling, this enables to define a single, high-level compensation task for a block, rather than one for each task encompassed in this block [Ley95]. The notion of sphere of atomicity is similar to the recovery spheres identified in [Dav78]. The latter may be exploited for forward recovery purposes in that a failure can be handled by applying compensation only to the current recovery sphere, followed by its re-execution.

The separation of isolation from the other ACID properties has been subject to the largest number of approaches aiming at decoupling transactional properties. In order to allow isolation to be applied independently and at different granularities smaller than global transactions or processes, the notion of *spheres of isolation* has been coined [SR96, Alo97, AHST97b]. Most approaches, however, are very restrictive in that they implement conventional distributed transactions based on two phase commit protocols and two phase locking (e.g., C-units [TV95] or atomic units [DD96]), or even follow ideas which are close to concepts of mutual exclusion as they are present, for instance, in operating systems, rather than applying the traditional notions of serializability for these spheres [Lyn83, FÖ89, AAA96a]. In [Lyn83] and [FÖ89], semantic knowledge is exploited to decompose a transaction into a set of steps which form indivisible groups of basic operations. Between these steps, breakpoints can be placed which specify when and by whom the execution of a transaction may be interfered. Hence, the concurrent execution of a set of transactions is equivalent to some serial execution of steps but does not necessarily induce serializability in the traditional sense. In [BL93, BGLL98], a formal approach on how to consistently decompose a transaction into steps is discussed. In contrast to the former two approaches decomposing transactions into steps, transactional workflows are rather synthesized from such units of execution [RS95].

Although the notion of *sphere of consistency* is not explicitly introduced, all approaches intuitively consider a global transaction or process, respectively, as the unit for which consistency has to hold. However, the discussion of the previous section has shown that in some cases, especially in the presence of a relaxed notion of isolation, additional manual operations by some administrator are considered which, of course, have to be seen as part of the implicit sphere of consistency spanned by a transaction or process.

Finally, the aforementioned ideas of relaxing persistence for certain parts of transactions or processes can be captured by the notion of *spheres of persistence* [Alo97, AHST97b]. These spheres explicitly specify which intermediate states are to be made persistent while the state reached by subtransactions or tasks that do not belong to any sphere of persistence are only kept transiently. Since spheres of persistence affect the way recovery is performed in the case of system failures, they are similar to the system recovery spheres discussed in [Dav78]. The latter identify certain checkpoints from where execution can be resumed after system failures since the appropriate states are made persistent.

9.1.5 Agent-Based Process Management

The rise of agent technology and the increasing popularity of multiagent systems has led to a new paradigm for building distributed applications based on autonomous components, so-called agents. In contrast to transactional process management which is characterized by the dualism between a central process manager and additional coordination agents, these approaches exclusively rely on agents for the enactment of processes. In general, multiagent systems modularize the functionality of workflow management systems and, in most approaches, focus on a fully distributed approach to process management rather than imposing a centralized component for this purpose. However, this decentralized approach complicates the task of gathering a global view on a composite system and therefore may induce severe drawbacks, especially in terms of transactional execution guarantees that can be provided for processes in multiagent systems.

9.2 Introduction and Discussion of Related Approaches

This section provides a detailed discussion of related work. More precisely, the models on which these approaches are based as well as the correctness criteria they support are analyzed. In particular, the impact of potential relaxations and/or decompositions of transactional properties on the notion of correctness is considered.

Although we have previously identified a set of features in which transactional workflows differ from advanced transaction models, a clear distinction is sometimes hardly possible in practice. Some approaches have started in the area of multidatabase systems and have evolved towards transactional workflows. Hence, certain approaches listed under the caption of transactional workflows could also be classified as advanced transaction models and vice versa.

9.2.1 Classification Scheme

Before we go into the details of related approaches, we first work out a classification scheme which will be exploited later on in order to relate all these approaches and to facilitate their comparison.

To this end, we start with the characterization of the underlying *model* of each approach. In here, we are interested in the following aspects and related questions:

i.) System Model:

- Which levels are considered?
- Is there any differentiation between global and local levels?

ii.) Subtransaction/Task Model:

- What are the basic units of execution?
- What termination properties are they supposed to have?
- Is compensation explicitly considered?

iii.) Transaction/Process Model:

- How is control flow specified?

— Is failure handling part of the transaction/process model?
— Does the possibility of alternative executions exist?

In addition to the underlying model, we are particularly interested in the different notions of *correctness* which are supported by related approaches from advanced transaction models and transactional workflows and especially the influences on relaxations of ACID properties. To this end, we will mainly focus on concurrency control and recovery:

i.) Concurrency Control:

— Is commutativity at subtransaction/task level introduced and if so, how is it defined?
— What notion of correctness with respect to concurrency control is supported?

ii.) Recovery:

— What is the default strategy for recovery?
— Is forward recovery possible and if so, when and based on which requirements?

iii.) Joint Criterion for Concurrency and Recovery:

— Is there a joint criterion or are both problems addressed independently?

9.2.2 Advanced Transaction Models

In this section, we introduce several advanced transaction models that are characterized by a certain vicinity to the process model which is employed in transactional process management. All these approaches have in common that they address distribution, heterogeneity, and autonomy of component systems [BGS92, BGS95]. In what follows, we restrict the discussion to advanced transaction models that i.) are closely related to the model of transactional processes and ii.) address correctness issues in sufficient detail. Some other approaches like polytransactions [SRK92], although presenting interesting concepts in terms of coordinating different heterogeneous and distributed databases by ad-hoc composition of global transactions based on dependency specifications are not considered since neither concurrency control not recovery issues for this type of advanced transaction model are discussed.

Sagas and Extended Sagas

Sagas have been proposed as a means to implement long lived transactions (LLT's) by decoupling them into an ordered sequence of semantically related operations, called subtransactions [GS87]. Following the open nested paradigm, each subtransaction of a LLT is allowed to commit as early as possible. In order to generalize the saga model, additional control flow dependencies allowing intra-saga parallelism and nesting are introduced [GGK+91a, GGK+91b].

In terms of the model, two levels are differentiated: the global, saga level and the local level at which subtransactions are settled (for extended sagas with deeper nesting, the local level is further decomposed). Subtransactions of a saga, the basic units of execution, have to correspond to conventional ACID transactions. In particular, they have to follow the "all-or-nothing" semantics of atomicity.

Moreover, each subtransaction has to be compensatable, and the appropriate compensating subtransaction has ubiquitously to be available. However, in case compensating subtransactions fail, manual intervention may be required. In addition to backward recovery, the possibility to define save-points between subtransactions exists and can be exploited for forward recovery purposes. Aside of the extensions of the basic saga model which explicitly introduce control flow constructs, sagas may also consider alternative executions (so-called secondary blocks) to overcome persisting failures of subtransactions in the presence of forward recovery.

The most important requirement for decoupling LLT's into sagas is that all subtransactions pairwise commute such that each subtransaction can be committed prior to the commit of the top-level saga without introducing inconsistencies in the presence of concurrency. That is, the isolation property trivially holds for any interleaved multi-saga execution. When failures occur, compensation of all committed subtransactions is possible. Moreover, by exploiting the notion of save-points which allow to make the current state of a saga persistent, partial backward recovery (to the most recent save-point) combined with forward recovery (re-execution of failed subtransactions) is possible. To extend the potential of forward recovery, also alternative executions which are part of the saga model can be exploited. Since concurrency control can be neglected with the assumption of pairwise commutativity for all subtransactions as it has to hold in the saga case, there is no need for a joint correctness criterion for concurrency control and recovery.

Migrating Transactions

The *migrating transactions (MTA)* model [KR88] can be considered as a generalization of the saga model for distributed environments. The name is coined since an MTA seems to migrate from one site to another in the network during its execution. An MTA corresponds to a long-lived transaction (called activity) and consists of a set of ACID subtransactions that reside at different nodes of a distributed system. The execution order of regular subtransactions (called actions) is defined via conditions on the termination states of preceding actions. Since not only the commit of actions but also their abort may be exploited in these conditions, failure handling strategies and alternative executions are part of the model. All actions of an MTA have to be compensatable, except for the last one, i.e., the one that does not appear in the condition of any other action, which is allowed to be even non-compensatable.

After execution, each action establishes some predicate (invariant) that specifies the necessary conditions for subsequent actions to be executed correctly. These invariants are the basis for implementing concurrency control in that an action of some MTA is only allowed to commit if it does not violate the invariant of any other active MTA. By this means, it is guaranteed that single MTAs can be completed correctly, even in the presence of concurrency. Each MTA is required to provide semantic atomicity. Hence, all actions of exactly one action set (consisting of all actions of one possible alternative execution) have to be committed or their effects have to be semantically undone (denoted as correct termination). The default strategy to cope with failures is backward recovery which does not require compensation to be applied in reverse order of the original actions but allows all previously committed actions of an MTA to be compensated concurrently. When some compensating subtransaction fails, manual intervention is required to re-establish consistency. In addition to backward recovery, restart points can be defined which allow partial backward recovery to these points, followed by forward recovery or alternative executions. Yet, a joint criterion for concurrency control and recovery does not exist.

Flexible Transactions

The model of *flexible transactions* has already been introduced in Section 3.4 in the context of extensions and generalizations of the conventional transaction model. In here, we briefly summarize the characteristics of flexible transactions and discuss the notions of correctness that are exploited in this model.

A flexible transaction as top-level transaction consists of a set of subtransactions between which two orders, a precedence order and a preference order are imposed [ELLR90]. Each of these subtransactions can be classified by exactly one of the termination properties compensatable, retriable, or pivot [LKS91, MRKS92, MRSK92]. For each compensatable subtransaction, the appropriate inverse has to exist. The precedence order can be regarded as a means to specify control flow; the preference order allows for a specification of alternative executions. Zhang et al. [ZNBB94] have finally presented a criterion to formally verify whether or not a single flexible transaction is correctly defined (semi-atomicity), even in the presence of multiple pivot subtransactions.

In the context of the flexible transaction model, a criterion for concurrency control, called *serializability with respect to compensation (SRC)* has been introduced [MRKS92, MRSK92]. In SRC, regular global transactions and their compensating transactions are treated independently. Whenever transactions exist that are globally serialized between a regular transaction and its compensation, SRC requires that they must not have any sites in common (that is, they do not access shared data objects), independently of the access characteristics of the associated subtransactions at these common sites. Yet, SRC implicitly assumes that all pairs of subtransactions being executed at the same site are in conflict. In terms of recovery, various strategies are possible: pure backward recovery (in case only compensatable subtransactions have been executed), partial backward recovery and alternative execution, as well as pure forward recovery (by repeated invocation of retriable subtransactions) [ZNBB94]. The strategy that is actually applied has to be determined dynamically based on the state of a flexible transaction. However, there is no joint criterion for concurrency control and recovery; although recovery of flexible transactions is elaborated in depth [ZNBB94], concurrency control is either neglected or, if present, treated independently [MRKS92, MRSK92].

S–Transactions

The *S–transaction* model (as an abbreviation for semantic transaction model) has been originally designed for multidatabases in banking environments and particularly considers autonomy in various flavors [Vei90, VEH92]. The basic units of execution of S-transactions are traditional ACID transactions provided by component databases. Each of these local subtransactions is required to be compensatable. An S-transactions consists of a set of sub-S-transactions; each of these sub-S-transactions either corresponds to a single local transaction or is formed recursively by a set of sub-S-transactions, thereby allowing an arbitrary deep nesting. The flow of control for the top-level S-transaction is defined via the S-transaction definition language (STDL) which also considers failure handling strategies such as alternative executions.

In terms of global correctness, state transitions induced by sub-S-transactions and top-level S-transactions are considered. While each local subtransaction follows the ACID paradigms, its state changes are valid. In addition, each combination of such local state changes is considered as correct at global level. Hence, S-transactions follow the same assumptions as sagas, namely that all local subtransactions pairwise commute. This allows each local subtransaction to be committed immediately without affecting global consistency. Recovery is performed by applying compensation. However, due to the autonomy of sites, compensating subtransactions may fail (leading to the notion of semantical crash of a S-transaction) and require subsequent manual intervention. Since, by the absence of conflicts, concurrency control is trivially ensured, there is no joint criterion for concurrency control and recovery.

NT/PV Transactions

The *NT/PV* model (nested transactions with predicates and versions) has been introduced in a general context [KS88, KS94] but it has been shown that it is well-suited for long-running, cooperative transactions as they occur, for instance, in computer aided software engineering (CASE) [KS90]. NT/PV transactions consist of nested transactions which are successively mapped to basic read/write operations. However, distribution is not addressed in that a centralized database system is required which, in turn, must be able to keep multiple versions of each data object. Failure handling or even alternative executions are not considered in the NT/PV model.

Assigned with each transaction as well as with each subtransactions is a pair of predicates specifying both the state in which the transaction can be executed and the state achieved after execution. Since multiple versions exist, a consistent version of the data objects accessed —for which the input conditions hold (version function)— can be chosen, prior to the execution of each subtransaction. Hence, the criterion for concurrency control is much more liberal than the traditional notion of serializability and can be tailored to the application-specific needs (depending on the version function exploited and the predicates assigned to (sub)transactions, it may range between CPSR and arbitrary non-serializable executions). Although the NT/PV model follows the open nested transaction paradigm, recovery is not addressed; even the requirement that each subtransaction should be compensatable is not stated explicitly.

M–Serializability

The approach of *M–serializability* [RKC92] follows the ideas of relaxing and decoupling transactional properties while, at the same time, applying them at different levels of granularity. M–serializability extends traditional multidatabase transactions by allowing to specify execution-atomic units that consist of a set of subtransactions but must not necessarily span the whole global transaction. Hence, concurrency control has only to consider the serializable execution of these execution-atomic units such that the sphere of isolation may not equal but rather be included in the sphere of atomicity (the global transaction). For recovery purposes, conventional backward recovery based on compensation is applied.

Open Publication Transactions

In [MRKN92], a transaction model for publication environments is introduced, based on multi-level transactions. These environments are characterized by the exploitation of semantically rich operations on documents which are mapped, using different intermediate levels of abstraction, to read/write operations. Hence, traditional ACID transactions are the basic units of execution (applications which do not provide transactions have to be extended). In addition, each document operation must have an appropriate undo operation for compensation purposes. In compliance with the multilevel transaction model, a transaction is a sequence of semantically rich operations, without information on failure handling and/or alternative executions. Extensions of the model of open publication transactions are present in the TransCoop model [RKT+95, KTWK98] which considers additional operations that occur in publication applications and which require, for instance, the consistent merge of different schedules.

Concurrency control is based on information about the commutativity of operations. Since multiple versions of each document exist, this cannot be specified statically but has always to dynamically consider the versions currently accessed. The criterion for concurrency control, called object-oriented serializability, follows the notion of level-by-level serializability (cf. Section 3.3.1). Recovery strategies only include the successive appliance of undo operations in reverse order.

9.2.3 Transactional Workflows

While advanced transaction models provide a first step towards correct executions in heterogeneous, autonomous, and distributed environments, transactional workflows extend these approaches by further relaxing some of the restrictions present in advanced transaction models. While all advanced transaction models require databases as underlying systems, most transactional workflow models consider not only databases but application systems in a more general sense [GHS95], thereby introducing an increased degree of heterogeneity [AAA+96b].

In general, two types of transactional workflows can be differentiated: system-oriented and human-oriented workflows [GHS95]. While the latter can be characterized by the integration of users, programs, data, and organizational structures [AM97], the former category strongly requires the enforcement of transactional properties, i.e., correctness with respect to both concurrency control and recovery [SR93, RS95, KR96b, ED97, CHRW98] but must also address the correctness of single processes and tasks [GHS95]. A further, commonly quoted important feature of transactional workflows is the possibility of forward recovery [RS95, Ley96, WS97] which can be rather barely found in advanced transaction models. Based on these features, the overall goal of transactional workflows is to provide a generic environment in which advanced applications can be developed, rather than introducing special advanced transaction models for each single application [AAA+96b].

Inter–Process Communication in OPERA

The process support system *OPERA* [AHST97a, AHST97b, Hag99], developed at ETH, can shortly be characterized by the support of both sophisticated exception handling strategies [HA98b, HA98c] and event-based intra-process and inter-process communication mechanisms [HA98a, HA99a]. Processes in OPERA consist of activities, blocks (which encompass sets of activities), and/or subprocesses, thereby allowing processes to be nested. Activities correspond to arbitrary service invocations or even require user interaction, thus, they are not assumed to be transactional in nature. Yet, various termination characteristics are differentiated with respect to atomicity, compensation, and retriability of single activities, thereby extending the termination characteristics identified by the flex transaction model. Processes are specified based on the OPERA canonical representation (OCR) which not only considers activity, control flow, and data flow specification but also exception handling strategies as well as explicit event specification and processing.

OPERA supports the notion of spheres to set the boundaries for certain transactional properties within processes. The most important spheres supported by OPERA are spheres of atomicity

[Alo97], based on the notion of blocks [Hag99]. Failure recovery in OPERA is based on exception handling mechanisms [HA98b, HA98c]. To this end, specialized blocks —exception handlers— are defined within processes. These handlers contain the specification of strategies determining the reaction to failures which can lead from switching to other activities (i.e., alternatives) to the compensation of activities having generated a failure. In the presence of subprocess hierarchies, these exception handling mechanisms are even well-suited for propagating failures in upward direction such that they can be handled at higher levels of abstraction.

In the traditional transaction model as well as in the diverse extensions and relaxations, each transaction is considered to form an independent unit and flow of information between different transactions is only possible via shared data objects. This basic assumption has led to the notion of serializability which addresses the controlled access to these shared data. OPERA, however, follows a different approach: information flow between processes is made explicit (inter-process communication) in that it is transferred via events (and associated parameters) that are published by one process and consumed by others [HA98a, HA99a]. To this end, event types have to be specified during process definition and to be associated with activities which act either as sender or consumer. In general, the signaling of such an event can be exploited for the start of activities (consumers) of other processes. Hence, this event-based communication allows to implement user-defined mechanisms for controlling concurrency in process support systems. However, special consideration is needed in the presence of failures, i.e., when some activity is compensated after having signaled an event that has already been consumed. To cope with these cases, an additional recovery mode has to be defined with each consumption in order to specify corrective actions. This recovery mode may span the whole spectrum between ignoring the failure of a signaling activity (e.g., in the case the consumer cannot be compensated once it has terminated successfully), over partial compensation of the consumer process back to a state prior to the consumption of the invalidated event and its subsequent re-execution to the cascading abort of the consumer process. In general, the explicit inter-process communication allows to decouple atomicity from isolation. Yet, event-based communication and appropriate recovery modes jointly consider recovery aspects and the special, user-defined restriction of concurrency although this joint treatment is not intended to coincide with the traditional correctness criteria of the unified theory of concurrency control and recovery.

ConTracts

The *ConTract model* [Wäc91, WR92, Wäc96, RSS97] aims at bringing together elements of programming languages (control flow specifications, iterations, conditional branching, etc.) and transaction processing. A ConTract is equivalent to a long-running transaction, or process, and consists of a set of steps that are combined by a script which specifies the execution dependencies between them (static control flow specification) and which allows to encompass single steps in atomic units of work (called transactions). Each step defines basic computations and follows the ACID properties [WR92]. This restriction is later relaxed in that steps may also be arbitrary program invocations (semi-transactional steps) [RSS97]. Compensation must exist for each step, or, if steps are grouped into transactions, for each transaction. If compensation does not succeed, a compensation step may be submitted repeatedly. However, the case in which it never leads to success is also possible; the definitive failure of compensation is then considered as a special case of "semantical compensation" and leads at most to a notification of a ConTract administrator. Moreover, the script also allows the specification of alternative executions for failure handling purposes.

Associated with each single step is an entry invariant and an exit invariant; furthermore, each step is required to be compensatable. The entry invariant reflects the conditions that must be true in order to start the execution of a step. The exit invariant of a step contains the post conditions that hold after its successful execution. If this condition is present in the entry invariant of a subsequent step, it must not be violated in between, i.e., by steps of concurrent ConTracts (= establishment of an invariant). The concurrency control mechanism exploited for ConTracts is therefore called invariant-based serializability. In order to ensure compensation, the invariant established by a step must also encompass the preconditions that have to hold prior to the execution of its compensation. In spite of the existence of compensation for each step or transaction, the default strategy for dealing with failures is forward recovery, based on the persistently stored ConTract state and the context of the current execution. If backward recovery by compensation is to be performed, this has to be stated explicitly by a user. A joint criterion for fault-tolerant concurrent ConTract executions exists [RSS97] which exploits the notion of expansion of the original unified theory of concurrency control and recovery. However, forward recovery —although it is the default mechanism for recovery— is not present in this joint criterion which considers only backward recovery.

Spheres of Isolation – Extensions of the Basic ConTract Model

The core model of the *Spheres of Isolation* approach [SR96] is strongly related to the ConTract model. Basic elements are activities having ACID properties. Moreover, each activity is required to be compensatable. Control flow within processes is defined on events specifying when activities have to be started. In particular, these events contain the termination state of preceding activities such that their failure can be handled by alternative executions.

Similar to the ConTract model, concurrency control is based on invariants. However, unlike ConTracts, constraints in the spheres of isolation approach are settled at object level, rather than being defined within steps. Hence, this technique to limit concurrency is closely related to the Escrow transaction model [O'N86] which is exploited to decrease parallelism in long-running transactions accessing hot-spot data objects. A single process is executed correctly if no violation of any object constraint occurred. The goal of a concurrent execution of processes is to provide two properties: success and correctness. The success of a process execution denotes the possibility to successfully terminate a process even in the presence of concurrency, i.e., that no object constraints are invalidated, called "object-local" concurrency control. The notion of correctness guarantees the availability of compensation until the end of a process. Correctness and successful termination is treated differently by assigning a (symbolic) Sphere of Isolation (SoI) to each property, i.e., success and correctness. Although forward recovery is considered as default recovery strategy, only backward recovery by compensation is present in the formal treatment based on the notion of correctness SoI. Although no joint criterion for concurrency control and recovery has been explicitly introduced, the simultaneous consideration of both SoIs treats both problems jointly while, however, being limited to backward recovery.

Activities/Transaction Model (ATM)

The *Activities/Transaction Model (ATM)* [DHL90, DHL91], which is the basis of the prototype system Pegasus [DS93] that has been developed at HP Labs, relies on ECA rules (Event – Condition – Action) as means of dynamic control flow specification of transactions, extended by additional scripting language elements [DHL91]. Events are either database operations or others signaled by external processes. Conditions can be either queries over the database and/or predicates over the parameters of events. Actions, finally, may be database operations and/or invocations of external applications. These actions can be either compensatable or critical [DHL91] where the latter cannot be compensated. Transactions can be nested, i.e., they contain not only actions but, recursively, also transactions. Failure handling is part of the model in that rules can be exploited to catch failures by specifying appropriate alternative executions.

In ATM, several possibilities exist for the coupling of consecutive rule elements (that is E-C and C-A couplings), namely immediate, deferred, and decoupled, which are combined with the closed nested transaction model [Mos85, Mos87], except for decoupled nested transactions which actually become independent top-level transactions. Due to the exploitation of the closed nested paradigm, effects of critical activities do not become visible until the top-level transaction commits. In terms of concurrency control, serializability is required. Special care is needed for causally dependent decoupled transactions which must be serialized after their original parents. For recovery purposes, the individual strategies specified via ECA rules are applied. The nested structure of transactions requires in some cases the upward propagation of failures until an appropriate rule is found. A joint criterion for correct concurrency control and recovery does not exist.

Open Process Management

Open process management (OPM) [CD96, CD97b] extends the ATM approach [DHL90, DHL91] by enriching the nested activity model with a combination of closed nested [Mos85, Mos87] and open nested transactions [WS92]. Each process consists of single activities and/or blocks; the latter consist recursively again of activities and blocks. Similar to ATM, activities correspond either to ACID transactions or to arbitrary service invocations. Moreover, they may be either compensatable or critical, that is non-compensatable. Control flow within processes is defined by a combination of ECA rules and inter-activity dependencies, i.e., constraints on the states of preceding activities.

Activities within a process are open, i.e., they are allowed to commit prior to the commit of a process although these changes are only visible to activities of the same process and not to the outside (these activities are called in–process open). That is, in–process open activities are open nested transactions within the scope of a closed transaction, the associated process. The goal of these activities is to increase parallelism compared with closed nested transactions but, at the same time, to avoid the relaxation of atomicity as given by the open nested transaction model. In the presence of in-process openness, critical activities must be deferred until the commit of the corresponding process. Serializability is exploited as correctness criterion for concurrency control. In terms of recovery, the process model allows both compensation (which is required in the presence of in-process open activities) and explicit alternative executions within blocks, defined by inter-activity constraints and ECA rules. When an activity fails, it is first checked whether in block alternative executions exist in the current block. If these do not exist, failure handling is propagated to the block hierarchy. By activity dependencies between processes, recovery is extended to multi-process executions. However, concurrency control and recovery are not considered jointly.

Panta Rhei

Panta Rhei [EG96, EGL97] is a workflow management system built on top of an active DBMS. Basic units of execution are tasks which correspond to arbitrary service invocations in underlying systems. Processes contain both tasks and activities (subprocesses) which consist of tasks and/or, recursively, of activities, thus allowing arbitrary deep nesting. In terms of process and activity specifications, information on the characteristics (transactional aspects) of tasks are required [EL95, EL96]. These include a task's potential property to succeed after repeated invocation (Force) and its compensation behavior (Storno-Type). The latter may include the availability of a compensation task but addresses also the case where compensation of a task is not available (critical task). The Workflow Activity Definition Language (WADL) [EL95], which is based on the ACTA transaction framework [CR90, CR91, CR94], allows for the specification of alternative executions in case of (expected) failures.

Each activity and each task is characterized by a vitality specification. A vital task (or activity) is one whose failure requires appropriate failure handling within its process; the failure of a non-vital task or activity, however, does not affect the correct execution of the associated process. Therefore, only failures of vital activities have to be considered for recovery purposes. The way recovery is performed is defined by the Storno-Type and the Force property of each activity. Due to the possibility to encompass failure handling strategies for (expected) failures in the process model, pure backward recovery, partial backward recovery combined with alternative executions, and forward recovery by re-execution is possible. However, recovery is not required to succeed (e.g., a compensation activity may fail or the repeated execution of an activity may not lead to success). In all these cases, manual intervention is necessary. In addition, a correctness validation at build-time is possible, indicating whether a process model is unsafe or not. A process is unsafe when a possible execution exists in which a critical task is vital, i.e., would have to be compensated; otherwise, a process specification is said to be safe. In the Panta Rhei approach, correctness in the presence of concurrency, which is based on the notion of semantic serializability [BDS+93], is treated independently of recovery.

Spheres of Joint Compensation

The *spheres of joint compensation* approach addresses the fault-tolerant execution of single processes [Ley95, Ley96]. Processes consist of activities which themselves correspond to arbitrary service invocations (steps). Moreover, the process model includes various constructs for the specification of control flow, e.g., conditional branching, forks, joins, and loops. Each activity does not necessarily have to provide ACID guarantees but its has to be compensatable. In addition, it is possible to assign one single compensation activity to groups of activities; these groups are called spheres of joint compensation. Either all activities of such a sphere have to be executed successfully or all have to be compensated. Different spheres may intersect or be even contained within each other. For recovery purposes, various strategies exist (and have to be specified at build-time): pure backward recovery, partial compensation combined with the re-invocation of failed activities, or even the repeated invocation of the whole process without preceding compensation can be applied. Partial backward recovery, however, may even necessitate cascading aborts of spheres of joint compensation in case they do overlap. Concurrency control is not addressed in this approach.

CREW

The *CREW* (correct & reliable execution of workflows) approach [KR98] explicitly addresses failure handling as well as intra- and inter-workflow coordination. Processes are specified by means of the language for workflow specification (LAWS) and consist of steps which correspond to arbitrary service invocations that are required to be compensatable. LAWS addresses both data flow dependencies and control flow dependencies for regular execution, but no alternatives for failure handling purposes. In terms of concurrency control, conflict behavior between steps has to be specified manually. In addition, order constraints between conflicting steps (both within processes and between independent processes) have to be specified explicitly ("coordinated execution specification") by a workflow designer such that serializability is not automatically guaranteed but would require exhaustive manual specification. Recovery encompasses both compensation and re-execution of steps. In order to determine the scope of recovery, so-called compensation dependent steps (similar to the spheres of joint compensation) can be defined. Moreover, the effort for compensation and re-execution of steps can, in some cases, be reduced by either incremental re-execution or partial compensation. These two options allow to apply changes to the effects of already completed steps which are required, for instance, after input parameters have changed, without undoing and repeatedly invoking them. These variants are captured under the notion of "opportunistic compensation".

The METU Approach to Transactional Workflows

The *METU model* [AHAD99] is closely related to the ConTract model. It avoids semantically rich operations and exploits the traditional read/write model. Activities, the basic units of execution within processes, have to be defined by their read/write characteristics and a so-called activity specification which consists of a set of input and output conditions. Input conditions describe the state in which an activity can be started and output conditions are post-conditions that hold after the execution of an activity. Additionally, basic (global) and inter-activity constraints exist. The latter reflect dependencies between input and output constraints of activities of one process. Control flow definition is based on a graphical workflow specification which is, however, restricted to regular executions and does neither address failure handling nor alternatives. The correct execution of a single process is defined by the compliance of all basic constraints prior to the start of the process and after its termination, in addition to the input constraints that must hold prior to the execution of each activity. The semantics of inter-activity constraints in combination with the activity specification (input and output condition) leads to the notion of "constraint-based concurrency control" and is similar to the invariant-based concurrency control of the ConTract model. The concurrent execution of processes is considered to be correct when each process is executed correctly, when all basic constraints are valid before the start of the first process and are (again) valid in the final state (at the end of an execution history), and when no inter-activity constraints are violated. The METU approach does not consider recovery.

Isolation Units

The goal of this approach is to automatically identify independent units within processes, so-called *Isolation Units (IUs)* [AAHD97, DGA$^+$97] and to apply serialization concepts at the level of these IUs. Tasks, the basic elements of processes, correspond to semantically rich operations which are successively mapped to read/write operations. Each task is assumed to be transactional in nature. The process model considers two kinds of dependencies: data flow dependencies and serial control flow dependencies. An IU consists of all tasks of a process that are connected by both data flow and serial control flow dependencies. The correctness criterion for concurrency control is serializability of Isolation Units. Hence, these isolation units follow the spheres ideas of shrinking the logical boundaries for isolation although a rather syntactical approach for decomposing processes is used which does not consider application-specific dependencies between tasks between which no data flow occurs. Failure handling is not part of the model; recovery is not addressed.

9.2.4 Commercial Workflow Management Systems

Most of the previously introduced models are only of theoretical nature and only few of the advanced transaction models and transactional workflow models are actually implemented in research prototypes. When taking a look at commercial workflow management systems, it becomes obvious that the focus of these systems is more on aspects like document flow, multi-platform support, worklist and user management, application and office integration, GUIs, and so forth, rather than providing sophisticated transactional properties. However, some systems, especially those that have grown from a database context or that are strongly related to database applications, at least provide rudimentary support for transactional execution guarantees. In what follows, we will briefly introduce these systems and the particular notion of correctness they support.

Oracle Workflow

Oracle Workflow [Ora99, SVM98] of Oracle Corporation [Ora] is tightly integrated into the Oracle8 database server. The Oracle Workflow engine is implemented by PL/SQL procedures which exploit meta information that is stored in database tables and views. Activities of Oracle Workflows can either be user-defined PL/SQL procedures or arbitrary external applications which are invoked via their API by queuing mechanisms (i.e., Oracle's pipes). Failures of activities occurring during process executions are handled on a per-process basis: an additional error process which contains information on the failure handling strategy (either ignore the failure, abort the failed process, i.e., stop its execution, or its re-invocation) has to be assigned to each regular process. When a failure occurs, the regular process is frozen and the error process is started. The latter notifies an administrator who has to initiate the pre-defined failure handling strategy manually. Hence, no recovery related action is performed automatically. Similarly, no restriction on concurrency control is imposed per default. Processes are assumed to be independent, and each activity of a process is executed within a single transaction. Yet, only two concurrent activities are serialized by the underlying database if they access shared data. If isolation between concurrent processes has to be enforced, it has to be specified explicitly by so-called block activities which stop the execution of a process until other concurrent activities have terminated.

MQSeries Workflow

MQSeries Workflow [MQS99] of IBM [IBM] has emerged from the workflow management system FlowMark. It is built on top of two separate relational database systems, a built-time database for process specifications and a run-time database for the persistent storage of the states of active processes and of process execution histories. Activities, the basic units of execution, can correspond to the execution of arbitrary applications. Processes can be nested, i.e., multiple levels of subprocesses are allowed such that activities can be grouped at different levels of abstraction for reuse. In terms of application integration, the interaction of two components is essential. First, application agents at the corresponding site are required which manage the start of the associated application. Second, communication between workflow system and application agent is performed via MQSeries persistent message queues which guarantee that activities are executed exactly once and that acknowledgments will not get lost. Such acknowledgments are dequeued and subsequently stored in the run-time database within one single distributed transaction (by using a 2PC protocol) in order to guarantee the integrity of the run-time database. This avoids the repeated execution of successfully terminated activities, even in the case of system crashes. Based on the persistent process state stored in the run-time database, system failures can be handled by forward recovery, i.e., the continuation of a process execution based on the latest state information. While system failures can be handled automatically, the handling of activity failures has to be specified explicitly in a process. Since MQSeries considers processes to be totally independent, no mechanisms for concurrency control are supported.

SAP R/3 Business Workflow

SAP R/3 Business Workflow [WFB+95, MB00] is, in contrast to the previous systems, not a stand-alone workflow management system but it is part of the enterprise resource planing (ERP) system SAP R/3 [Buc99, SAP00] of SAP AG [SAP]. Hence, it is tailored to the execution of SAP internal transactions (which can be either performed automatically by accessing the underlying database but they may also require user interaction) as basic units of execution. Yet, SAP Business Workflows also support the execution of external applications which have to be registered at the R/3 gateway. Failures that occur when executing a SAP Business Workflow raise a pre-defined exception. During process specification, exception handling strategies can be defined. For activity failures, these strategies allow the specification of alternatives which are executed automatically after an exception is raised. When an exception is raised for which no appropriate handler is defined, the process is frozen and an administrator is notified who has to manually apply corrective actions. Since activities correspond to SAP transactions, their concurrent execution is handled by SAP's locking mechanism (although the latter has to be implemented explicitly within each transaction). Synchronization of concurrent processes, however, has to be done manually by integrating so-called waiting steps into the process. Then, the execution of a process can be deferred until certain events occur, i.e., the termination of other processes or activities. Hence, this only allows for a rather restrictive concurrency control by mutually excluding parts of processes.

9.2.5 Agent–Based Process Management

In the area of multiagent systems for process support, two different architectural paradigms can be distinguished [Hay99]. Some approaches impose a centralized component for this purpose while others follow a purely distributed approach. In the centralized approach, global knowledge is available that can be exploited for enforcing execution guarantees of processes. The decentralized approach, in contrast, avoids certain overhead but has to cope with the problem that individual agents do not have a global view on processes which therefore affects the task of enforcing globally correct multi-process executions. In what follows, we briefly introduce and compare multiagent approaches following the different paradigms to agent-based process management.

Scheduling Agents

The *scheduling agent* approach [HSK98] follows the centralized multiagent paradigm. Hence, it is characterized by the existence of a dedicated agent that controls the execution of processes. This component, called schedule processing agent, is extended by a family of additional agents, each dedicated to a specific task. The core part of this architecture is formed, aside of the schedule processing agent, by a scheduling agent and a schedule repairing agent. The scheduling agent is responsible for the rule-based generation of processes, given a specification by some user (via a dedicated GUI agent). The execution of this schedule, which corresponds to a process program in the terminology of transactional process management, is controlled by the schedule processing agent. In the case of failures, recovery by compensation or by repeated execution is initiated by the schedule repairing agent. Obviously, the differences of this approach to transactional process management are more on a terminological level than on a conceptual one, aside of the fact that the functionality provided by the process manager is split into two independent components, namely the schedule processing agent and the schedule repairing agent. This approach addresses failure handling, but it does not consider any support for concurrency control.

MARCAs

A rather hybrid approach combining both centralized and distributed aspects can be found in the MARCA agent-based architecture for process management [DBT+99]. The system comprises a set of agents, called MARCAs, one for each site where an activity is to be executed and, in addition, a centralized component, the coordinating MARCA. The latter does not participate in the execution of processes but is only required to manage process models and to configure the individual MARCAs, the actual units of execution. This configuration includes information on which service a MARCA has to execute, given certain incoming messages, and which other MARCA has to be notified in the case of success or failure of this service. Hence, each component possesses only local process information. A process is executed without central control, in that each MARCA directly notifies, by message transfer, the MARCA which is responsible for the subsequent activity and, in addition, attaches to this message the data that has to be shipped. Although some limited form of failure handling is possible by alternative messages that can be send when an activity fails, compensation is not considered. Even worse, this distributed process execution does not allow for any global view on the system which would be required to support concurrency control. In the terminology of transactional process management, MARCAs are closely related to TCAs which interact, after configuration, among each other, without any control of a process manager.

ADEPT

A decentralized approach where no pre-determined process programs exist but where processes are rather settled dynamically at run-time by inter-agent negotiation and the subsequent placement of contracts between agents can be found in the ADEPT (advanced decision environment for process tasks) approach to process management [NJFM96, JNF98, JFN+00]. When a process is to be executed, the agent via which the process is requested by some user may offer distinct tasks or the whole process to other agents. By deciding to which agent the offer is granted to, certain characteristics like process cost or service quality can be optimized. In case the requesting agent negotiates with other agents on a per-task basis, it keeps the responsibility to control the execution of the whole process. In case some bidding agent commits to control the whole set of tasks, control is switched to this agent which can then either, if possible, provide these tasks locally or can issue again an offer to search for other agents providing the tasks that cannot be provided locally. Since there is no global control, the correct concurrent execution of processes cannot be enforced. Even worse, also support for the correct execution of single processes is limited (even in the case no failures exist, this is strongly dependent on the negotiation strategies used, the degree of detail in which services are described, and the way, the fulfillment of contracts is controlled).

Mobile Agents

Another approach to agent-based process management is to exploit mobile agent technology [MLL97]. These agents, which encapsulate code, data, and process state are transferred through a network to some site where the code wrapped within the agent is executed, thereby exploiting the data that comes along with it. After successful execution, state information is updated and, if necessary, the agent continues wandering through the network so as to perform the subsequent task at another site. Although this approach has been proposed especially for inter-organizational business processes [MLL97], it may face, due to security reasons, severe problems since foreign code is in general not allowed to be executed behind the firewall of an enterprise. In addition, this mobile agent approach to process management neglects the fact that activities are complex, i.e., require application services to be invoked, which exceeds, in most cases, the power of what can be achieved by transferring some piece of code to a site and execute it there.

9.3 Summarizing Comparison and Classification

The above discussion of related approaches from advanced transaction models, transactional workflows, and multiagent systems for process support has given insights in the variety of models and the different notions of correctness that are supported. In this section, we briefly summarize the major aspects of these approaches and relate them to transactional process management.

In Table 9.1, a summary of the main characteristics of all advanced transaction models introduced in Section 9.2.2 is presented. Similarly, Table 9.2 summarizes the properties of the underlying models of the diverse transactional workflow approaches and Table 9.3 summarizes the basic characteristics of all multiagent systems for process support. In addition, Table 9.2 also comprises the characterization of the model of transactional process management. All tables contain the model-related aspects of the classification scheme that has been introduced in Section 9.2.1.

In terms of the system model, most approaches address a two level configuration while others allow deeper levels of nesting, either by considering nested transactions at the local level (i.e., S–transactions, open publication transactions, and NT/PV transactions) or by allowing special constructs such as subprocesses or blocks to recursively group basic units of execution. Only the totally distributed ADEPT and mobile agents approaches do not consider multiple levels. The model of transactional processes, as introduced in Chapter 4, has been restricted to a two-level configuration. However, no assumption is made about the structure of subsystem transactions which can, in effect, be implemented by nested transactions. Moreover, by their special semantics, multi-activity nodes which are a substantial part of the process model are closely related to the notion of blocks as it is present in some transactional workflow models. Hence, the $(*)$ superscript placed in the corresponding field in Table 9.2 is used to indicate that associating a two level configuration to transactional process management is induced by the degree of abstraction applied, rather than being an inherent property.

Obviously, all advanced transaction models require ACID transactions as basic units of execution, thereby limiting their applicability to database environments while some transactional workflow

	System Model	Subtransaction/Task Model		Transaction/Process Model		
	Levels	Basic Units	Termination Properties	Control Flow	Failure Handling	Alter–natives
Sagas	two levels: saga & local txns	ACID trans-actions	each subtrans-action must be compensatable	appli-cation program	save-points and second-ary blocks	✓
Migrating Transactions	two levels: MTA & actions (local)	ACID trans-actions	each action com-pensatable, except for the last one	state condi-tions	conditions on aborted actions	✓
Flexible Transactions	two levels: flexible tx & local txns	ACID trans-actions	compensa-table, pivot, or retriable	pre-cedence order	prefer-ence order	✓
S–Transactions	multiple levels: S-tx & local txns (can be nested)	ACID trans-actions	each subtrans-action must be compensatable	STDL	explicitly specified in STDL	✓
NT/PV Transactions	multiple levels: NT/PV & local (nested) txns	ACID trans-actions	N/A	partial intra-tx order	—	—
M–Serializability	two levels: global & local	ACID trans-actions	each subtrans-action must be compensatable	intra tx order	—	—
Open Publication Transactions	multiple levels: document ops as nested txns	ACID trans-actions	undo operation for each regular operation required	intra-tx order	—	—

Table 9.1: Overview and Comparison of Advanced Transaction Models

models address more general contexts by allowing activities to be associated with arbitrary service invocations. In terms of transactional process management, we have identified ACA and CPSR as axiomatic requirement for subsystem transactions. But, as indicated by the (†) subscript in Table 9.2, this does not necessarily exclude applications whose services do not follow this requirement; it rather necessitates special treatment —as discussed in Chapter 8— which allows the functionality of these systems to be extended yet to meet the required criteria. Multiagent systems, however, allow arbitrary application services to be invoked, without the requirement that these are executed in a transactional context. Mobile agents, finally, encapsulate the code which is shipped to the site where it is to be executed.

Termination properties of subtransactions are rather treated restrictively, both in advanced transaction models and transactional workflows. Most advanced transaction models follow the concept of open nested transactions, thus requiring each subtransaction to be compensatable. While migrating transactions at least allow one subtransaction to be non-compensatable, only flexible transactions allow for a substantial generalization in advanced transaction models. Similarly, ATM and OPM require non-compensatable activities to be deferred, while only Panta Rhei, OPERA, and transactional process management provide more freedom on the usage of non-compensatable activities. In the presence of diverse termination properties of activities, the possibility for validating processes is crucial. However, only flexible transactions (semi-atomicity), OPERA (by the availability of exception handlers), and transactional process management (guaranteed termination) provide sufficient criteria for these purposes. Panta Rhei also comes along with the possibility of validating processes

	System Model	Subtransaction/Task Model		Transaction/Process Model		
	Levels	Basic Units	Termination Properties	Control Flow	Failure Handling	Alter–natives
Transactional Process Management	two levels: processes & subsystem txns*	ACA & CPSR services†	compensatable/ pivot; retriability is orthogonal†	pre-cedence order	pre-ference order	✓
OPERA	multiple levels: processes & sub-proc's/activities	arbit-rary services	fine-grained specification possible	OCR	exception handlers	✓
ConTracts	two levels: ConTracts & steps (local)	ACID & semi-tx steps	each step/ tx must be compensatable	script	alternatives defined via script	✓
Spheres of Isolation	two levels: processes & activities	ACID trans-actions	each activity must be compensatable	by events (states of activities)	events on aborted activities	✓
ATM	multiple levels: transactions & subtxns/actions	ACID txns or services	compensatable & non-compen-satable actions	ECA rules & scripts	alternatives via ECA rules	✓
OPM	multiple levels: processes & activities/blocks	ACID txns or services	compensatable & non-compen-satable activities	ECA rules & depend-encies	via rules/ depend-encies	✓
Panta Rhei	multiple levels: processes & tasks/activities	arbit-rary services	compensatable & non-compen-satable tasks	WADL	alternatives and/or re-execution	✓
Spheres of Joint Com-pensation	multiple levels: process & sub-proc's/activities	arbit-rary services	each activity must be compensatable	scrip-ting language	re-execution of failed activities	—
CREW	two levels: processes & steps	arbit-rary services	each step must be compensatable	LAWS	re-execution (complete/ incremental)	—
METU	two levels: processes & activities	ACID trans-actions	N/A	graphical specifi-cation	—	—
Isolation Units	multiple levels: processes & sem. rich operations	ACID trans-actions	N/A	serial flow depend-encies	—	—

Table 9.2: Overview and Comparison of Transactional Workflow Models

but in a less powerful framework (non-compensatable activities are allowed if they are not vital, i.e., if their presence does not hinder a process to be aborted correctly). In contrast to advanced transaction models and transactional workflows, multiagent systems (except for scheduling agents) do not differentiate between termination properties of services.

In most transactional workflow approaches, failure handling strategies are integrated into the core model while this can be found much less often in advanced transaction models. Similarly, alternative executions rather belong to transactional workflows than to advanced transaction models (the support of alternative executions for failure handling purposes is denoted by ✓). Yet, alternative executions are also considered to be an important feature in commercial workflow management

	System Model	Subtransaction/Task Model		Transaction/Process Model		
	Levels	Basic Units	Termination Properties	Control Flow	Failure Handling	Alter–natives
Scheduling Agents	two levels: scheduling & application agents	arbitrary application services	compensation possible, but not mandatory	schedu-ling agent	alternatives and/or re-execution	✓
MARCAs	two levels: Coord. MARCA & MARCAs	arbitrary application services	N/A	Coord. MARCA	alternatives via rules	✓
ADEPT	single level	arbitrary application services	N/A	dynami-cally, by negotiation	alternatives via negotiation	✓
Mobile Agents	single level	own code	N/A	part of the agent	—	—

Table 9.3: Overview and Comparison of Models of Multiagent Systems for Process Support

systems (and can, in effect, be found in all commercial systems we have discussed). Similar concepts can also be found in multiagent systems for process support. Scheduling agents consider both forward recovery by alternatives and backward recovery by compensation. ADEPT, in contrast, supports rather rudimentary failure handling strategies in that an agent can offer tasks to other agents when it detects that they cannot be provided locally, or when they have failed. Similarly, the MARCAs consider only alternative executions (which have to be specified explicitly by the coordinating MARCA), hence allow only to apply forward recovery. In the mobile agent approach, failure handling is not considered at all. Dynamic approaches such as ADEPT have the advantage that they can seamlessly cope with the unavailability of sites or agents which then simply do not participate in the bidding procedure. Although this support is not natively provided in the case of pre-determined process programs, it is usually addressed by appropriate, explicitly specified alternatives. Most agent-based approaches claim to be more flexible and more reliable than process-centered approaches since they do not have to consider a dedicated component controlling the execution of processes which is seen as single point of failure. However, this claim cannot be accepted in its generality. First, sophisticated backup mechanisms as proposed in [KAGM96, HA99b] can be applied to process-centered approaches in order to increase their availability. Second, in decentralized approaches like mobile agents or ADEPT, the failure of active agents may induce that processes are immediately stopped, without the possibility of being resumed. This is reinforced by the fact that backup mechanisms in these approaches are rather difficult to provide, due to decentralization, ad-hoc interactions, and/or mobility.

While the characteristics of all models —except for multiagent systems— have been proven to be quite similar, the notions of correctness supported by the advanced transaction models and transactional workflows show a broader variety. Table 9.4 summarizes concurrency control and recovery issues that can be found in advanced transaction models and Table 9.5 considers the transactional workflow models presented in Section 9.2.3. The characteristics of transactional process management have been added to the latter table. For the sake of completeness, also the correctness criteria used in multiagent systems for process management are summarized in Table 9.6, although they lack considerable support for concurrency control (and in some cases even for recovery).

	Concurrency Control (CC)		Recovery (Rec)		CC & Rec
	Commutativity	Notion for correct CC	Default Strategy	Forward Recovery	Joint Criterion
Sagas	all subtransactions must commute	no need for consideration (CC trivially holds; no conflicts)	backward recovery	✓ (savepoints)	—
Migrating Transactions	defined implicitly via invariants	invariant–based CC	backward recovery	✓ (restart points)	—
Flexible Transactions	subtxns at the same site are implicitly assumed to conflict	serializability with respect to compensation (SRC)	state–dependent	✓	—
S–Transactions	all subtransactions must commute	no need for consideration (CC trivially holds; no conflicts)	backward recovery	—	—
NT/PV Transactions	defined implicitly via predicates	can be customized via predicates & version function	N/A	—	—
M–Serializability	derived from basic operations	M–serializability	backward recovery	—	—
Open Publication Transactions	explicitly defined between semantically rich operations	OO–serializability	backward recovery	—	—

Table 9.4: Overview and Comparison of Correctness Notions in Advanced Transaction Models

Except for spheres of joint compensation, all approaches from advanced transaction models and transactional workflows support some notion of concurrency control. While most of them follow the traditional assumption that flow of information between global transactions or processes, respectively, takes place via shared data, OPERA makes this information flow explicit by passing messages between processes. However, the differences between the various strategies that exist for concurrency control purposes are already becoming obvious by taking a look at the different notions of commutativity: ConTracts, migrating transactions, NT/PV transactions, and the METU approach associate predicates to subtransactions or activities, respectively, thereby specifying constraints (invariants) that must not be violated by concurrent processes; similar predicates are considered in the spheres of isolation approach, although these predicates are not attached to single activities but, in an Escrow-like style, to data objects. In all these cases, concurrency control is defined via the compliance with these constraints. Sagas and S transactions on the one hand and flexible transactions on the other hand follow the two extreme cases with respect to commutativity. Sagas and S-transactions require that all subtransactions pairwise commute such that concurrency control is trivially ensured by each arbitrary concurrent execution. Flexible transactions, however, restrictively consider subtransactions being executed at the same site to pairwise conflict, thus leading to the quite restrictive criterion of serializability with respect to compensation. Unlike transactional workflows and advanced transaction models, none of the agent-based approaches considers concurrency control. Yet, only the system architecture of the scheduling agents approach would allow to support concurrency control as part of the schedule processing agent although, due to the separation of schedule processing and schedule repairing agent, a joint consideration of both

	Concurrency Control (CC)		Recovery (Rec)		CC & Rec
	Commutativity	Notion for correct CC	Default Strategy	Forward Recovery	Joint Criterion
Transactional Process Management	defined by the effects of pairs of activities	Process-Serializability (P-SR)	state-dependent (P-RC)	✓	Correct Termination (CT)
OPERA	defined implicitly via signaling/consumption of events	user-defined	can be specified individually	✓	[restricted to CC via event mechanisms]
ConTracts	defined implicitly via invariants	invariant-based CC	forward recovery	✓	[considers only backward recovery]
Spheres of Isolation	defined implicitly via object constraints	object-local CC (success SoI)	forward recovery	✓	[both SoIs, but only backward recovery]
ATM	N/A	serializability, respecting causal dependencies	can be specified individually	✓	—
OPM	N/A	serializability	can be specified individually	✓	—
Panta Rhei	N/A	semantic serializability	defined in WADL via Storno-Type	✓	—
Spheres of Joint Compensation	—	—	has to be specified at build-time	✓	—
CREW	explicit step conflict specification	explicit "coordinated execution specification"	backward recovery	✓	—
METU	defined implicitly via inter-activity constraints	constraint-based CC	N/A	—	—
Isolation Units	derived from r/w operations at the leaf level	serializability of isolation units	N/A	—	—

Table 9.5: Overview and Comparison of Correctness Notions in Transactional Workflows

isolation and atomicity is not possible. Even worse, all other agent-based approaches to process management do not consider any global control by which inter-process dependencies and thus the correct parallelization of multi-process executions can be enforced. The latter fact, the lack of global control, has also been identified by Papazoglou as a key drawback of agent-based approaches compared to process-centric ones: "business transaction characteristics are better addressed by a process-centered approach to transaction management that supports long-lived, concurrent, nested, multi-threaded activities" [Pap99].

Most approaches consider a default strategy for recovery purposes such that all other strategies, that might be supplementarily supported, have to be requested explicitly. However, only flexible

	Concurrency Control (CC)		Recovery (Rec)		CC & Rec
	Commutativity	Notion for correct CC	Default Strategy	Forward Recovery	Joint Criterion
Scheduling Agents	N/A	[—]	depends on individual process	✓	—
MARCAs	N/A	—	forward recovery	✓	—
ADEPT	N/A	—	forward recovery	✓	—
Mobile Agents	N/A	—	N/A	—	—

Table 9.6: Overview and Comparison of Correctness Notions in Multiagent Systems for Process Support

transactions and transactional process management, which are closely related, treat all different recovery strategies equally and choose the appropriate one dynamically, based on the process state.

As we have previously seen in the general comparison of advanced transaction models and transactional workflows, a frequently quoted difference between the two notions is the support for forward recovery in transactional workflows while this is supposed to be rather unusual in the context of advanced transaction models. When taking a look at Tables 9.4 and 9.5, this characterization can be confirmed: from the approaches we have classified under the term advanced transaction models, only sagas, migrating transactions and flexible transactions support forward recovery while this is neglected by the METU approach and by isolation units. Also most of the agent-based approaches (aside of mobile agents) support forward recovery.

A crucial characteristics of the quality of a model is the existence of a joint criterion for concurrency control and recovery. While the support of such a joint criterion has been proven to be essential in the context of the conventional, single-level transaction model, it is even more important in generalized models. However, it has to be noted that certain approaches do not even address both problems independently (spheres of joint compensation does not consider concurrency control while the METU approach, isolation units, and NT/PV transactions neglect recovery). ConTracts exploit the unified theory of concurrency control, but only in the context of backward recovery (as required by the original notion of the unified theory). Forward recovery, although being the default strategy for failure handling, does not appear in the joint criterion. Similarly, the spheres of isolation approach addresses both problems simultaneously but also only in combination with backward recovery. In addition, the inter-process communication of OPERA also considers parallelism in the presence of recovery; however, the approach followed by explicitly exchanging data between processes is not related to the traditional notion of concurrency control. Since ConTracts, spheres of isolation, and OPERA, although considering atomicity and isolation simultaneously, restrict one of these notions in their joint criterion, the latter appear in brackets in Table 9.5. Hence, transactional process management is the only approach that provides a powerful criterion (correct termination, CT) that allows to address both problems simultaneously and, at the same time, considers the full strength of different recovery strategies.

Finally, we highlight certain special features of multiagent systems for process support. In transactional process management, dedicated coordination agents, TCAs, were introduced so as to allow the integration of arbitrary applications and the invocations of their services. Similar mechanisms are also present in most of the agent-based approaches, either as functionality integrated into the core components (e.g., MARCAs or the ADEPT agents) or as additional components, i.e., specialized application agents in the scheduling agents approach. However, in the case of mobile agents where code to be executed comes along with the agent itself, heterogeneity, access rights, etc., may limit or even circumvent the integration of arbitrary applications.

An inherent property of process programs in transactional process management is that they can be proven correct, prior to their execution. However, similar functionality cannot be found in any of the agent-based approaches. But, the verification of processes could, in general, be provided by all approaches where a dedicated component is responsible for the generation of process specifications (such as the the coordinating MARCA and the scheduling agent). However, this feature can definitively not be supported when processes are determined dynamically at run-time as it is the case in ADEPT. There, it may turn out at some point during process execution that the activities needed for the correct completion of a process are not available such that a process may end up in an inconsistent state.

According to Table 9.6, agent-based approaches are clearly limited in providing the necessary execution guarantees for transactional coordination. Recalling the agent classification we have introduced in Chapter 8, all approaches to agent-based process management, namely MARCAs, the ADEPT agents, mobile agents, and scheduling agents belong to the category of non-transactional cooperative coordination agents, i.e., agents for process enactment. However, since all these approaches avoid the large system footprint induced by process-centered approaches, they may be well-suited for certain classes of applications where transactional execution guarantees are not of primary importance. Yet, an interesting and open problem is the combination of both paradigms such that the different technologies converge. From an agent point of view, this would include the extension of a distributed agent-based approach by some thin global component that allows for transactional execution guarantees depending on the degree and the kind of correctness that is globally required (this global component is just one approach to provide execution guarantees in a distributed multiagent system rather than being an intrinsic requirement; execution guarantees can also be provided when agents synchronize themselves by means of bilateral, peer-to-peer communication). From the process-centered perspective, this would imply the need for modularizing process manager functionality and for making it available independently via agents. The combination of both paradigms then would allow to build transactional cooperative coordination agents, the subclass of coordination agents that is, so far, not populated.

10 Conclusion

"Il est vain, si l'on plante un chêne, d'espérer s'abriter bientôt sous son feuillage."

Antoine de Saint-Exupéry, Terres des Hommes

10.1 Summary

This thesis has introduced and elaborated the concept of *transactional process management* for the development of distributed applications in composite systems which consist of heterogeneous, autonomous, and distributed component systems. Transactional process management addresses the correct concurrent and fault-tolerant execution of processes. A process is a sequence of activities; each of these activities corresponds to an invocation of a transactional service in one of the components of a composite system. Yet, this paradigm allows to relate different services of originally independent systems and to integrate them into processes as applications at a higher semantical level. Hence, transactional process management provides the basic framework to coordinate systems by making their interdependencies explicit in appropriate processes and by enforcing the correct execution of the latter.

The core part of the thesis is dedicated to the development of a comprehensive theory of transactional process management. The notion of *process program* is used as a means to specify distributed applications over the components of a composite system. Transactional processes follow the paradigm of hyperdatabases in which transactional functionality is provided at a semantically higher level of abstraction. Each process reflecting the execution of a process program is considered as a hyperdatabase transaction which is built out of transactions of the underlying subsystems as basic elements. In particular, and in contrast to most advanced transaction models and transactional workflow approaches, process programs account for the characteristics of the components of composite systems and the special semantics of their services by differentiating between termination properties of services and by allowing the invocation of alternative services for failure handling purposes. To this end, the process programs model extends and generalizes ideas of flexible transactions. Most importantly, single process programs can be proven correct which implies that each failure can be handled correctly by either applying backward recovery by compensation or by executing alternative activities that are guaranteed to commit. This inherent feature of process programs, called *guaranteed termination*, considerably exceeds and generalizes the traditional "all-or-nothing" semantics of atomicity.

The main challenge in developing a theory of transactional process management was to establish a framework to jointly reason about correct concurrency control and recovery, based on the correctness of single process programs. In addition, the theory of transactional process management makes intensive use of basic ideas that have been introduced in the context of the composite systems theory. Essentially, the interaction between hierarchical schedulers when executing transactional processes is taken into account so as to increase parallelism by applying the weak conflict order to conflicting activities. Moreover, due to the fact that both reasoning about serializability and recoverability is more complex in transactional processes than in traditional transactions, the unified theory of concurrency control and recovery has been extended and generalized in order to be made applicable to transactional processes. This has led to the notion of *correct termination* (CT) which is enforced by a process manager when executing process programs concurrently. Correct termination can be characterized by the following features:

i.) It accounts for the special structure of process programs and ensures the flexible handling of failures with appropriate alternative executions, thus enforces the guaranteed termination property.

ii.) It enforces correct interleavings of parallel processes according to dependencies stemming from both serializability and recoverability, while considering at the same time the different termination properties of single activities. Unlike other approaches addressing only parts of this problem, transactional process management covers both atomicity and isolation simultaneously and considers concurrency control and recovery at the appropriate level, the scheduling of processes.

However, a fundamental difference between the unified theory of concurrency control and recovery in traditional transactions and in transactional process management is implied by the semantics of activities. While the traditional notion assumes that a transaction can be aborted at any point in time prior to its commit, transactional process management has to consider also activities that require a process to proceed correctly after they have committed, since these activities cannot be compensated. To this end, the notion of expansion which is central to the traditional unified theory cannot be applied to transactional processes. Expansion allows to consider undo operations that would be required for failure handling purposes, only based on information about the operations of a partial schedule. But since forward recovery by the execution of (alternative) activities that are not known in advance is an important feature of transactional process management, information needed for the completion cannot be deduced from the activities of partial process schedules such that expansion cannot be applied to processes. Therefore, appropriate mechanisms to guarantee that each partial process schedule can be completed correctly without leaving to unresolvable situations have been identified and are a vital aspect of the correct termination criterion.

In addition to the theoretical part, the work presented in this thesis has also shown how a process manager supporting CT process schedules can be implemented. To this end, the *process locking* protocol has been introduced which allows dynamic scheduling while following the restrictions that have to be applied in order to guarantee the correct termination of partial process schedules. Due to the special semantics of transactional processes, traditional approaches based on exclusive and shared locks on data objects cannot be applied. Yet process locking relaxes the strong restrictions that can be found in traditional two phase locking protocols and exploits concepts from locks with constrained sharing. Additionally, locking techniques are applied at activity level, by mapping disallowed interleavings of processes with conflicting activities to non-compatible locks. In order to immediately verify the conformance of the order in which locks are shared between processes, process locking combines ordered shared locks with timestamp ordering techniques. An interesting extension to process locking —which requires additional information on the execution costs and on the failure probabilities of single activities— has led to the cost-based scheduling of transactional processes. This allows to apply special treatment to valuable, complex and thus expensive activities and to disallow cascading aborts involving processes encompassing such activities. By considering cost information, the degree of flexibility of a process manager is considerably increased since, within the same framework, cascading aborts are allowed for certain processes while, at the same time, this is avoided for all others. Based on the WISE process support system [AFH+99], a process manager supporting the dynamic cost-based scheduling of transactional processes which is, in turn, based on the process locking protocol has actually been implemented. The process manager is part of a comprehensive framework that also supports the modeling and verification of processes. To this end, the commercial process modeling and simulation tool IvyFrame of IvyTeam [Ivy] has been extended such that cost information and failure probabilities can be assigned to single activities. Most importantly, these extensions also address the crucial requirements imposed on process programs as higher order transactions, namely the support for their correctness validation as added value service. Based on the specification of single activities, processes can be proven correct with respect to guaranteed termination at built-time, by calculating the expected cost of a process.

A further goal of this thesis is to broaden the applicability of transactional process management. While the design and implementation of a dynamic scheduling protocol provides the basis for the execution of transactional processes in composite systems, the distribution, heterogeneity, and autonomy of the component systems on top of which processes are defined and are being executed still has to be taken into account. In particular, the theory of transactional process management imposes strong restrictions on the components of a composite system in that they have to provide key transactional functionality. However, many systems that can be found in practice do not meet these requirements. The concept of transactional coordination agents (TCAs) allows to enhance subsystems and to make them transactional such that the combination of subsystem and TCA provides the necessary functionality, even when this is not the case for the individual subsystems. With these extensions, transactional process management can be applied to a broad range of composite systems and especially to various kinds of non-transactional component systems. To this end, each TCA has to support the following tasks:

i.) It has to provide support for the interaction with the subsystem it is tailored to, thereby providing a common interface towards the process manager.

ii.) It has to support the different termination properties of activities, especially compensation and retriability.

iii.) It has to guarantee the atomicity of service invocations and to provide support for correct concurrent executions in the underlying subsystems.

iv.) Finally, the tasks of a TCA also include the enforcement of orders imposed by the process manager and the guarantee of avoiding cascading aborts.

Based on the notion of CT, we have identified both the properties that have to be provided by applications or their TCAs from the point of view of the process manager as well as the minimal set of properties of applications in order to allow TCAs to implement the missing functionality.

The main benefit of the work presented in this theses is the formation of a comprehensive framework by combining all the above concepts, namely the theory of transactional process management, the process locking protocol and its cost-based extensions for dynamic process scheduling, and the transactional coordination agents for making transactional process management applicable to arbitrary non-transactional systems. This framework supports various applications, thereby considerably exceeding the functionality of current approaches and making existing solutions applicable to more complex environments. Hence, this framework has been successfully applied in various areas. First, it allows the coordination of components of composite systems consisting of different, originally independent heterogeneous, autonomous, and distributed applications. In general, coordination is required in systems in which dependencies between different components exist, for instance in the form of replicated or semantically related data, such that services executed in one system must be accompanied by the execution of services in other systems. The notion of process program allows to materialize these dependencies and to execute corresponding processes so as to enforce consistency in composite systems. Second, this framework also allows for the development of new kinds of truly distributed applications.

In terms of subsystem coordination, transactional process management has been successfully applied to computer integrated manufacturing environments as presented in Example 2.1 [MLZ+98], especially with respect to the implementation of transactional coordination agents for application systems that can be found in this area [SSAS99]. In addition, transactional process management has also been applied to the coordination of subsystems in hospital information systems [SSS00] where —aside of dependencies between applications that have to be enforced— the transfer of large volumes of data has to be taken into account. Applications of transactional process management can also be found in the area of geographic information systems [RSS98], especially when external data is managed by —albeit outside of— database systems such that consistency has to be enforced by appropriate processes. Similarly, the management of multimedia data and the generation of sophisticated index structures based on features that have to be extracted from these multimedia objects also necessitate the application of transactional processes [WBGS99]. The transactional process management approach to subsystem coordination not only allows to seamlessly encompass the diverse dependencies between systems in process programs and thus covers a large variety of applications, the basic framework, when used for coordination purposes, is also completely transparent to the user.

In terms of application development, the paradigm of transactional processes has been intensively used in the field of electronic commerce. The WISE approach to business-to-business electronic commerce [AFH+99] supports the reliable and correct concurrent and fault-tolerant execution of business processes in virtual enterprises [AFL+99, LASS00], based on the concepts of transactional process management. Furthermore, transactional processes have been proven to be well-suited for the implementation of distributed payment transactions in business-to-customer and business-to-business electronic commerce [SPS99a, SPS99b]. While transactional execution guarantees (such as, for instance, different levels of atomicity in the exchange of money and goods between clients and merchants) have been previously identified as crucial requirement for such payment interactions [CHTY96, Tyg96, Tyg98], the implementation of payments as transactional processes has considerably increased the degree of flexibility [SPS00]. Moreover, it has been shown that new kinds of applications can be supported by transactional payment processes, involving more complex interactions and accounting for a larger degree of distribution than existing approaches and protocols for payments in electronic commerce. In particular, the possibility to prove the correctness of dynamically generated payment processes —both semantically with respect to the specific constraints of payment interactions in electronic commerce as well as structurally with respect to guaranteed termination— provides key functionality which, together with correct termination that is enforced by the process manager, meets the special requirements imposed by this kind of applications [PSS00].

Finally, the theory of transactional process management has been subject to a detailed and profound comparison with related work based on a thorough classification of approaches from the areas of advanced transaction models, transactional workflows, and multiagent systems for process support. This comparison has shown that none of these existing approaches supports a joint criterion for concurrency control and recovery while, at the same time, taking into account the various constraints that can be found when executing processes on top of arbitrary components of composite systems.

10.2 Outlook

The work presented in this thesis has addressed transactional process management in composite systems following a two level fork configuration where a process manager controls the execution of processes on top of component systems. However, the type of composite systems that has been addressed in [AFPS99a, AFPS99b] allows a deeper nesting of components and arbitrary configurations. In the composite systems theory, a scheduler is associated with each component and is considered to control the execution of transactions following the traditional assumption that aborts are possible at any point in time prior to the transaction's commit. The seamless combination of both approaches, i.e., the kind of arbitrary configurations that is subject to the composite systems theory and the concept of processes as generalized transactions along with the special semantics that can be found in processes as addressed by the theory of transactional process management, is an interesting field for future work and would yet allow to build even more general and more complex applications.

The application of transactional process management to these arbitrarily nested configurations then induces a set of process managers, each associated with one component of the system. Each component is responsible for enacting processes that access local resources but that also integrate services (processes) provided by other components. Hence, each process may, in turn, be part of processes enacted by other components. When considering each of these process managers as an autonomous component, or agent, this kind of processing is strongly related to agent-based approaches to process management. In effect, each process manager would then follow the concept of *transactional cooperative coordination agent* — and would fill the gap we have detected in the classification of agent-based approaches to process management. A similar and yet comparably promising approach is to implement transactional processes by means of mobile agents. Each agent moves from component to component in order to locally invoke the process activities there. However, enforcing correct concurrent and fault-tolerant process executions in the absence of a centralized process manager then requires considerable extensions, for instance in that the individual mobile process enactment agents have to synchronize their execution by peer-to-peer communication.

Eventually, not all kinds of applications require full support for concurrency control and recovery. The generalization of transactional process management to arbitrary configurations could also be accompanied with the modularization and decomposition of the functionality of a process manager. Then, based on the requirements of applications, the necessary degree of system support, much like isolation levels in SQL, can be chosen and the overhead imposed by a process manager can be reduced for certain kinds of applications.

Finally, when considering further types of applications, the framework for supporting transactional process management on top of the components of composite systems may have to be extended. In particular, when new application systems have to be integrated, appropriate TCAs must be implemented. However, new types of applications may also require the extension of the basic framework, similar to the special requirements imposed by payment processes in electronic commerce, i.e., the support for the dynamic generation of processes and for sophisticated correctness validation.

Bibliography

"Denn obgleich die mündliche Rede lebendiger und unmittelbarer wirken mag, so hat doch das geschriebene Wort den Vorzug, daß es mit Muße gewählt und gesetzt werden konnte, daß es feststeht und in dieser vom Schreibenden wohl erwogenen und berechneten Form und Stellung wieder und wieder gelesen werden und gleichmäßig wirken kann."

Thomas Mann, Die Buddenbrooks

[AA90] D. Agrawal and A. El Abbadi. Locks with Constrained Sharing. In *Proceedings of the 9th ACM Symposium on Principles of Database Systems (PODS'90)*, pages 85–93, Nashville, Tennessee, USA, April 1990. ACM Press.

[AAA96a] G. Alonso, D. Agrawal, and A. El Abbadi. Process Synchronization in Workflow Management Systems. In *Proceedings of the 8th IEEE Symposium on Parallel and Distributed Processing (SPDP'96)*, New Orleans, Louisiana, USA, October 1996.

[AAA+96b] G. Alonso, D. Agrawal, A. El Abbadi, M. Kamath, R. Günthör, and C. Mohan. Advanced Transaction Models in Workflow Contexts. In *Proceedings of the 12th International Conference on Data Engineering (ICDE'96)*, pages 574–581, New Orleans, Louisiana, USA, February 1996. IEEE Computer Society Press.

[AAHD97] B. Arpinar, S. Arpinar, U. Halici, and A. Doğaç. Correctness of Workflows in the Presence of Concurrency. In *Proceedings of the 3rd Next Generation Information Technologies and Systems Conference (NGITS'97)*, Neve Ilan, Israel, June 1997.

[ABC+76] M. Astrahan, M. Blasgen, D. Chamberlin, K. Eswaran, J. Gray, P. Griffiths, W. King, R. Lorie, P. McJones, J. Mehl, G. Putzolu, I. Traiger, B. Wade, and V. Watson. System R: Relational Approach to Database Management. *ACM Transactions on Database Systems (TODS)*, 1(2):97–137, June 1976.

[ABC+95] M. Ajmone-Marsan, G. Balbo, G. Conte, S. Donatelli, and G. Francheschinis. *Modelling with Generalized Stochastic Petri Nets.* John Wiley & Sons, Chichester, England, 1995.

[Abe90] O. Abeln. *The CA...–Technologies in Industrial Practice.* Carl Hanser Verlag, 1990. In German.

[ABFS97] G. Alonso, S. Blott, A. Feßler, and H.-J. Schek. Correctness and Parallelism in Composite Systems. In *Proceedings of the 16th ACM Symposium on Principles of Database Systems (PODS'97)*, pages 197–208, Tucson, Arizona, USA, May 1997. ACM Press.

[ABSS00] G. Alonso, C. Beeri, H.-J. Schek, and H. Schuldt. Atomicity and Isolation for Transactional Processes. Final Report of the Work Package: "Architectural Design for Data Consistency and Execution Guarantees" of the ESPRIT project MARIFlow (A Workflow Management System for Maritime Industry), April 2000.

[AFH+99] G. Alonso, U. Fiedler, C. Hagen, A. Lazcano, H. Schuldt, and N. Weiler. WISE: Business to Business E-Commerce. In *Proceedings of the 9th International Workshop on Research Issues in Data Engineering. Information Technology for Virtual Enterprises (RIDE-VE'99)*, pages 132–139, Sydney, Australia, March 1999. IEEE Computer Society Press.

[AFL+99] G. Alonso, U. Fiedler, A. Lazcano, H. Schuldt, C. Schuler, and N. Weiler. WISE: An Infrastructure for E–Commerce. In *Proceedings of the Informatik'99 GI-Workshop Enterprise-wide and Cross-enterprise Workflow Management: Concepts, Systems, Applications*, pages 2–9, Paderborn, Germany, October 1999. Technical Report Nr. 99-07, University of Ulm, Department of Computer Science.

[AFPS99a] G. Alonso, A. Feßler, G. Pardon, and H.-J. Schek. Correctness in General Configurations of Transactional Components. In *Proceedings of the 18th ACM Symposium on Principles of Database Systems (PODS'99)*, pages 285–293, Philadelphia, Pennsylvania, USA, May/June 1999. ACM Press.

[AFPS99b] G. Alonso, A. Feßler, G. Pardon, and H.-J. Schek. Transactions in Stack, Fork, and Join Composite Systems. In *Proceedings of the 7th International Conference on Database Theory (ICDT'99)*, pages 150–168, Jerusalem, Israel, January 1999. Springer LNCS, Vol. 1540.

[AHAD99] B. Arpinar, U. Halici, S. Arpinar, and A. Doğaç. Formalization of Workflows and Correctness Issues in the Presence of Concurrency. *Journal of Distributed and Parallel Databases*, 7(2):199–248, April 1999.

[AHST97a] G. Alonso, C. Hagen, H.-J. Schek, and M. Tresch. Distributed Processing over Standalone Systems and Applications. In *Proceedings of the 23rd International Conference on Very Large Databases (VLDB'97)*, pages 575–579, Athens, Greece, August 1997. Morgan Kaufmann Publishers.

[AHST97b] G. Alonso, C. Hagen, H.-J. Schek, and M. Tresch. *Towards a Platform for Distributed Application Development*, pages 195–221. In: [DKÖS98]. Istanbul, Turkey, August 1997.

[Alo97] G. Alonso. Processes + Transactions = Distributed Applications. In *Proceedings of the 7th International Workshop on High Performance Transaction Systems (HPTS'97)*, Asilomar, California, USA, September 1997.

[AM97] G. Alonso and C. Mohan. *Workflow Management: The Next Generation of Distributed Processing Tools*, chapter 2. In: [JK97]. Kluwer Academic Publishers, 1997.

[AS96a] G. Alonso and H.-J. Schek. Database Technology in Workflow Environments. *Informatik/Informatique. Journal of the Swiss Computer Science Society*, 2(2):19–22, April 1996. Special Issue on Databases.

[AS96b] G. Alonso and H.-J. Schek. Research Issues in Large Workflow Management Systems. In *Proceedings of the NSF Workshop on Workflow and Process Automation: State-of-the-Art and Future Directions*, Athens, Georgia, USA, May 1996.

[AVA+94a] G. Alonso, R. Vingralek, D. Agrawal, Y. Breitbart, A. El Abbadi, H.-J. Schek, and G. Weikum. Unifying Concurrency Control and Recovery of Transactions. *Information Systems*, 19(1):101–115, March 1994.

[AVA+94b] G. Alonso, R. Vingralek, D. Agrawal, Y. Breitbart, A. El Abbadi, H.-J. Schek, and G. Weikum. A Unified Approach to Concurrency Control and Transaction Recovery. In *Proceedings of the 4th International Conference on Extending Database Technology (EDBT'94)*, pages 123–130, Cambridge, England, March 1994. Springer LNCS, Vol. 779.

[BBG+83] C. Beeri, P. Bernstein, N. Goodman, M. Lai, and D. Shasha. A Concurrency Control Theory for Nested Transactions. In *Proceedings of the 2nd Annual ACM Symposium on Principles of Distributed Computing (PODC'83)*, pages 45–62, Montréal, Canada, August 1983. ACM Press.

[BBG89] C. Beeri, P. Bernstein, and N. Goodman. A Model for Concurrency in Nested Transaction Systems. *Journal of the ACM*, 36(2):230–269, April 1989.

[BDG+94] A. Biliris, S. Dar, N. Gehani, H. Jagadish, and K. Ramamritham. ASSET: A System for Supporting Extended Transactions. In *Proceedings of the ACM SIGMOD International Conference on Management of Data (SIGMOD'94)*, pages 44–54, Minneapolis, Minnesota, USA, May 1994. ACM Press.

[BDS+93] Y. Breitbart, A. Deacon, H.-J. Schek, A. Sheth, and G. Weikum. Merging Application-centric and Data-centric Approaches to Support Transaction-oriented Multi-system Workflows. *ACM SIGMOD Record*, 22(3):23–30, September 1993.

[Bee00] C. Beeri. A Theory of Isolation and Atomicity. March 2000.

[Ber96] P. Bernstein. Middleware: A Model for Distributed System Services. *Communications of the ACM*, 39(2):86–98, February 1996.

[BGLL98] A. Bernstein, D. Gerstl, W.-H. Leung, and P. Lewis. Design and Performance of an Assertional Concurrency Control System. In *Proceedings of the 14th International Conference on Data Engineering (ICDE'98)*, pages 436–445, Orlando, Florida, USA, February 1998. IEEE Computer Society Press.

[BGRS91] Y. Breitbart, D. Georgakopoulos, M. Rusinkiewicz, and A. Silberschatz. On Rigorous Transaction Scheduling. *IEEE Transactions on Software Engineering*, 17(9):954–960, September 1991.

[BGS92] Y. Breitbart, H. Garcia-Molina, and A. Silberschatz. Overview of Multidatabase Transaction Management. *The VLDB Journal*, 2(1):181–239, October 1992.

[BGS95] Y. Breitbart, H. Garcia-Molina, and A. Silberschatz. *Transaction Management in Multidatabase Systems*, chapter 28. In: [Kim95]. Addison-Wesley, 1995.

[Bha87] B. Bhargava, editor. *Concurrency Control and Reliability in Distributed Systems.* Van Nostrand Reinhold Company, New York, USA, 1987.

[BHG87] P. Bernstein, V. Hadzilacos, and N. Goodman. *Concurrency Control and Recovery in Database Systems.* Addison-Wesley, 1987.

[BK96] F. Bause and P. Kritzinger. *Stochastic Petri Nets.* Vieweg, Wiesbaden, Germany, 1996.

[BL93] A. Bernstein and P. Lewis. High Performance Transaction Systems Using Transaction Semantics. Technical Report TR No. 93/05, Department of Computer Science, State University of New York at Stony Brook, July 1993.

[BN97] P. Bernstein and E. Newcomer. *Principles of Transaction Processing.* Morgan Kaufmann Publishers, 1997.

[Box98] D. Box. *Essential COM.* Addison-Wesley, 1998.

[BP95] R. Barga and C. Pu. A Practical and Modular Implementation of Extended Transaction Models. In *Proceedings of the 21st International Conference on Very Large Databases (VLDB'95)*, pages 206–217, Zürich, Switzerland, September 1995. Morgan Kaufmann Publishers.

[BR92] B. Badrinath and K. Ramamritham. Semantics-Based Concurrency Control: Beyond Commutativity. *ACM Transactions on Database Systems (TODS)*, 17(1):163–199, March 1992.

[BS87] I. Bronstein and A. Semendjajew. *Compendium of Mathematics.* B. G. Teubner Verlagsgesellschaft, Leipzig, Germany, 23rd edition, 1987. In German.

[BSW79] P. Bernstein, D. Shipman, and W. Wong. Formal Aspects of Serializability in Database Concurrency Control. *IEEE Transactions on Software Engineering*, SE-5(3):203–216, May 1979.

[BSW88] C. Beeri, H.-J. Schek, and G. Weikum. Multi–Level Transaction Management, Theoretical Art or Practical Need? In *Proceedings of the 1st International Conference on Extending Database Technology (EDBT'88)*, pages 134–154, Venice, Italy, March 1988. Springer LNCS, Vol. 303.

[Buc99] R. Buck-Emden. *The Technology of the SAP R/3 System.* Addison Wesley, 4th edition, 1999. In German.

[CD96] Q. Chen and U. Dayal. A Transactional Nested Process Management System. In *Proceedings of the 12th International Conference on Data Engineering (ICDE'96)*, pages 566–573, New Orleans, Louisiana, USA, February/March 1996. IEEE Computer Society Press.

[CD97a] S. Chaudhuri and U. Dayal. An Overview of Data Warehousing and OLAP Technology. *ACM SIGMOD Record*, 26(1):65–74, March 1997.

[CD97b] Q. Chen and U. Dayal. Failure Handling for Transaction Hierarchies. In *Proceedings of the 13th International Conference on Data Engineering (ICDE'97)*, pages 245–254, Birmingham, England, April 1997. IEEE Computer Society Press.

[CGH+94] S. Chawathe, H. Garcia-Molina, J. Hammer, K. Ireland, Y. Papakonstantinou, J. Ullman, and J. Widom. The TSIMMIS Project: Integration of Heterogeneous Information Systems. In *Proceedings of the 10th Meeting of the Information Processing Society of Japan (IPSJ'94)*, pages 7–18, Tokyo, Japan, October 1994.

[CHN+95] W. Cody, L. Haas, W. Niblack, M. Arya, M. Carey, R. Fagin, M. Flickner, D. Lee, D. Petkovic, P. Schwarz, J. Thomas, M. Tork Roth, J. Williams, and E. Wimmers. Querying Multimedia Data from Multiple Repositories by Content: The Garlic Project. In *Proceedings of the 3rd IFIP Conference on Visual Database Systems (VDB'95)*, pages 17–35, Lausanne, Switzerland, March 1995. Chapman & Hall.

[CHRW98] A. Cichocki, A. Helal, M. Rusinkiewicz, and D. Woelk. *Workflow and Process Automation: Concepts and Technology.* Kluwer Academic Publishers, 1998.

[CHS+95] M. Carey, L. Haas, P. Schwarz, M. Arya, W. Cody, R. Fagin, M. Flickner, A. Luniewski, W. Niblack, D. Petkovic, J. Thomas, J. Williams, and E. Wimmers. Towards Heterogeneous Multimedia Information Systems: The Garlic Approach. In *Proceedings of the 5th International Workshop on Research Issues in Data Engineering. Distributed Object Management (RIDE-DOM'95)*, pages 124–131, Taipei, Taiwan, March 1995. IEEE Computer Society Press.

[CHTY96] J. Camp, M. Harkavy, D. Tygar, and B. Yee. Anonymous Atomic Transactions. In *Proceedings of the 2nd USENIX Workshop on Electronic Commerce*, pages 123–133, Oakland, California, USA, November 1996. The USENIX Association.

[Cia95] G. Ciardo. Discrete-Time Markovian Stochastic Petri Nets. Technical Report NASA CR-195039, ICASE Report No. 95-9, NASA Langley Research Center, Institute for Computer Applications in Science and Engineering (ICASE), Hampton, Virginia, USA, February 1995.

[Clo00] Cloverleaf: Functional Specification. White Paper, 2000. Healthcare.com, Marietta, Georgia, USA. `http://www.healthcare.com`.

[CoC96] CoCreate Software. *WorkManager, Release 3.5*, 1996. `http://www.cocreate.com`.

[CR90] P. Chrysanthis and K. Ramamritham. ACTA: A Framework for Secifying and Reasoning About Transaction Structure and Behavior. In *Proceedings of the ACM SIGMOD International Conference on Management of Data (SIGMOD'90)*, pages 194–203, Atlantic City, New Jersey, USA, May 1990. ACM Press.

[CR91] P. Chrysanthis and K. Ramamritham. A Formalism for Extended Transaction Models. In *Proceedings of the 17th International Conference on Very Large Databases (VLDB'91)*, pages 103–112, Barcelona, Spain, September 1991. Morgan Kaufmann Publishers.

[CR94] P. Chrysanthis and K. Ramamritham. Synthesis of Extended Transaction Models Using ACTA. *ACM Transactions on Database Systems (TODS)*, 19(3):450–491, May 1994.

[Dav78] C. Davies. Data Processing Spheres of Control. *IBM Systems Journal*, 17(2):179–198, 1978.

[dBKV98] R. de By, W. Klas, and J. Veijalainen, editors. *Transaction Management Support for Cooperative Applications*. Kluwer Academic Publishers, 1998.

[DBT+99] A. Doğaç, C. Beeri, A. Tumer, M. Ezbiderli, N. Tatbul, C. Icdem, G. Erus, O. Cetinkaya, and N. Hamali. *MARIFlow: A Workflow Management System for Maritime Industry*, pages 33–51. In: [SB99]. Edicoes Salamandra Lda, 1999.

[DD96] L. Do and P. Drew. Interactions of Concurrent Workflow Processes over Shared Information. In *Proceedings of the NSF Workshop on Workflow and Process Automation in Information Systems*, Athens, Georgia, USA, May 1996.

[Dea95] A. Deacon. *Transactional Workflows Support using Middleware*, pages 205–214. In: [HSW95]. Springer-Verlag, 1995.

[Der70] C. Derman. *Finite State Markovian Decision Processes*, volume 67 of *Mathematics in Science and Engineering*. Academic Press, New York, USA, 1970.

[DGA+97] A. Doğaç, E. Gokkoca, S. Arpinar, P. Koksal, I. Cingil, B. Arpinar, N. Tatbul, P. Karagoz, U. Halici, and M. Atinel. *Design and Implementation of a Distributed Workflow Management System: METUFlow*, pages 60–90. In: [DKÖS98]. Istanbul, Turkey, August 1997.

[DHL90] U. Dayal, M. Hsu, and R. Ladin. Organizing Long-Running Activities with Triggers and Transactions. In *Proceedings of the ACM SIGMOD International Conference on Management of Data (SIGMOD'90)*, pages 204–214, Atlantic City, New Jersey, USA, May 1990. ACM Press.

[DHL91] U. Dayal, M. Hsu, and R. Ladin. A Transactional Model for Long–Running Activities. In *Proceedings of the 17th International Conference on Very Large Databases (VLDB'91)*, pages 113–122, Barcelona, Spain, September 1991. Morgan Kaufmann Publishers.

[DKÖS98] A. Doğaç, L. Kalinichenko, T. Özsu, and A. Sheth, editors. *Workflow Management Systems and Interoperability*, volume 164 of *NATO ASI Series F: Computer and System Sciences*. Springer-Verlag, 1998. Proceedings of the NATO Advanced Study Institute (ASI) on Workflow Management Sysytems. Istanbul, Turkey, August 1997.

[DS93] U. Dayal and M.-C. Shan. Issues in Operation Flow Management for Long-Running Acivities. *Bulletin of the IEEE Technical Committee on Data Engineering*, 16(1):41–44, March 1993. Special Issue on Workflow and Extended Transaction Systems.

[DSW94] A. Deacon, H.-J. Schek, and G. Weikum. Semantics-Based Multilevel Transaction Management in Federated Systems. In *Proceedings of the 10th International Conference on Data Engineering (ICDE'94)*, pages 452–461, Houston, Texas, USA, February 1994. IEEE Computer Society Press.

[ED97] A. Elmagarmid and W. Du. *Workflow Management: State of the Art Versus State of the Products*, pages 1–17. In: [DKÖS98]. Istanbul, Turkey, August 1997.

[EG96] J. Eder and H. Groiss. *A Workflow Management System Based on Active Databases*, chapter 22. In: [VB96]. International Thompson Publishing, 1996. In German.

[e*G00] e*Gate Integrator — The eBusiness Integration Platform. White Paper, April 2000. Software Technologies Corporation. `http://www.stc.com`.

[EGL97] J. Eder, H. Groiss, and W. Liebhart. *The Workflow Management System Panta Rhei*, pages 129–144. In: [DKÖS98]. Istanbul, Turkey, August 1997.

[EGLT76] K. Eswaran, J. Gray, R. Lorie, and I. Traiger. The Notions of Consistency and Predicate Locks in a Database System. *Communications of the ACM*, 19(11):624–633, November 1976.

[EL95] J. Eder and W. Liebhart. The Workflow Activity Model WAMO. In *Proceedings of the 3rd International Conference on Cooperative Information Systems (CoopIS'95)*, pages 87–98, Vienna, Austria, May 1995.

[EL96] J. Eder and W. Liebhart. Workflow Recovery. In *Proceedings of the 1st IFCIS International Conference on Cooperative Information Systems (CoopIS'96)*, pages 124–132, Brussels, Belgium, June 1996. IEEE Computer Science Press.

[eLi00] Enterprise Application Integration (EAI): Providing Stability in the Whirlwind of E–Commerce. White Paper, May 2000. BEA Systems, Inc., E-Commerce Integration Division.

[ELLR90] A. Elmagarmid, Y. Leu, W. Litwin, and M. Rusinkiewicz. A Multidatabse Transaction Model for InterBase. In *Proceedings of the 16th International Conference on Very Large Databases (VLDB'90)*, pages 507–518, Brisbane, Australia, August 1990. Morgan Kaufmann Publishers.

[Elm92] A. Elmagarmid, editor. *Database Transaction Models for Advanced Applications*. Morgan Kaufmann Publishers, 1992.

[ERS99] A. Elmagarmid, M. Rusinkiewicz, and A. Sheth, editors. *Management of Heterogeneous and Autonomous Database Systems*. Morgan Kaufmann Publishers, 1999.

[Feß99] A. Feßler. *A Generalized Transaction Theory for Database and Non-Database Tasks*. PhD thesis, Swiss Federal Institute of Technology Zürich, 1999. Diss. ETH Nr. 13445. In German.

[FFM94] T. Finin, R. Fritzson, and D. McKay. KQML as an Agent Communication Language. In *Proceedings of the 3rd International Conference on Information and Knowledge Management (CIKM'94)*, pages 456–463, Gaithersburg, Maryland, USA, November/December 1994. ACM Press.

[FG96] S. Franklin and A. Graesser. Is it an Agent, or Just a Program?: A Taxonomy for Autonomous Agents. In *Proceedings of the 3rd International Workshop on Intelligent Agents: Agent Theories, Architectures, and Languages (ATAL'96)*, pages 21–35, Budapest, Hungary, August 1996. Springer LNAI, Vol. 1193.

[FÖ89] A. Farrag and T. Özsu. Using Semantic Knowledge of Transactions to Increase Concurrency. *ACM Transactions on Database Systems (TODS)*, 14(4):503–525, December 1989.

[FS99] A. Feßler and H.-J. Schek. A Generalized Transaction Theory for Database and Non-database Tasks. In *Proceedings of the 5th International Euro-Par Conference (Euro-Par'99)*, pages 459–468, Toulouse, France, August/September 1999. Springer LNCS, Vol. 1685. Topic 05: Parallel and Distributed Databases.

[GGK$^+$91a] H. Garcia-Molina, D. Gawlick, J. Klein, K. Kleissner, and K. Salem. Coordinating Activities Through Extended Sagas: A Summary. In *Proceedings of the 36th IEEE Computer Society International Conference (COMPCON SPRING'91)*, pages 568–573, San Francisco, California, USA, February/March 1991. IEEE Computer Society Press.

[GGK$^+$91b] H. Garcia-Molina, D. Gawlick, J. Klein, K. Kleissner, and K. Salem. Modeling Long-Running Activities as Nested Sagas. *Bulletin of the IEEE Technical Committee on Data Engineering*, 14(1):14–18, March 1991.

[GH94] D. Georgakopoulos and M. Hornick. A Framework for Enforceable Specification of Extended Transaction Models and Transaction Workflows. *International Journal of Cooperative Information Systems (IJCIS)*, 3(3):599–617, 1994.

[GHK93] D. Georgakopoulos, M. Hornick, and P. Krychniak. An Environment for the Specification and Management of Extended Transactions in DOMS. In *Proceedings of the 3rd International Workshop on Research Issues in Data Engineering. Interoperability in Multidatabase (RIDE-IMS'93)*, pages 253–257, Vienna, Austria, April 1993. IEEE Computer Society Press.

[GHKM94] D. Georgakopoulos, M. Hornik, P. Krychniak, and F. Manola. Specification and Management of Extended Transactions in a Programmable Transaction Environment. In *Proceeding of the 10th International Conference on Data Engineering (ICDE'94)*, pages 462–473, Houston, Texas, USA, February 1994. IEEE Computer Society Press.

[GHM$^+$93] D. Georgakopoulos, M. Hornick, F. Manola, M. Brodie, S. Heiler, F. Nayeri, and B. Hurwitz. An Extended Transaction Environment for Workflows in Distributed Object Computing. *Bulletin of the IEEE Technical Committee on Data Engineering*, 16(2):24–27, March 1993. Special Issue on Workflow and Extended Transaction Systems.

[GHM96] D. Georgakopoulos, M. Hornick, and F. Manola. Customizing Transaction Models and Mechanisms in a Programmable Environment Supporting Reliable Workflow Automation. *IEEE Transactions on Knowledge and Data Engineering (TKDE)*, 8(4):630–649, August 1996.

[GHS95] D. Georgakopoulos, M. Hornick, and A. Sheth. An Overview of Workflow Management: From Process Modeling to Workflow Automation Infrastructure. *Distributed and Parallel Databases*, 3(2):119–153, April 1995.

[GK94] M. Genesereth and S. Ketchpel. Software Agents. *Communications of the ACM*, 37(7):48–53, July 1994.

[GM83] H. Garcia-Molina. Using Semantic Knowledge for Transaction Processing in a Distributed Database. *ACM Transactions on Database Systems (TODS)*, 8(2):186–213, June 1983.

[GMB+81] J. Gray, P. McJones, M. Blasgen, B. Lindsay, R. Lorie, T. Price, F. Putzolu, and I. Traiger. The Recovery Manager of the System R Database Manager. *ACM Computing Surveys*, 13(2):223–243, June 1981.

[GPQ+97] H. Garcia-Molina, Y. Papakonstantinou, D. Quass, A. Rajaraman, Y. Sagiv, J. Ullman, V. Vassalos, and J. Widom. The TSIMMIS Approach to Mediation: Data Models and Languages. *Journal of Intelligent Information Systems*, 8(2):117–132, March/April 1997.

[GR93] J. Gray and A. Reuter. *Transaction Processing: Concepts and Techniques*. Morgan Kaufmann Publishers, 1993.

[Gra80] J. Gray. A Transaction Model. In *Proceedings of the 7th Colloquium on Automta, Languages and Programming*, pages 282–298, Noordwijkerhout, The Netherlands, July 1980. Springer LNCS, Vol. 85.

[Gra81] J. Gray. The Transaction Concept: Virtues and Limitations. In *Proceedings of the 7th International Conference on Very Large Databases (VLDB'81)*, pages 144–154, Cannes, France, September 1981. IEEE Computer Society Press. Invited paper.

[Gra99] J. Gray. What Next? A Dozen Information-Technology Research Goals. Technical Report MS-TR-99-50, Microsoft Research, Advanced Technology Division, Redmond, Washington, USA, June 1999. Turing Lecture.

[GRS91] D. Georgakopoulos, M. Rusinkiewicz, and A. Sheth. On Serializability of Multidatabase Transactions Through Forced Local Conflicts. In *Proceedings of the 7th International Conference on Data Engineering (ICDE'91)*, pages 314–323, Kobe, Japan, April 1991. IEEE Computer Society Press.

[GRS94] D. Georgakopoulos, M. Rusinkiewicz, and A. Sheth. Using Tickets to Enforce the Serializability of Multidatabase Transactions. *IEEE Transactions on Knowledge and Data Engineering (TKDE)*, 6(1):166–180, February 1994.

[GS87] H. Garcia-Molina and K. Salem. Sagas. In *Proceedings of the ACM SIGMOD International Conference on Management of Data (SIGMOD'87)*, pages 249–259, San Francisco, California, USA, May 1987. ACM Press.

[HA98a] C. Hagen and G. Alonso. Beyond the Black Box: Event-based Inter-Process Communication in Process Support Systems. Technical Report No. 303, Department of Computer Science, Swiss Federal Institute of Technology Zürich, July 1998.

[HA98b] C. Hagen and G. Alonso. Flexible Exception Handling in Process Support Systems. Technical Report No. 290, Department of Computer Science, Swiss Federal Institute of Technology Zürich, February 1998.

[HA98c] C. Hagen and G. Alonso. Flexible Exception Handling in the OPERA Process Support System. In *Proceedings of the 18th International Conference on Distributed Computing Systems (ICDCS'98)*, pages 526–533, Amsterdam, The Netherlands, September 1998. IEEE Computer Society Press.

[HA99a] C. Hagen and G. Alonso. Beyond the Black Box: Event-based Inter-Process Communication in Process Support Systems. In *Proceedings of the 19th International Conference on Distributed Computing Systems (ICDCS'99)*, pages 450–457, Austin, Texas, USA, June 1999. IEEE Computer Society Press.

[HA99b] C. Hagen and G. Alonso. Highly Available Process Support Systems: Implementing Backup Mechanisms. In *Proceedings of the 18th Symposium on Reliable Distributed Systems (SRDS'99)*, pages 112–121, Lausanne, Switzerland, October 1999. IEEE Computer Society Press.

[Had83] V. Hadzilacos. An Operational Model for Database System Reliability. In *Proceedings of the 2nd ACM Symposium on Principles of Database Systems (PODS'83)*, pages 244–257, Atlanta, Georgia, USA, March 1983. ACM Press.

[Hag99] C. Hagen. *A Generic Kernel for Reliable Process Support.* PhD thesis, Swiss Federal Institute of Technology (ETH) Zürich, 1999. Diss. ETH Nr. 13114.

[Has96] H. Hasse. *A Unified Theory for Correct Parallelization and Fault-Tolerant Execution of Database Transactions.* PhD thesis, Swiss Federal Institute of Technology Zürich, 1996. Diss. ETH Nr. 11569. In German.

[Hay99] C. Hayes. Agents in a Nutshell — A Very Brief Introduction. *IEEE Transactions on Knowledge and Data Engineering (TKDE)*, 11(1):127–132, January/February 1999.

[HBS73] C. Hewitt, P. Bishop, and R. Steiger. A Universal Modular ACTOR Formalism for Artificial Intelligence. In *Proceedings of the 3rd International Joint Conference on Artificial Intelligence (IJCAI'73)*, pages 235–245, Stanford, California, USA, August 1973.

[HGW+95] J. Hammer, H. Garcia-Molina, J. Widom, W. Labio, and Y. Zhuge. The Stanford Data Warehousing Project. *Bulletin of the IEEE Technical Committee on Data Engineering*, 18(2):41–48, June 1995. Special Issue on Materialized Views and Data Warehousing.

[Hol95] D. Hollingsworth. *Workflow Management Coalition: The Workflow Reference Model.* Workflow Management Coalition, January 1995. Document TC00-1003. http://www.wfmc.org.

[HR83] T. Härder and A. Reuter. Principles of Transaction–Oriented Database Recovery. *ACM Computing Surveys*, 15(4):287–317, December 1983.

[HS96] H. Hasse and H.-J. Schek. Unified Theory for Classical and Advanced Transaction Models. In *Proceedings of the Dagstuhl Seminar "Object Orientation with Parallelism and Persistence"*, pages 127–150, Schloss Dagstuhl, Germany, April 1996. Kluwer Academic Publishers.

[HS98a] M. Huhns and M. Singh. *Agents and Multiagent Systems: Themes, Approaches and Challenges*, chapter 1, pages 1–27. In: [HS98b]. Morgan Kaufmann Publishers, 1998.

[HS98b] M. Huhns and M. Singh, editors. *Readings in Agents.* Morgan Kaufmann Publishers, 1998.

[HSK98] M. Huhns, M. Singh, and T. Ksiezyk. Global Information Management via Local Autonomous Agents. In *[HS98b]*, pages 36–45. Morgan Kaufmann Publishers, 1998.

[HSW95] F. Huber-Wäschle, H. Schauer, and P. Widmeyer, editors. *GISI 95 — Challenges of a Global Information Network for Computer Science*, Informatik Aktuell, Zürich, Switzerland, September 1995. German Society for Computer Science (GI) and Swiss Computer Science Society (SI), Springer-Verlag. In German.

[IBM] IBM, International Business Machines Corporation. `http://www.ibm.com`.

[Ivy] IvyTeam, Zug, Switzerland. `http://www.ivyteam.com`.

[JB96] S. Jablonski and C. Bußler. *Workflow Management: Modeling Concepts, Architecture, and Implementation.* International Thomson Computer Press, 1996.

[JFN+00] N. Jennings, P. Faratin, T. Norman, P. O'Brien, and B. Odgers. Autonomous Agents for Business Process Management. *International Journal of Applied Artificial Intelligence*, 14(2):145–189, 2000.

[JK97] S. Jajodia and L. Kerschberg, editors. *Advanced Transaction Models and Architectures.* Kluwer Academic Publishers, 1997.

[JNF98] N. Jennings, T. Norman, and P. Faratin. ADEPT: An Agent-Based Approach to Business Process Management. *ACM SIGMOD Record*, 27(4):32–39, December 1998.

[KAGM96] M. Kamath, G. Alonso, R. Günthör, and C. Mohan. Providing High Availability in Very Large Workflow Management Systems. In *Proceedings of the 5th International Conference on Extending Database Theory (EDBT'96)*, pages 427–442, Avignon, France, March 1996. Springer LNCS, Vol. 1057.

[Kim95] W. Kim, editor. *Modern Database Systems: The Object Model, Interoperability and Beyond.* Addison-Wesley, 1995.

[Kle91] J. Klein. Advanced Rule Driven Transaction Management. In *Proceedings of the 36th IEEE Computer Society International Conference (COMPCON SPRING'91)*, pages 562–567, San Francisco, California, USA, February/March 1991. IEEE Computer Society Press.

[KLS90] H. Korth, E. Levy, and A. Silberschatz. A Formal Approach to Recovery by Compensating Transactions. In *Proceedings of the 16th International Conference on Very Large Databases (VLDB'90)*, pages 95–106, Brisbane, Australia, August 1990. Morgan Kaufmann Publishers.

[Klu96] M. Klusch. *Rational-Cooperative Discovery of Inter-Database Dependencies.* PhD thesis, Christian-Albrechts University of Kiel, December 1996. In German.

[Klu99] M. Klusch, editor. *Intelligent Information Agents — Agent-Based Information Discovery and Management on the Internet.* Springer-Verlag, 1999.

[KR88] J. Klein and A. Reuter. Migrating Transactions. In *Proceedings of the International Workshop on the Future Trends of Distributed Computing Systems in the 1990s*, pages 512–520, Hong Kong, September 1988. IEEE Computer Society Press.

[KR96a] M. Kamath and K. Ramamritham. Bridging the Gap between Transaction Management and Workflow Management. In *Proceedings of the NSF Workshop on Workflow and Process Automation in Information Systems*, Athens, Georgia, USA, May 1996.

[KR96b] M. Kamath and K. Ramamritham. Correctness Issues in Workflow Management. *Distributed Systems Engineering Journal*, 3(4):213–221, December 1996.

[KR98] M. Kamath and K. Ramamritham. Failure Handling and Coordinated Execution of Concurrent Workflows. In *Proceedings of the 14th International Conference on Data Engineering (ICDE'98)*, pages 334–341, Orlando, Florida, USA, February 1998. IEEE Computer Society Press.

[KS88] H. Korth and G. Speegle. Formal Model of Correctness Without Serializability. In *Proceedings of the ACM SIGMOD International Conference on Management of Data (SIGMOD'88)*, pages 379–386, Chicago, Illinois, USA, June 1988. ACM Press.

[KS90] H. Korth and G. Speegle. Long-Duration Transactions in Software Design Projects. In *Proceedings of the 6th International Conference on Data Engineering (ICDE'90)*, pages 568–574, Los Angeles, California, USA, February 1990. IEEE Computer Society Press.

[KS94] H. Korth and G. Speegle. Formal Aspects of Concurrency Control in Long-Duration Transaction Systems Using the NT/PV Model. *ACM Transactions on Database Systems (TODS)*, 19(3):492–535, September 1994.

[KTWK98] J. Klingemann, T. Tesch, J. Wäsch, and W. Klas. *The TransCoop Transaction Model*, chapter 7. In: [dBKV98]. Kluwer Academic Publishers, 1998.

[Kum96] V. Kumar, editor. *Performance of Concurrency Control Mechanisms in Centralized Database Systems*. Prentice Hall, New Jersey, 1996.

[LASS00] A. Lazcano, G. Alonso, H. Schuldt, and C. Schuler. The WISE Approach to Electronic Commerce. *International Journal of Computer Systems Science & Engineering*, 15(5):343–355, September 2000. Special Issue on Flexible Workflow Technology Driving the Networked Economy.

[Ley95] F. Leymann. Supporting Business Transactions via Partial Backward Recovery in Workflow Management Systems. In *Proceedings of Datenbanksysteme in Büro, Technik und Wissenschaft (BTW'95)*, Informatik Aktuell, pages 51–70, Dresden, Germany, March 1995. Springer Verlag.

[Ley96] F. Leymann. *Transaction Concepts for Workflow Management Systems*, chapter 19. In: [VB96]. International Thompson Publishing, 1996. In German.

[Lin99] D. Linthicum. Enterprise Application Integration from the Ground Up. *Software Development Magazine*, April 1999. `http://www.sdmagazine.com`.

[Lin00] D. Linthicum. EAI — Application Integration Exposed. *Software Magazine*, February/March 2000. `http://www.softwaremag.com`.

[LKS91] E. Levy, H. Korth, and A. Silberschatz. A Theory of Relaxed Atomicity. In *Proceedings of the 10th Annual ACM Symposium on Principles of Distributed Computing (PODC'91)*, pages 95–109, Montréal, Canada, August 1991. ACM Press.

[LMR90] W. Litwin, L. Mark, and N. Roussopoulos. Interoperability of Multiple Autonomous Databases. *ACM Computing Surveys*, 22(3):267–293, September 1990.

[LSV95] F. Leymann, H.-J. Schek, and G. Vossen, editors. *Transactional Workflows*, Dagstuhl Seminar Report No. 152, Schloss Dagstuhl, Germany, July 1995.

[LV00] J. Lechtenbörger and G. Vossen. On Herbrand Semantics and Conflict Serializability of Read-Write Transactions. In *Proceedings of the 19th ACM Symposium on Principles of Database Systems (PODS'00)*, pages 187–194, Dallas, Texas, USA, June 2000. ACM Press.

[Lyn83] N. Lynch. Multilevel Atomicity – A New Correctness Criterion for Database Concurrency Control. *ACM Transactions on Database Systems (TODS)*, 8(4):484–502, December 1983.

[MB00] U. Mende and A. Berthold. *SAP Business Workflow — Concepts, Development, Application.* Addison-Wesley, 2nd edition, 2000. In German.

[MEN98] M. Magnanelli, A. Erni, and M. Norrie. A Web Agent for the Maintenance of a Database of Academic Contacts. *INFORMATICA — International Journal of Computing and Informatics*, 22(4), December 1998.

[MHL+92] C. Mohan, D. Haderle, B. Lindsay, H. Pirahesh, and P. Schwarz. ARIES: A Transaction Recovery Method Supporting Fine-Granularity Locking and Partial Rollbacks Using Write-Ahead Logging. *ACM Transactions on Database Systems (TODS)*, 17(1):94–162, March 1992.

[MLL97] M. Merz, B. Liberman, and W. Lamersdorf. Using Mobile Agents to support Interorganizational Workflow Management. *International Journal of Applied Artificial Intelligence*, 11(6):551–569, September 1997.

[MLZ+98] M. Meier, U. Leonhardt, E. Zwicker, M. Norrie, A. Kobler, H.-J. Schek, and H. Schuldt. Computer Integrated Methods based on Federated Databases to Improve Product Modularity and Document Flow in Design Processes. Final Report of Project 3008.2, Swiss Commission of Technology and Innovation (KTI), Zürich, Switzerland, July 1998.

[MN00] M. Magnanelli and M. Norrie. Databases for Agents and Agents for Databases. In *Proceedings of 2nd International Bi-Conference Workshop on Agent-Oriented Information Systems (AOIS'00)*, Stockholm, Sweden, June 2000.

[Mos85] J. Moss. *Nested Transactions: An Approach to Reliable Distributed Computing.* The MIT Press, 1985.

[Mos87] J. Moss. *Nested Transactions: An Introduction*, chapter 14, pages 395–425. In: [Bha87]. Van Nostrand Reinhold Company, 1987.

[MQS99] *MQSeries Workflow — Concepts and Architecture, Version 3.2.1*, third edition, September 1999. IBM, International Business Machines Corporation.

[MQS00a] MQSeries Adapters. White Paper, March 2000. IBM, International Business Machines Corporation.

[MQS00b] MQSeries Integrator: A Technical Overview. White Paper, 2000. IBM, International Business Machines Corporation.

[MQS00c] MQSeries Publish/Subscribe User's Guide. IBM Red Book, No. GC34-5269-05, 2000. IBM, International Business Machines Corporation.

[MR99] R. Müller and E. Rahm. Rule-Based Dynamic Modification of Workflows in a Medical Domain. In *Proceedings of Datenbanksysteme in Büro, Technik und Wissenschaft (BTW'99)*, pages 429–448, Freiburg, Germany, March 1999. Springer Verlag.

[MRKN92] P. Muth, T. Rakow, W. Klas, and E. Neuhold. *A Transaction Model for an Open Publication Environment*, chapter 6. In: [Elm92]. Morgan Kaufmann Publishers, 1992.

[MRKS92] S. Mehrotra, R. Rastogi, H. Korth, and A. Silberschatz. A Transaction Model for Multidatabase Systems. Technical Report TR-92-14, Department of Computer Science, University of Texas at Austin, USA, March 1992.

[MRSK92] S. Mehrotra, R. Rastogi, A. Silberschatz, and H. Korth. A Transaction Model for Multidatabase Systems. In *Proceedings of the 12th International Conference on Distributed Computing Systems (ICDCS'92)*, pages 56–63, Yokohama, Japan, June 1992. IEEE Computer Society Press.

[Mül93] J. Müller, editor. *Distributed Artificial Intelligence: Techniques and Applications.* BI Wissenschaftsverlag, 1993. In German.

[MWGW99] P. Muth, J. Weißenfels, M. Gillmann, and G. Weikum. Integrating Light-Weight Workflow Management Systems within Existing Business Environments. In *Proceedings of the 15th International Conference on Data Engineering (ICDE'99)*, pages 286–293, Sydney, Australia, March 1999. IEEE Computer Society Press.

[Nel95] B. Nelson. *Stochastic Modeling – Analysis and Simulation.* Mc Graw-Hill, New York, USA, 1995.

[NJFM96] T. Norman, N. Jennings, P. Faratin, and E. Mamdani. Designing and Implementing a Multi-Agent Architecture for Business Process Management. In *Proceedings of the 3rd International Workshop on Intelligent Agents: Agent Theories, Architectures, and Languages (ATAL'96)*, pages 261–275, Budapest, Hungary, August 1996. Springer LNAI, Vol. 1193.

[NSSW94a] M. Norrie, W. Schaad, H.-J. Schek, and M. Wunderli. CIM Through Database Coordination. In *Proceedings of the 4th International Conference on Data and Knowledge Systems for Manufacturing and Engineering (DKSME'94)*, volume 2, pages 668–673, Hong Kong, May 1994.

[NSSW94b] M. Norrie, W. Schaad, H.-J. Schek, and M. Wunderli. Exploiting Multidatabase Technology for CIM. Technical Report No. 219, Department of Computer Science, Swiss Federal Institute of Technology Zürich, July 1994.

[NW96] M. Norrie and M. Wunderli. Agent–Based Tool Integration for Distributed Information Systems. In *Proceedings of the 8th International Conference on Advanced Information System Engineering (CAiSE'96)*, pages 383–401, Heraklion, Greece, May 1996. Springer LNCS, Vol. 1080.

[NW97] M. Norrie and M. Wunderli. Tool Agents in Coordinated Information Systems. *Information Systems*, 22(2):59–77, June 1997.

[NWM+94] M. Norrie, M. Wunderli, R. Montau, U. Leonhardt, W. Schaad, and H.-J. Schek. Coordination Approaches for CIM. In *Proceedings of the European Workshop on Integrated Manufacturing Systems Engineering*, pages 223–232, Grenoble, France, December 1994.

[OHE96] R. Orfali, D. Harkey, and J. Edwards. *The Essential Distributed Objects Survival Guide*. John Wiley & Sons, 1996.

[OHE99] R. Orfali, D. Harkey, and J. Edwards. *Client/Server Survival Guide*. John Wiley & Sons, 3rd edition, 1999.

[OMG] The Object Management Group. `http://www.omg.org`.

[O'N86] P. O'Neil. The Escrow Transaction Model. *ACM Transactions on Database Systems (TODS)*, 11(4):405–430, December 1986.

[Ora] Oracle Corporation. `http://www.oracle.com`.

[Ora99] Oracle Corporation. *Oracle Workflow Server & Client, Release 2.5.1*, 1999.

[Pap79] C. Papadimitriou. The Serializability of Concurrent Database Updates. *Journal of the ACM*, 26(4):631–653, October 1979.

[Pap86] C. Papadimitriou. *Database Concurrency Control*. Computer Science Press, 1986.

[Pap99] M. Papazoglou. The Role of Agent Technology in Business to Business Electronic Commerce. In *Proceedings of the 3rd International Workshop on Cooperative Information Agents (CIA'99)*, pages 245–264, Stockholm, Sweden, July 1999. Springer LNAI Vol. 1652.

[PGGU95] Y. Papakonstantinou, A. Gupta, H. Garcia-Molina, and J. Ullman. A Query Translation Scheme for Rapid Implementation of Wrappers. In *Proceedings of the 4th International Conference on Deductive and Object-Oriented Databases (DOOD'95)*, pages 161–186, Singapore, December 1995. Springer LNCS, Vol. 1013.

[PLS92] M. Papazoglou, S. Laufmann, and T. Sellis. An Organizational Framework for Cooperating Intelligent Information Systems. *International Journal of Intelligent and Cooperative Information Systems*, 1(1):169–202, March 1992.

[PSS00] A. Popovici, H. Schuldt, and H.-J. Schek. Generation and Verification of Heterogeneous Purchase Processes. In *Proceedings of the International Workshop on Technologies for E-Services (TES'00)*, Cairo, Egypt, September 2000.

[Raz92] Y. Raz. The Principle of Commitment Ordering, or Guaranteeing Serializability in a Heterogeneous Environment of Multiple Autonomous Resource Managers Using Atomic Commitment. In *Proceedings of the 18th International Conference on Very Large Databases (VLDB'92)*, pages 292–312, Vancouver, Canada, August 1992. Morgan Kaufmann Publishers.

[RC96] K. Ramamritham and P. Chrysanthis. A Taxonomy of Correctness Criteria in Database Applications. *The VLDB Journal*, 5(1):85–97, January 1996.

[RD98] M. Reichert and P. Dadam. $\text{ADEPT}_{\text{flex}}$ — Supporting Dynamic Changes of Workflows Without Losing Control. *Journal of Intelligent Information Systems*, 10(2):93–129, March 1998.

[Red96] J.-P. Redlich. *Corba 2.0 — A Practical Introduction for C++ and Java.* Addison-Wesley, 1996. In German.

[RELL90] M. Rusinkiewicz, A. Elmagarmid, Y. Leu, and W. Litwin. Extending the Transaction Model to Capture more Meaning. *ACM SIGMOD Record*, 19(1):3–7, March 1990.

[RKC92] M. Rusinkiewicz, P. Krychniak, and A. Cichocki. Towards a Model for Multidatabase Transactions. *International Journal of Intelligent and Cooperative Information Systems*, 1(3 & 4):570–617, December 1992.

[RKT+95] M. Rusinkiewicz, W. Klas, T. Tesch, J. Wäsch, and P. Muth. Towards a Cooperative Transaction Model – The Cooperative Activity Model. In *Proceedings of the 21st International Conference on Very Large Databases (VLDB'95)*, pages 194–205, Zürich, Switzerland, September 1995. Morgan Kaufmann Publishers.

[RN95] S. Russell and P. Norvig. *Artificial Intelligence: A Modern Approach.* Prentice-Hall, 1995.

[RS95] M. Rusinkiewicz and A. Sheth. *Specification and Execution of Transactional Workflows*, chapter 29. In: [Kim95]. Addison-Wesley, 1995.

[RSL78] D. Rosenkrantz, R. Stearns, and P. Lewis. System Level Concurrency Control for Distributed Database Systems. *ACM Transactions on Database Systems (TODS)*, 3(2):178–198, June 1978.

[RSS97] A. Reuter, K. Schneider, and F. Schwenkreis. *ConTracts Revisited*, chapter 5, pages 127–151. In: [JK97]. Kluwer Academic Publishers, 1997.

[RSS98] L. Relly, H. Schuldt, and H.-J. Schek. Exporting Database Functionality – The CONCERT Way. *Bulletin of the IEEE Technical Committee on Data Engineering*, 21(3):43–51, September 1998. Special Issue on Interoperability.

[SAP] SAP AG, Walldorf, Germany. `http://www.sap.com`.

[SAP00] SAP AG. *SAP R/3 Online Documentation, Release 4.5b*, 2000.

[SAS99] H. Schuldt, G. Alonso, and H.-J. Schek. Concurrency Control and Recovery in Transactional Process Management. In *Proceedings of the 18th ACM Symposium on Principles of Database Systems (PODS'99)*, pages 316–326, Philadelphia, Pennsylvania, USA, May/June 1999. ACM Press.

[SB99] C. Guedes Soares and J. Brodda, editors. *Applications of Information Technology to the Maritime Industries.* Edicoes Salamandra Lda, June 1999. MAREXPO Consortium.

[SBG+00] H.-J. Schek, K. Böhm, T. Grabs, U. Röhm, H. Schuldt, and R. Weber. Hyperdatabases. In *Proceedings of the 1st International Conference on Web Information Systems Engineering (WISE'00)*, pages 14–23, Hong Kong, China, June 2000. IEEE Computer Society Press.

[Sch96a] W. Schaad. *Transactions in Heterogeneous Federated Database Systems*. PhD thesis, Swiss Federal Institute of Technology Zürich, 1996. Diss. ETH Nr. 11425. In German.

[Sch96b] H.-J. Schek. Improving the Role of Future Database Systems. *ACM Computing Surveys*, 28(4), December 1996. Position Statement.

[SGA87] K. Salem, H. Garcia-Molina, and R. Alonso. Altruistic Locking: A Strategy for Coping with Long Lived Transactions. In *Proceedings of the 2nd International Workshop on High Performance Transaction Systems (HPTS'87)*, pages 175–198, Asilomar, California, USA, September 1987. Springer LNCS, Vol. 359.

[SL90] A. Sheth and J. Larson. Federated Database Systems for Managing Distributed, Heterogeneous, and Autonomous Databases. *ACM Computing Surveys*, 22(3):183 – 236, September 1990.

[SPS99a] H. Schuldt, A. Popovici, and H.-J. Schek. Execution Guarantees in Electronic Commerce Payments. In *Proceedings of the 8th International Workshop on Foundations of Models and Languages for Data and Objects: Transactions and Database Dynamics (TDD'99)*, pages 193–202, Schloss Dagstuhl, Germany, September 1999. Springer LNCS, Vol. 1773.

[SPS99b] H. Schuldt, A. Popovici, and H.-J. Schek. Give me all I pay for – Execution Guarantees in Electronic Commerce Payments. In *Proceedings of the Informatik'99 GI-Workshop Enterprise-wide and Cross-enterprise Workflow Management: Concepts, Systems, Applications*, pages 10–17, Paderborn, Germany, October 1999. Technical Report Nr. 99-07, University of Ulm, Department of Computer Science.

[SPS00] H. Schuldt, A. Popovici, and H.-J. Schek. Automatic Generation of Reliable E-Commerce Payment Processes. In *Proceedings of the 1st International Conference on Web Information Systems Engineering (WISE'00)*, pages 434–441, Hong Kong, China, June 2000. IEEE Computer Society Press.

[SR93] A. Sheth and M. Rusinkiewicz. On Transactional Workflows. *Bulletin of the IEEE Technical Committee on Data Engineering*, 16(1):37–40, March 1993. Special Issue on Workflow and Extended Transaction Systems.

[SR96] F. Schwenkreis and A. Reuter. *Synchronizing Long-Lived Computations*, chapter 12, pages 336–355. In: [Kum96]. 1996.

[SRK92] A. Sheth, M. Rusinkiewicz, and G. Karabatis. *Using Polytransactions to Manage Interdependent Data*, chapter 14. In: [Elm92]. Morgan Kaufmann Publishers, 1992.

[SS93] W. Schaad and H.-J. Schek. Federated Transaction Management Using Open Nested Transactions. In *Proceedings of the DBTA Workshop on Interoperability of Database Systems and Database Applications*, Fribourg, Switzerland, October 1993.

[SSA99] H. Schuldt, H.-J. Schek, and G. Alonso. Transactional Coordination Agents for Composite Systems. In *Proceedings of the 3rd International Database Engineering and Applications Symposium (IDEAS'99)*, pages 321–331, Montréal, Canada, August 1999. IEEE Computer Society Press.

[SSAS99] C. Schuler, H. Schuldt, G. Alonso, and H.-J. Schek. Workflows over Workflows: Practical Experiences with the Integration of SAP R/3 Business Workflows in WISE. In *Proceedings of the Informatik'99 GI-Workshop Enterprise-wide and Cross-enterprise Workflow Management: Concepts, Systems, Applications*, pages 65–71, Paderborn, Germany, October 1999. Technical Report Nr. 99-07, University of Ulm, Department of Computer Science.

[SSS00] C. Schuler, H. Schuldt, and H.-J. Schek. Transactional Execution Guarantees for Data–Intensive Processes in Medical Information Systems. In *Proceedings of the 1st European Workshop on Computer-based Support for Clinical Guidelines and Protocols (EWGLP'2000)*, Leipzig, Germany, November 2000.

[SST98] H. Schuldt, H.-J. Schek, and M. Tresch. Coordination in CIM: Bringing Database Functionality to Application Systems. In *Proceedings of the 5th European Concurrent Engineering Conference (ECEC'98)*, pages 223–230, Erlangen, Germany, April 1998.

[SSW95] W. Schaad, H.-J. Schek, and G. Weikum. Implementation and Performance of Multi-level Transaction Management in a Multidatabase Environment. In *Proceedings of the 5th International Workshop on Research Issues in Data Engineering. Distributed Object Management (RIDE-DOM'95)*, pages 108–115, Taipei, Taiwan, March 1995. IEEE Computer Society Press.

[SVM98] R. Stieber, N. Vecchiarelli, and S. Mackay. The Wonders of Workflow. *Oracle Magazine*, 12(3):105–115, May/June 1998.

[SWS91] H.-J. Schek, G. Weikum, and W. Schaad. A Multi-Level Transaction Approach to Federated DBMS Transaction Management. In *Proceedings of the 1st International Workshop on Research Issues on Data Engineering. Interoperability in Multidatabase Systems (RIDE-IMS'91)*, pages 280–287, Kyoto, Japan, April 1991. IEEE Computer Society Press.

[SWY93] H.-J. Schek, G. Weikum, and H. Ye. Towards a Unifying Theory of Concurrency Control and Recovery. In *Proceedings of the 12th ACM Symposium on Principles of Database Systems (PODS'93)*, pages 300–311, Washington D.C., USA, June 1993. ACM Press.

[SZB+96] A. Silberschatz, S. Zdonik, J. Blakeley, P. Buneman, U. Dayal, T. Imielinski, S. Jajodia, H. Korth, G. Lohman, D. Lomet, D. Maier, F. Manola, T. Özsu, R. Ramakrishnan, K. Ramamritham, H.-J. Schek, R. Snodgrass, J. Ullman, and J. Widom. Strategic Directions in Database Systems – Breaking Out of the Box. *ACM Computing Surveys*, 28(4):764–778, December 1996.

[Tho79] R. Thomas. A Majority Consensus Approach to Concurrency Control for Multiple Copy Databases. *ACM Transactions on Database Systems (TODS)*, 4(2):180–209, June 1979.

[TIB] TIBCO Software Inc. `http://www.tibco.com`.

[TIB99] TIB/Rendezvous. White Paper, 1999. TIBCO Software Inc.

[Tij94] H. Tijms. *Stochastic Models – An Algorithmic Approach*. John Wiley & Sons, Chichester, England, 1994.

[Tre96] M. Tresch. Middleware: Key Technology for the Development of Distributed Information Systems. *Informatik Spektrum*, 19(5):249–256, October 1996. In German.

[TV95] J. Tang and J. Veijalainen. Transaction-oriented Work-flow Concepts in Inter-organizational Environments. In *Proceedings of the 4th International Conference on Information and Knowledge Management (CIKM'95)*, pages 250–259, Baltimore, Maryland, USA, November 1995. ACM Press.

[Tyg96] D. Tygar. Atomicity in Electronic Commerce. In *Proceedings of the 15th Annual ACM Symposium on Principles of Distributed Computing (PODC'96)*, pages 8–26, Philadelphia, Pennsylvania, USA, May 1996. ACM Press.

[Tyg98] D. Tygar. Atomicity versus Anonymity: Distributed Transactions for Electronic Commerce. In *Proceedings of the 24th International Conference on Very Large Databases (VLDB'98)*, pages 1–12, New York, USA, August 1998. Morgan Kaufmann Publishers.

[VB96] G. Vossen and J. Becker, editors. *Business Process Modeling and Workflow Management: Models, Methods, and Tools*. International Thomson Publishing, 1996. In German.

[VEH92] J. Veijalainen, F. Eliassen, and B. Holtkamp. *The S–Transaction Model*, chapter 12. In: [Elm92]. Morgan Kaufmann Publishers, 1992.

[Vei90] J. Veijalainen. *Transaction Concepts in Autonomous Database Environments*. Number 183 in GMD Reports, Gesellschaft für Mathematik und Datenverarbeitung. R. Oldenbourg Verlag, 1990.

[VHBS98] R. Vingralek, H. Hasse-Ye, Y. Breitbart, and H.-J. Schek. Unifying Concurrency Control and Recovery of Transactions with Semantically Rich Operations. *Theoretical Computer Science*, 190(2):363–396, January 1998.

[Vos97] G. Vossen. The CORBA Specification for Cooperation in Heterogeneous Information Systems. In *Proceedings of the 1st International Workshop on Cooperative Information Agents (CIA'97)*, pages 101–115, Kiel, Germany, February 1997. Springer LNAI, Vol. 1202.

[VW92] J. Veijalainen and A. Wolski. Prepare and Commit Certification for Decentralized Transaction Management in Rigorous Heterogeneous Multidatabases. In *Proceedings of the 8th International Conference on Data Engineering (ICDE'92)*, pages 470–479, Tempe, Arizona, USA, February 1992. IEEE Computer Society Press.

[VYBS95] R. Vingralek, H. Ye, Y. Breitbart, and H.-J. Schek. Unified Transaction Model for Semantically Rich Operations. In *Proceedings of the 5th International Conference on Database Theory (ICDT'95)*, pages 148–161, Prague, Czech Republic, January 1995. Springer LNCS, Vol. 893.

[Wäc91] H. Wächter. ConTracts: A Means for Improving Reliability in Distributed Computing. In *Proceedings of the 36th IEEE Computer Society International Conference (COMPCON SPRING'91)*, pages 574–578, San Francisco, California, USA, February/March 1991. IEEE Computer Society Press.

[Wäc96] H. Wächter. *An Architecture for the Reliable Execution of Distributed Applications on Shared Resources*. PhD thesis, University of Stuttgart, 1996. In German.

[WBGS99] R. Weber, J. Bolliger, T. Gross, and H.-J. Schek. Architecture of a Networked Image Search and Retrieval System. In *Proceedings of the 8th International Conference on Information and Knowledge Management (CIKM'99)*, pages 430–441, Kansas City, Missouri, USA, November 1999. ACM Press.

[WDSS93] G. Weikum, A. Deacon, W. Schaad, and H.-J. Schek. Open Nested Transactions in Federated Database Systems. *Bulletin of the IEEE Technical Committee on Data Engineering*, 16(1):4–7, March 1993. Special Issue on Workflow and Extended Transaction Systems.

[Wei87] G. Weikum. *Transaction Management in Database Systems with Layered Architectures*. PhD thesis, University of Darmstadt, 1987. In German.

[Wei88] G. Weikum. *Transactions in Database Systems: Fault-tolerant Control of Parallel Executions*. Addison-Wesley, 1988. In German.

[Wei91] G. Weikum. Principles and Realization Strategies of Multilevel Transaction Management. *ACM Transactions on Database Systems (TODS)*, 16(1):132–180, March 1991.

[WFB+95] H. Wächter, F. Fritz, A. Berthold, B. Drittler, H. Eckert, R. Gerstner, R. Götzinger, R. Krane, A. Schaeff, C. Schlögel, and R. Weber. *Modeling and Execution of Flexible Business Processes with SAP Business Workflow 3.0*, pages 197–204. In: [HSW95]. Springer-Verlag, 1995. In German.

[WfM] Workflow Management Coalition. `http://www.wfmc.org`.

[WfM98] Workflow Management Coalition. *Workflow Management Application Programming Interface (Interface 2 & 3) Specification*, July 1998. Document WFMC-TC-1009. `http://www.wfmc.org`.

[WGL+96] J. Wiener, H. Gupta, W. Labio, Y. Zhuge, H. Garcia-Molina, and J. Widom. A System Prototype for Warehouse View Maintenance. In *Proceedings of the Workshop on Materialized Views: Techniques and Applications (VIEWS'96)*, pages 26–33, Montréal, Canada, June 1996.

[Wie92] G. Wiederhold. Mediators in the Architecture of Future Information Systems. *IEEE Computer*, 25(3):38–49, March 1992.

[WR92] H. Wächter and A. Reuter. *The ConTract Model*, chapter 7, pages 219–263. In: [Elm92]. Morgan Kaufmann Publishers, 1992.

[WS92] G. Weikum and H.-J. Schek. *Concepts and Applications of Multilevel Transactions and Open Nested Transactions*, chapter 13. In: [Elm92]. Morgan Kaufmann Publishers, 1992.

[WS97] D. Worah and A. Sheth. *Transactions in Transactional Workflows*, chapter 1. In: [JK97]. Kluwer Academic Publishers, 1997.

[Wun96] M. Wunderli. *Database Technology for the Coordination of CIM Subsystems.* PhD thesis, Swiss Federal Institute of Technology Zürich, 1996. Diss. ETH Nr. 11718.

[WV90] A. Wolski and J. Veijalainen. 2PC Agent Method: Achieving Serializability in Presence of Failures in a Heterogeneous Multidatabase. In *Proceedings of the International Conference on Databases, Parallel Architectures, and their Applications (PARBASE'90)*, pages 321–330, Miami Beach, Florida, USA, March 1990. IEEE Computer Society Press.

[WWC92] G. Wiederhold, P. Wegner, and S. Ceri. Towards Megaprogramming. *Communications of the ACM*, 35(11):89–99, November 1992.

[ZNBB94] A. Zhang, M. Nodine, B. Bhargava, and O. Bukhres. Ensuring Relaxed Atomicity for Flexible Transactions in Multidatabase Systems. In *Proceedings of the ACM SIGMOD International Conference on Management of Data (SIGMOD'94)*, pages 67–78, Minneapolis, Minnesota, USA, May 1994. ACM Press.

Curriculum Vitae

Name:	Heiko Schuldt
Date of Birth:	October 20, 1969
Place of Birth:	Karlsruhe, Germany
Citizenship:	German

School

1976 – 1980	Primary School, Karlsruhe-Neureut
1980 – 1989	Gymnasium Neureut
04/1989	Abitur
06/1989 – 08/1990	Military Service, Dillingen/Donau, Germany

University

10/1990 – 07/1996	Studies of Computer Science at the University of Karlsruhe
09/1993 – 01/1994	Student Research Project at the Ecole Nationale Supérieure d'Informatique et de Mathématiques Appliquées de Grenoble (ENSIMAG) in Grenoble, France
12/1995 – 07/1996	Diploma Thesis at the Heidelberg Scientific Center (WZH) of IBM in Heidelberg, Germany
07/1996	Diplom-Informatiker, University of Karlsruhe

Employment

02/1992 – 03/1992 and 08/1992 – 10/1992	Internship with Siemens GmbH, Karlsruhe
09/1994 – 07/1996	ISB GmbH (Institute of Software Development and IT Consulting), Karlsruhe
since 08/1996	Research and Teaching Assistant, ETH Zürich, Institute of Information Systems, Database Research Group (Prof. H.-J. Schek)